The Cognitive Development of Reading and Reading Comprehension

Learning to read may be the most complex cognitive operation that children are expected to master, and the latest research in cognitive development has offered important insights into how children succeed or fail at this task. *The Cognitive Development of Reading and Reading Comprehension* is a multidisciplinary, evidence-based resource for teachers and researchers that examines reading comprehension from a cognitive development perspective, including the principal theories and methods used in the discipline. The book combines research into basic cognitive processes—genetics, perception, memory, executive functioning, and language—with an investigation of the effects that context and environment have on literacy outcomes, making clear how factors such as health, family life, community, policy, and ecology can influence children's cognitive development.

Carol McDonald Connor is Chancellor's Professor, School of Education, University of California, Irvine, USA, Senior Research Scientist at the Institute for the Science of Teaching and Learning at Arizona State University, and a Distinguished Research Associate at the Florida Center for Reading Research, Florida State University, USA.

The Cognitive Development of Reading and Reading Comprehension

Edited by Carol McDonald Connor

Routledge
Taylor & Francis Group

LONDON AND NEW YORK

First published 2016
by Routledge
711 Third Avenue, New York, NY 10017

and by Routledge
2 Park Square, Milton Park, Abingdon, Oxon OX14 4RN

Routledge is an imprint of the Taylor & Francis Group, an informa business

Library of Congress Cataloging in Publication Data

Names: Connor, Carol McDonald, editor.
Title: The cognitive development of reading and reading comprehension /
edited by Carol McDonald Connor.
Description: New York, NY : Routledge, 2016. | Includes bibliographical
references and index.
Identifiers: LCCN 2015036128| ISBN 9781138908420 (hardback) | ISBN
9781138908437 (pbk.) | ISBN 9781315694429 (ebook)
Subjects: LCSH: Reading–Psychological aspects. | Reading comprehension. |
Cognition in children.
Classification: LCC BF456.R2 C565 2016 | DDC 418/.4019–dc23
LC record available at http://lccn.loc.gov/2015036128

ISBN: 978-1-138-90842-0 (hbk)
ISBN: 978-1-138-90843-7 (pbk)
ISBN: 978-1-315-69442-9 (ebk)

Typeset in Bembo
by Cenveo Publisher Services

Printed and bound in the United States of America by Publishers Graphics,
LLC on sustainably sourced paper.

Contents

Acknowledgements

This book was written by students for students who are interested in cognitive development and reading. Except for the chapters in which I am the first author, the first author in every case was a student in my graduate seminar in cognitive development, which I taught in fall of 2013 at Arizona State University. Each of them recruited a co-author who is also an expert in the field. In my opinion, the result is a highly approachable book that presents seminal as well as cutting-edge research about cognitive development, how children learn to read, and the multiple sources of influence that affect their learning. Thus, I would like to thank each of the students in the class who contributed a chapter. I would also like to thank the expert mentors, many of whom are close friends and colleagues, who helped them craft and improve their chapters. It is our hope that this book will be useful to students, faculty, and practitioners who want to learn more about reading in the context of children's cognitive development.

We hope you enjoy this book. It has been a learning experience for all of us.

Chapter 1

Introduction to the Cognitive Development of Reading

Carol McDonald Connor and
Jennifer L. Weston

The study of cognitive development has been essential in understanding how children learn to read, what has to happen for them to learn to read proficiently, and the sources of influence on reading development. Learning to read may be the most complex cognitive task we expect all children to master—it is much like expecting all children to become chess masters. And the stakes are much higher. Children who do not read well are more likely to drop out of high school, become teen parents, or enter the criminal justice system (Reynolds, Temple, Robertson, & Mann, 2002). Research in cognitive development has offered important insights into how children succeed or fail learning to read. For example, one might believe that learning to talk is more difficult than learning to read but research shows that we are essentially hardwired to learn how to talk (Dunbar, 1996). We are not wired to learn to read. Reading is a human invention that is between 5000 and 3500 years old (Campbell, 2013) whereas we humans have been talking for over 100,000 years at least. Because reading is an invention, learning to read essentially coopts parts of the brain originally designed for other tasks, like language, memory, and perception.

Therefore, children need careful and highly technical instruction if they are to learn to read and write well (Adams, 1990). First they must master the alphabetic principle—that letters stand for sounds and that these letters combine to create words that have meaning. Then they have to learn how to make sense of what they have decoded, which is even more difficult. Unfortunately, because it is a polyglot, English is among the most difficult languages to read and write: the spelling is irregular and the vocabulary is vast. That said, cognitive development research indicates that virtually all children *can* learn to read and write. The study of reading and writing offers a window into understanding the breadth and depth of research in cognitive development. This edited book is developed to be a resource for researchers, teachers, and for university courses on reading and/or cognitive development. For this edited volume, we are focusing on reading comprehension rather than more basic processes such as phonological awareness, phonics, and fluency. At the same time, unless these more fundamental processes are fluent and automatic, children with have a great deal of difficulty understanding what it is they are trying to decode.

Learning Theories and Learning to Read

How a 6-year-old reads and understands is very different than the way a college student reads and understands. Hence, as we think about reading and cognitive development, learning is a critical aspect of developing proficient reading comprehension skills. Webster's dictionary defines learning as "the activity or process of gaining knowledge or skill by studying, practicing, being taught, or experiencing something: the activity of someone who learns." Throughout the ages, philosophers have discussed learning. Soon after psychology was established as a science, the empirical study of learning began. Many early psychologists subscribed to the experimental method of introspection, a self-analysis of one's own perceptions. Behaviorism and the behaviorist theories of learning developed in response to the limitations of introspection techniques. In direct comparison to introspection, behaviorists relied on observable behavior assuming that an individual's *feelings* of mastery or learning were not as important as his actual *behavior*.

Three theories of learning came out of the behaviorist school of thought: connectionism, classical conditioning, and operant conditioning. Modern learning theories have grown out of these early learning theories. At the same time, cognitive theories of learning expanded on social psychology theories. Although there are many learning theories, here we focus on three that can help us understand how children learn to read: social learning theory (Bandura, 1977b); Anderson's cognitive skill theory (Anderson, 1982, 1996); and the model of domain learning (Alexander, 2006).

Social Learning Theory

The theory of social learning postulated by Bandura (1977b) was one of the first cognitive theories of learning. Social cognitive theory holds that knowledge, skills, strategies, beliefs, and attitudes, along with how to behave correctly in situations, may be learned by observing others. This theory makes a distinction between learning and performance, and hypothesizes that what we learn depends on a variety of internal and external factors. Bandura (1977a) stressed the social nature of learning, hypothesizing two types of learning: *enactive* and *vicarious* learning. Enactive learning is learning by enacting a behavior and observing the consequences. In contrast to operant conditioning, social cognitive theory holds that consequences inform and motivate behavior rather than simply strengthen behavior. Vicarious learning is learning without overt completion of a behavior. Vicarious learning is done by watching or listening to models of instruction. These models may take many forms and include human models, text, and even television. The advantage of vicarious learning is that it allows the learning of information and skills that might be difficult to learn from interactions with the environment. Cycles of vicarious and enactive learning, along with corrective feedback, are necessary for learning, according to social cognitive theory.

Thus, one way children learn to read is through modeling or imitating behaviors. Modeling is a combination of both vicarious and enactive learning. Social cognitive theory stresses that imitation is an instinct that is conditioned from birth (Bandura, 1977a). Modeling allows learners to acquire increasingly complex skills. For example, children who see their parents read for pleasure are more likely to enjoy reading themselves. Indeed, even before they learn to read, children pretend to read if they have been given a model (e.g., a parent or teacher) and are more likely to read well if their parents spend more time reading with them (Debaryshe, 1993; Whitehurst et al., 1988).

Zimmerman (1990) expanded on the social learning theory by being more specific about the nature of the internal and external factors that influence learning and performance. He defined *self-regulated learning* as active learning, with the learner not just performing actions but also taking an active role in their learning. One of the most important tenants of self-regulated learning is that the learner is aware of what they have and have not learned. Furthermore, self-regulated learners view their learning process as under their control. This makes it easier for them to overcome obstacles. The learning process in self-regulated learning involves the steps of planning, goal setting, self-monitoring and self-evaluation of learning. Being knowledgeable about one's own learning allows for the proper allocation of resources. For example, if children are aware that they are struggling, they may seek out help. Not only are self-regulated learners aware of their learning, they are also aware of the impact of their actions on their learning. Self-regulation falls along a continuum ranging from very high to very low. Moreover, levels of self-regulation may vary from task to task. The decision to self-regulate, or not, may depend on external factors, including explicit instruction in, for example, writing (Graham, Harris, & Mason, 2005).

Children can be taught how to regulate their own learning, particularly with regard to reading and writing. For example, Harris and Graham have developed an effective writing intervention that incorporates the explicit teaching of self-regulated strategy use (Graham, et al., 2005).

Cognitive Skill Theory

Anderson's cognitive skill theory (1982) differs from social cognitive theory both in scope and design by focusing on the nature of *changes* in developing skills over time. Basing his theory on work by Fitts (1964), Anderson postulates three stages of skill acquisition: the *declarative* stage, *knowledge* compilation, and the *procedural* stage. The first stage involves encoding the information necessary to complete a skill. The second stage is the transition phase; this includes the conversion of information into a procedure that can be practiced. The fixing of any errors present in the initial encoding of the skill also occurs during the compilation stage. The third stage continues indefinitely. It involves the continual practice and improvement of the skill. Skill acquisition theory is the basis of Anderson's ACT Model (1996) in which declarative knowledge is represented as a network, and procedural knowledge is represented as a series of production rules. Control over both cognition and behavior in this model is a result of production rules. Learning in cognitive skill theory is considered very differently than learning in the prior theories.

Initial skill learning involves the learning of facts, or the acquisition of declarative knowledge. This would be similar to learning the letters of the alphabet for a young child. Declarative knowledge is interpreted using general production rules. General rules are used because instruction rarely informs the learner about what procedures are to be used to apply the information. These general problem-solving rules are crucial to the skill acquisition theory, because these rules are universally used to bridge gaps between declarative knowledge and behaviors.

In the second stage, compilation is initially slow, as the general production rules are used to produce behavior and then speeds up as appropriate behaviors are found and the need for rehearsal is diminished. For example, children no longer need to sound out words letter by letter because they recognize the words automatically.

The procedural stage is the practice stage in which novices progress and begin to gain expertise. Increased practice results in both generalization and discrimination, although trial and error do play a part in the development of these processes. The cognitive skill theory is very good at explaining learning in well-defined domains, such as mathematics, and for understanding the acquisition of early decoding and comprehension skills. However, it is less useful when trying to explain reading comprehension when children are expected to read more critically, compare the meaning of various texts, and make inferences about what they are reading.

Model of Domain Learning

Alexander's model of domain learning brings together aspects of each of the prior theories of learning. Like Anderson's (1982) theory, the model of domain learning is a stage-based learning theory. Unlike the cognitive skill theory, the model of domain learning takes into account individual factors much like those considered in social learning theory (Bandura, 1977b). The model of domain learning is a model of the development of expertise and includes three stages: acclimation, competency, and proficiency or expertise.

The three stages of the model of domain learning can be explained by looking at the characteristics of learners in each of these categories and how their knowledge, interest and strategic processing differ. Individuals in the acquisition stage will have fragmented or incomplete knowledge of the task and the domain. These individuals might rely on situational interest, or their response to the aspects of the task that are enticing, including novelty and compensation (Mitchell, 1993). Strategies are used during the acclimation phase. However, strategy use is generally limited to surface strategies such as rereading or paraphrasing (Alexander, 2003). Once an individual has acquired a sufficient amount of knowledge as well as cohesive understanding of the domain, they enter the stage of competence. Readers in the acclimation phase may struggle with any or all aspects of reading including decoding, vocabulary knowledge, and comprehension. Readers in this stage may gravitate towards books on topics that interest them or that contain pictures that can aid in understanding.

In the stage of competence, situational interest decreases in influencing learning while individual interest increases. A change also occurs in strategy use, with individuals using a mix of surface level and deep processing strategies including such activities as critiquing texts and comparing them to other texts. The progression to expertise is not assured for any skill, including reading. Children may be competent but not expert readers into adulthood. For readers to be successful in today's society it is necessary that they read at a minimum of the competency level. This level of expertise allows individuals to, for instance, compare the labels of three medications to choose the best one for their ailment.

Expertise (Ericsson, 2006) is marked by possessing a broad principled knowledge base and requires that the individual contributes to the domain—for example, successful novelists might be consider expert readers under this definition. Experts are highly interested (i.e., individual interest). Situational interest is less important. Experts rely heavily on deep processing strategies. Of course, an expert in one field (the novelist) may be in the acclimation stage in another field (e.g., writing textbooks). Expertise may be either domain specific or domain general. For example, if a child is an expert reader, this expertise may generalize to other domains in which they have to read text (e.g., reading Harry Potter versus a history textbook). However, this expertise may not transfer to other less related domains, such as art or music.

Cognitive Theories of Reading

There are many theories about the processes underlying skilled reading, such as Chall's stage theory (Chall, 1996), the Construction-Integration Model (Kintsch, 1988), and the lexical quality hypothesis (Perfetti & Stafura, 2014) that are directly informed by cognitive theories on learning.

However, theories of language learning have also informed theories of reading, including the whole language theory of reading (Goodman, 1970), which purported that learning to read was like learning to talk. This theory has been largely abandoned as greater appreciation for the invented nature and neurological basis of reading and reading disabilities became clearer (Shaywitz, et al., 2002). Among the most influential and well-supported theories of reading is the simple view of reading (Hoover & Gough, 1990) where proficient reading comprehension is the product of fluent decoding and proficient listening comprehension (i.e., oral language). If either is weak, then reading comprehension is compromised. However, the role of instruction is missing in these theories and so emerging theories have started borrowing from developmental psychology and biology and applying dynamic systems theories (Mitchell, 2011; Yoshikawa & Hsueh, 2001). We briefly review Chall's (Chall, 1996) stage theory, the Construction-Integration Model, the lexical hypothesis theory, and finally emerging theories, such as the Lattice Model (Connor, et al., 2014), that borrow from dynamic systems theory and include the role of instruction.

Stage Theory

Chall's (1996) stage theory covers life span reading from acquisition through reading for a purpose where individuals progress through six stages of learning to read. Although originally Chall assigned ages to each stage, later research suggested that learning to read can transcend maturational milestones and that the stages are not strictly sequential and can be concurrent.

In stage 0, or pre-reading, children are not yet literate but they are becoming familiar with spoken language. Stage 1 involves learning the alphabetic principle as children become increasingly familiar with letters and the corresponding sounds. In stage 2, children have increased fluency and are able to read words and simple stories. Stage 3 consists of two parts: in the first part, children focus on the acquisition of vocabulary and knowledge through reading. The second part of stage 3 introduces the idea of critically analyzing texts. Stage 4 is marked by increases in the complexity of texts utilized by learners. In this stage, learners are presented with multiple viewpoints, complex concepts and are encouraged to think critically about text. The difference between stages 4 and 5 is the utility of reading. Individuals in stage 5 read for a purpose with an emphasis on analysis and synthesis of text.

While not as comprehensive as Chall's theory the model of domain learning (Alexander, 2006; Fox & Alexander, 2011) can be applied to learning to read. During the acquisition stage the focus would be on decoding, word-level processing and the acquisition of vocabulary. Learners in this stage would be subject to situational interest and may prefer texts with interesting characters or pictures (Silvia, 2003). Individuals in the competence stage would have a broad knowledge of language and vocabulary. These individuals would be fluent and utilize sophisticated strategies including meaning building, reflection, and evaluation of text. The texts read in the competence stage would likely be driven by individual interest, although situational interest would still influence reading choices. For example, an individual may choose to read science fiction due to individual interest but be compelled to read history texts for a class through situational interest, in this case, the interest in passing a class.

Construction-Integration Model

The Construction-Integration (C-I) Model (Kintsch, 1998) is the basis of many other models of reading comprehension. In this model, knowledge and memory are represented as a network. Construction is the activation of this network based on the information presented in the text and related knowledge. Activation comes from the current sentence, prior sentence, related knowledge, and related texts. Integration involves the spreading activation from these sources. The C-I Model relies on three levels of representation and comprehension: surface structure, propositional text base, and situation model. The surface structure is made up of words and syntactic structure of text. The propositional structure is where text is represented in the simplest propositional form. The situation model goes beyond the text and includes all information not explicit in the text. In the situation model inferences are divided into automatic and controlled, and retrieved and generated inferences

According to the C-I Model, coherence is based on the extent to which knowledge is activated and incorporated into mental representations. Coherence is also reliant on automaticity and the linking of propositions to discourse representation. Essentially, a text will be easier for a reader to comprehend if they have prior knowledge of the topic. Regardless of skill level, a computer science textbook will be more difficult for an English major to comprehend than a math or engineering major. This is due to existing prior knowledge and the relation or proximity between prior knowledge of the reader and targeted topic.

There have been many comprehension theories that have built on the C-I Model; for example, theories of dynamic text comprehension. One theory of dynamic text comprehension, the Landscape Model (Rapp, van den Broek, McMaster, Kendeou, & Espin, 2007) differs from the C-I Model in that activation of concepts can be both automatic and strategic. Passive activation is similar to activation in the C-I Model, whereas strategic activation (or coherence activation) involves the effortful search for meaning. This model makes no assumption about the levels of comprehension; rather it considers different levels of analysis ranging from the propositional level to whole texts. Important is the idea that, to the extent readers develop coherent mental representations of text, their comprehension of the text will be greater.

Lexical Quality Hypothesis

The lexical quality hypothesis holds that the quality of readers' word knowledge and their fluent access to word meanings will directly influence their reading comprehension. High lexical quality includes well-specified and partly redundant representations of the written form (orthography) and the sounds that the letters represent (phonology) along with flexible understanding of the meaning of the text, allowing for rapid and reliable meaning retrieval. Low-quality representations lead to specific word-related problems in comprehension. This hypothesis has been supported through neurological studies (Perfetti & Stafura, 2014) and elucidates the connections between foundational (i.e., decoding) and higher order skills (e.g., lexical representation).

The Lattice Model

The Lattice Model (Connor, et al., 2014) is an emerging and evolving model that attempts to capture the dynamic and interactive nature of learning to read (see Figure 1.1). It borrows from bioecological and

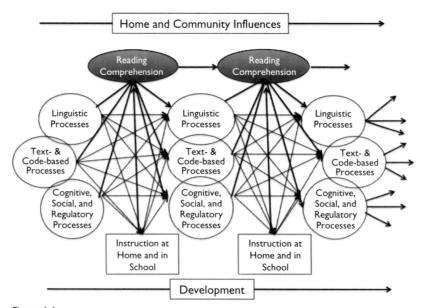

Figure 1.1

dynamic systems frameworks (Bronfenbrenner & Morris, 2006; Yoshikawa & Hsueh, 2001) as well as the stage, C-I, and lexical quality hypothesis models. The model "conceptualize[s] reading comprehension as a complex activity that requires the reader (in this case, the student) to call on the coordination of cognitive, regulatory, linguistic, and social mechanisms, as well as text specific processes, which are developing over time and that have reciprocal and interacting bootstrapping effects on one another (Gough & Tunmer, 1986; Kintsch, 1998; Perfetti & Stafura, 2014; Rapp & van den Broek, 2005). Moreover, the extent to which students successfully read for understanding is further influenced by their purpose for reading and characteristics of the text itself (Snow, 2001)" (Connor, et al., 2014, p. 4). The model acknowledges individual differences among children, including genetics, home environment, and life experiences. It also incorporates the notion of *specificity of learning*—that children tend to learn what is taught and that these skills do not typically generalize to other skills. Finally, the model aims to identify malleable sources of influence on reading compre- hension, which may be on a continuum from "under-the-hood" and largely automatic and unconscious (e.g., application of oral language) to more reflective and metacognitive (e.g., examining text structure). Key to this model is that instruction provided by knowledgeable others, including parents and teachers, plays an important role is the process of helping beginning readers become proficient readers. The model is developmental, suggesting that reading processes and how they interact may change as children mature, particularly as their brain develops. There are also boot- strapping (i.e., one skill helps build other skills) and reciprocal effects (e.g., that vocabulary supports stronger reading comprehension and, in turn, stronger reading comprehension supports developing vocabulary skills). According to this model, improving only one aspect of reading (e.g., vocabulary) is unlikely to have an effect on the entire system. Rather, this model suggests that instruction in the multiple skills that underlie profi- cient reading comprehension is more likely to be effective in improving reading comprehension (NICHD, 2000). Moreover, borrowing from bio- ecological theory, the model proposes that proximal sources of influence, such as home and school, will have a greater impact than more distal sources of influence, such as district, state, and national policy, but that these distal sources are still important to consider.

Introduction to the Chapters

Working from these cognitive theories and the research that supports them, we will start with the genetics of reading. A large body of work demon- strates the substantial role of genetic influences on the development of reading comprehension. The purpose of Chapter 2, by Little, Wang, and Hart, is to review the behavioral and molecular genetic literature pertaining to the etiology and development of reading comprehension. Within the realm of the behavioral genetics literature, this chapter reviews literature demonstrating that genetic influences vary with development; the environment and gene-by-environment interactions play a role in the development of reading comprehension skills; individual differences play a role in moderating genetic influences; and reading comprehension and other cognitive skills share genetic influences. The literature on molecular genetics is also reviewed, highlighting the role of some of the most studied candidate genes, exploring the role of endophenotypes in this literature, and discussing future directions in this area of research. Although technical, this information is critical for teachers and others who support students' efforts to learn to read.

We then move to issues of perception, including digital media. Chapter 3, by Roschke and Radach, begins with an overview of the perception literature related to reading comprehension with an emphasis on the work by eye movement researchers. Discussion then turns to the increasing influence of technology in education and how factors unique to online environments may impact the underlying cognitive processes involved in reading comprehension.

Clearly, memory is a critical aspect of proficient reading comprehension. Chapter 4, by Russell and Connor, explores how memory, specifically working memory, affects reading comprehension ability. As a child matures and advances through elementary school, the cognitive skills required to be a skilled reader change and evolve. Beginning readers rely heavily on decoding and vocabulary skills to improve their reading comprehension, but by the time a child reaches the third grade, working memory begins to account for significant variance in measures of reading comprehension. In this chapter, they argue that working memory supports many of the component skills involved in reading comprehension and they review literature examining reading comprehension as children develop with particular focus on children with reading disabilities. The implications of this research and future directions are discussed. Of course, the Lattice Model suggests that these associations might be reciprocal and new research is discussed that shows that this might be the case.

Chapter 5, by Lin, Coburn, and Eisenberg, draws from research in developmental and educational sciences to describe relations between self-regulation and the acquisition of reading and other academic skills. Gaps in research that are emerging across disciplines are discussed, and future avenues of interdisciplinary research that may advance understanding about self-regulation are proposed.

In Chapter 6, the authors, Allen and McNamara, suggest that a close inspection of the literature on cognitive language development can expand our understanding of the relationship between language and reading comprehension skills. They describe the language acquisition process and how this relates to the overall development of the cognitive system. They then discuss how the higher level properties of language development may relate to our understanding of the reading comprehension process. Finally, they offer some suggestions for future research in the areas of language development and reading comprehension, as well as avenues for educational interventions aimed to improve reading skills.

Wynne and Connor discuss social cognitive theory and research on self-perception, self-efficacy, growth mindset, and theory of mind in Chapter 7. They discuss whether self-perception influences reading achievement in children and then examine how different self-perception abilities influence reading comprehension in youth.

In Chapter 8, Wolf proposes that although reading comprehension in children is frequently examined in the context of developmental milestones, neurological functioning, learning abilities, and academic abilities, it is equally important to consider the influences of emotional and physical experiences on reading comprehension. At the same time, children's reading comprehension development may be elucidated by examining the emotional and physical health, and environmental concerns, which affect a child's ability to learn, focus, and understand what they are reading.

Chapter 9, by Montano and Hindman, describes the different parenting practices that impact children's cognitive development, more specifically the development of reading and reading comprehension skills. The chapter is divided into sections that summarize the research findings on the specific parenting practices that are described. The literature shows that how and how much parents speak to their children, shared book reading, parent teaching, and other positive parent-child interactions have significant implications for the development of children as successful readers.

The purpose of Chapter 10, by Chiapa and Morrison, is to provide an overview of the current literature describing the relation between proximal and distal ecological factors, such as neighborhood environment, teacher instruction, and children's literacy outcomes. This chapter also aims to highlight potential buffering effects and provides a discussion to encourage new directions for future interventions promoting literacy. Chapter 11, by Mansion, Connor, and Duncan, on policy and learning to read explains that the fields of cognitive development and educational psychology have long been aware of the importance of teaching children how to read. However, the governments that legislate and decide scholastic policy, as well as the educational institutions that provide children with reading instruction, have been slower to utilize the rigorous approaches suggested by these fields. The purpose of this chapter is to review community and policy influences on how children learn to read.

In Chapter 12, Connor reviews the literature on literacy interventions and discusses how cognitive development theories have and will continue to influence how we teach children to read. Finally, in Chapter 13, Connor brings together the information in each chapter, highlights 12 conclusions, and discusses how this information can inform the implementation of more effective literacy instruction in early elementary school.

References

Adams, M. J. (1990). *Beginning to Read: Thinking and Learning about Print*. Cambridge, MA: MIT Press.

Alexander, P. A. (2003). The development of expertise: The journey from acclimation to proficiency. *Educational Researcher, 32*, 10–14.

Alexander, P. A. (2006). The path to competence: A lifespan developmental perspective on reading. *Journal of Literacy Research, 37*, 413–436.

Anderson, J. R. (1982). Acquisition of cognitive skill. *Psychological Review, 86*, 369–406.

Anderson, J. R. (1996). ACT: A simple theory of complex cognition. *American Psychologist, 51*, 355–365.

Bandura, A. (1977a). Self-efficacy: Toward a unifying theory of behavioural change. *Psychological Review, 84*, 191–215.

Bandura, A. (1977b). *Social Learning Theory*. Upper Saddle River, NJ: Prentice-Hall.

Bronfenbrenner, U., & Morris, P. A. (2006). The bioecological model of human development. In R. M. Lerner & W. Damon (Eds.), *Handbook of Child Psychology: Theoretical Models of Human Development* (6th ed., Vol. 1). Hoboken, NJ: John Wiley & Sons.

Campbell, L. (2013). *Historical Linguistics*. Edinburgh: Edinburgh University Press.

Chall, J. S. (1996). *Stages of Reading Development* (2nd ed.). Orlando, FL: Harcourt Brace.

Connor, C. M., Phillips, B., Kaschak, M., Apel, K., Kim, Y.-S., Al Otaiba, S., et al. (2014). Comprehension tools for teachers: Reading for understanding from prekindergarten through fourth grade. *Educational Psychology Review, 26*(3), 379–401.

Debaryshe, B. D. (1993). Joint picture-book reading correlates of early oral language skill. *Journal of Child Language, 20*, 455–461.

Dunbar, R. (1996). *Grooming, Gossip, and the Evolution of Language*. Cambridge, MA: Harvard University Press.

Ericsson, K. A. (Ed.). (2006). *The Cambridge Handbook of Expertise and Expert Performance*. New York: Cambridge University Press.

Fitts, P. M. (1964). Perceptual–motor skill learning. In A. W. Melton (Ed.), *Categories of Human Learning*. New York: Academic Press.

Fox, E., & Alexander, P. A. (2011). Learning to read. In R. E. Mayer & P. A. Alexander (Eds.), *Handbook of Research on Learning and Instruction*. New York: Routledge.

Goodman, K. (1970). Reading: A psycholinguistic guessing game. In H. Singer & R. B. Ruddell (Eds.), *Theoretical Models and Processes of Reading*. Newark, DE: International Reading Association.

Gough, P. B., & Tunmer, W. E. (1986). Decoding, reading, and reading disability. *Remedial and Special Education, 7*, 6–10.

Graham, S., Harris, K. R., & Mason, L. (2005). Improving the writing performance, knowledge, and self-efficacy of struggling young writers: The effects of self-regulated strategy development. *Contemporary Educational Psychology, 30*, 207–241.

Hoover, W. A., & Gough, P. B. (1990). The simple view of reading. *Reading and Writing*, *2*(2), 127–160.

Kintsch, W. (1988). The role of knowledge in discourse comprehension: A construction-integration model. *Psychological Review*, *95*(2), 163–182.

Kintsch, W. (1998). *Comprehension: A Paradigm for Cognitions*. New York: Cambridge University Press.

Mitchell, M. (1993). Situational interest: Its multifaceted structure in the secondary school mathematics classroom. *Journal of Educational Psychology*, *85*, 424–436.

Mitchell, M. (2011). *Complexity: A Guided Tour*. New York: Oxford University Press.

NICHD. (2000). National Institute of Child Health and Human Development, National Reading Panel report: Teaching children to read: An evidence-based assessment of the scientific research literature on reading and its implications for reading instruction. Washington, DC: U.S. Department of Health and Human Services, Public Health Service, National Institutes of Health, National Institute of Child Health and Human Development.

Perfetti, C., & Stafura, J. (2014). Word knowledge in a theory of reading comprehension. *Scientific Studies of Reading*, *18*(1), 22–37.

Rapp, D. N., & van den Broek, P. (2005). Dynamic text comprehension: An integrative view of reading. *Current Directions in Psychological Science*, *14*(5), 276–279.

Rapp, D. N., van den Broek, P., McMaster, K., Kendeou, P., & Espin, C. A. (2007). Higher-order comprehension processes in struggling readers: A perspective for research and intervention. *Scientific Studies of Reading*, *11*(4), 389–312.

Reynolds, A. J., Temple, J. A., Robertson, D. L., & Mann, E. A. (2002). Age 21 cost-benefit analysis of the Title I Chicago child-parent centers. *Educational Evaluation and Policy Analysis*, *24*(4), 267–303.

Shaywitz, B. A., Shaywitz, S. E., Pugh, K. R., Mencl, W. E., Fulbright, R. K., Skudlarksi, P., et al. (2002). Disruption of posterior brain systems for reading in children with developmental dyslexia. *Biological Psychiatry*, *52*, 101–110.

Silvia, P. (2003). Self-efficacy and interest: Experimental studies of optimal incompetence. *Journal of Vocational Behavior*, *62*, 237–249.

Snow, C. E. (2001). *Reading for Understanding*. Santa Monica, CA: RAND Education and the Science and Technology Policy Institute.

Whitehurst, G. J., Falco, F. L., Lonigan, C. J., Fischel, J. E., DeBaryshe, B. D., Valdez-Menchaca, M. C., et al. (1988). Accelerating language development through picture book reading. *Developmental Psychology*, *24*(4), 552–559.

Yoshikawa, H., & Hsueh, J. (2001). Child development and public policy: Toward a dynamic systems perspective. *Child Development*, *72*(6), 1887–1903.

Zimmerman, B. J. (1990). Self-regulated academic learning and achievement: The emergence of a social cognitive perspective. *Educational Psychology Review*, *2*, 173–201.

Chapter 2

Behavioral and Molecular Genetic Influences on Reading-Related Outcomes

Callie W. Little, Frances Wang, and Sara A. Hart

Reading comprehension is a multifaced construct that can be described as the ability to understand and employ text for learning (Cain & Oakhill, 2009). As the definition suggests, reading comprehension is an extremely valuable skill that not only must *be learned* but is also necessary in order for individuals *to learn*. Reading comprehension is inextricably tied to success in school and adequate functioning in today's society (Alfassi, 2004). Elucidating the etiology of processes driving the development of reading comprehension, such as genetics, can inform the implementation of more effective instructional and preventive interventions.

Reading comprehension is composed both of cognitive sub-processes such as executive functioning and working memory and several interdependent component reading skills that interact dynamically in the production of proficient reading comprehension abilities (Cutting, Materek, Cole, Levine, & Mahone, 2009; Sesma, Mahone, Levine, Eason, & Cutting, 2009). Component reading skills of reading comprehension most commonly studied include, decoding and phonological awareness, reading fluency, and vocabulary (Cain & Oakhill, 2009; de Jong & van der Leij, 2002; Kim, Wagner, & Foster, 2011; Quinn, Wagner, Petscher, & Lopez, 2014). Decoding and phonological awareness involve accurately mapping orthographic (written) representations of words onto their phonological (sound) counterparts (Hanna, 1965) and reading fluency is the ability to quickly decode text at both the word and passage level (Fuchs, Fuchs, Hosp, & Jenkins, 2001). In addition to knowledge of how to quickly and accurately decode text, comprehension of text relies on understanding the meanings of words and phrases (Beck, Perfetti, & McKeown, 1982). Skilled comprehenders on average display greater competencies in reading component skills and these component skills have been used to consistently predict reading comprehension ability (Kendeou, van den Broek, White, & Lynch, 2009; Kim, Petscher, Schatschneider, & Foorman, 2010; Priya, 2009). These component skills and reading comprehension will be collectively referred to as reading or reading skills within this chapter, unless explicitly labeled for purposes of discussing etiological influences on individual components of reading.

Multiple processes contribute to the etiology and development of reading, one of which is genetic influences. In fact, behavior genetic studies demonstrate that genetic influences on reading comprehension and its component skills generally account for about 50 percent of the variance in children's reading skills (e.g., Betjemann, et al., 2008; Byrne, et al., 2009; Harlaar, et al., 2010; Petrill, et al., 2007; Oliver & Plomin, 2007; Taylor, Roehrig, Hensler, Connor, & Schatschneider, 2010). Furthermore, specific genes have been identified that are significantly associated with reading (Grigorenko, 2013). This work demonstrates the substantial role that genetic influences play in reading development and highlights the importance of further exploring nuances in this relation. The purpose of this chapter is to review the behavioral and molecular genetic literature pertaining to the etiology and development of reading.

Behavioral Genetics Perspective

Behavioral genetic studies examine the genetic and environmental influences on outcomes by comparing family members of differing genetic relatedness (Neale & Cardon, 1992). One of the most common ways of doing so is to compare monozygotic (MZ) twins, who share 100 percent of their segregating genetic material, to dizygotic (DZ) twins, who share approximately 50 percent of their segregating genetic material. If MZ twins are more similar than DZ twins on a particular outcome, additive genetic influences, labeled heritability (h^2), are assumed. Alternatively, if MZ twins are less than two times as similar as DZ twins are on a particular outcome, shared environmental (c^2) influences are inferred. Shared environmental influences are those factors that make siblings more similar to each other, such as attending the same school and growing up in the same home. Lastly, to the extent to which MZ twins are not the same on a particular trait, non-shared environmental influences can be inferred (plus error; e^2). Non-shared environmental influences include factors that make siblings less similar to each other, such as having different friends or being in different classrooms.

As stated earlier, behavioral genetic studies have revealed that on average 50 percent of the variation in reading skills is accounted for by genetic influences (e.g., Betjemann, et al., 2008; Byrne, et al., 2009; Harlaar, et al., 2010; Oliver & Plomin, 2007; Petrill, et al., 2007; Taylor, et al., 2010). Genetic influences on reading may act either in a *generalist* fashion, in which the same genes are influencing multiple traits following the "generalist genes" hypothesis (Plomin & Kovas, 2005), or *uniquely*, in which different genes are enacting influences on separate traits or through both common and unique genetic influences.

Under the generalist genes hypothesis, common genes influence reading skills across the continuum of ability, suggesting that there are genetic influences on the component skills of reading comprehension, and, importantly, that these genetic influences are the same across the skills. Generalist genetic influences can also impact general cognitive skills associated with reading (e.g., executive functioning or working memory; Plomin & Kovas, 2005). Univariate behavior genetic analyses can decompose the variance of a single trait of interest into genetic and environmental influences. Following univariate analyses, multivariate behavior genetic analyses can partition the variance of multiple traits into genetic and environmental influences that overlap between the traits as well as genetic and environmental influences, which are specific to individual traits. Generalist genetic influences are thought to be present when overlapping genetic influences are found across traits. Genetically sensitive analyses of decoding and phonological awareness have found univariate heritability estimates ranging from .19–.84 in samples of elementary aged children (Betjemann, et al., 2008; Byrne, et al., 2002, 2007, 2008; Harlaar, Kovas, Dale, Petrill, & Plomin, 2012; Petrill, Deater-Deckard, Thompson, DeThorne, & Schatschneider, 2006). Similarly, previous genetic studies examining reading fluency (h^2 = .29–.82) have found a range of heritability estimates that is moderate to large and significant (Betjemann, et al., 2008; Byrne, et al., 2007; Hart, Petrill, & Thompson, 2010; Keenan, Betjemann, Wadsworth, DeFries, & Olson, 2006; Logan, et al., 2013).

For vocabulary, heritability estimates are slightly smaller, but range from small to large and are significant across samples from approximately 4 to 10 years of age (h^2=.12–.44; Byrne, et al., 2009; Hart, et al., 2009; Hayiou-Thomas, et al., 2006; Olson, et al., 2011; Spinath, Price, Dale, & Plomin, 2004). Reading comprehension estimates of heritability range from .32 to .82 across behavior genetics literature (Betjemann, et al., 2008; Byrne, et al., 2007; Hart, et al., 2010; Keenan, et al., 2006; Logan, et al., 2013). The average heritability for reading comprehension and its component skills further supports the large role that genetics play in reading and reading development. In addition, multivariate analyses have revealed significant overlapping genetic influences between decoding, fluency, vocabulary, and reading comprehension, suggesting generalist genetic influences among reading skills (Betjemann, et al., 2008; Byrne, et al., 2002, 2007, 2008; Harlaar, et al., 2012; Hart, et al., 2010; Keenan, et al., 2006, 2008; Petrill, et al., 2006). However, each of the reading skills examined through multivariate models also demonstrated influences from unique genetic sources after accounting for overlapping genetic influences. The presence of unique genetic influences indicates that reading skills, while highly related, are separable components subject to being differentially impacted. These studies provide an important jumping-off point for the field—they indicate that genetic influences are necessary to study in order to elucidate the etiology of reading skills and in what manner etiological influences determine how these skills develop or co-develop over time. By the same token, because genetic influences do not account for *all of the* variance in reading, these studies also demonstrate that shared environmental and non-shared environmental influences must also be considered. Indeed, one strength of behavioral genetic studies is in their ability to *tease apart* genetic from environmental influences as well as to elucidate the interactive influences between the two.

A large literature on this topic has burgeoned and provided vast insights into *how* and *for whom* genetic influences are important. Some of these new insights include, but are not limited to how: (a) genetic influences vary with development and (b) the environment and gene-by-environment interactions play a role in the development of reading comprehension skills. Each of these topics will be discussed in the following sections.

Genetic Influences Vary with Development

Learning to read relies on receiving direct instruction of the basic rules and processes, and as such reading skills are largely acquired during the school-age years when children have access to regular classroom instruction. Because dynamic biological and environmental changes occur during this time period, it is important to consider whether genetic and environmental influences on reading comprehension similarly demonstrate fluctuations as a result of development. Interestingly, studies show that genetic influences on various indices of reading comprehension, such as decoding and fluency, are quite stable from childhood through adolescence (Betjemann, et al., 2008; Harlaar, Dale, & Plomin, 2007a). That is, the same genetic influences that influence reading abilities for children appear to influence reading abilities for adolescents. Although these influences have been found to be quite stable, there is also evidence to suggest that reading is less heritable prior to the beginning of formal schooling and stabilizes after the beginning of formal schooling (Byrne, et al., 2009).

Furthermore, it might be expected that age-related differences in the heritability of certain reading skills would be observed, especially given the vast differences in cognitive and reading development with age. For instance, as children mature, successful reading likely involves the integration of more complex skills such as inference making, metacognitive knowledge and monitoring (Oakhill & Cain, 2003); these skills might be driven by new genetic influences not observed in younger children. Although age-specific genetic influences on reading-related outcomes have been found (Harlaar, Dale, & Plomin, 2007b; Hart, et al., 2013; Samuelsson, et al., 2008), other studies found no differences in the genetic influences on reading in childhood versus adolescence (Betjemann, et al., 2008; Wadsworth, Corley, Hewitt, & DeFries, 2001). While these studies have provided preliminary information about changes in reading skills over time, they have not utilized techniques that are best able to model developmental trends.

Improved methods for examining developmental fluctuations in the etiology of reading have recently been incorporated into behavior

genetics research. Latent growth curve models allow for more robust investigation of the etiological influences on growth in reading, and recent
applications of genetically sensitive latent growth models have found overlapping genetic influences between initial status and change in reading over
time (Christopher, et al., 2013a; Hart, et al., 2013; Logan, et al., 2013; Petrill,
et al., 2010a). These findings highlight the presence of stable genetic influences on reading development and provide additional evidence in support
of a generalist genes theory. Stable genetic influences across initial status
and growth can signify shared genes for reading skills or those for underlying skills related to broader cognitive functioning (Miller, Cutting, &
McCardle, 2013; Plomin & Kovas, 2005). Of equal importance is the detection of unique genetic influences on reading growth after accounting for
those that impact initial status in reading skills (Logan, et al., 2013), which
suggest that new genes are acting on reading growth above and beyond
those that influence initial reading ability. Beyond growth curve models,
behavior genetic research has also used simplex modeling to examine
incremental development of reading fluency. Simplex modeling differs
from latent growth curve modeling whereby ability status at one point in
time takes into account only the most recent previous time point rather
than all previous time points included together (Hart, et al., 2013). Findings
from this investigation were consistent with previous research indicating
stable as well as novel genetic influences on reading development in elementary grades (Hart, et al., 2013). In combination, the results of these
studies suggest that the influences of some genes on reading can have a
differential impact during different periods of development, with genes
coming "online" or going "offline" at certain times; nevertheless, there are
also some genetic influences that remain stable across the development of
reading, though it is unclear whether these genes are specific to reading
ability or whether they are shared with other cognitive abilities.

Multiple lines of behavioral genetic research in other fields (Dick, et al.,
2007; Fowler, et al., 2007; Haworth, et al., 2009; Meyers & Dick, 2010) have
demonstrated that genetic influences grow stronger with age because of
appropriate age-related increases in autonomy and niche picking (i.e., an
individual selecting an environment based on its suitability to his or her
genetic predispositions). This increase in autonomy and niche picking can
result in gene-environment covariation such that estimates of genetic
influences are magnified due to greater environmental opportunities for
genetic propensities to be expressed. Interestingly, Wadsworth, et al. (2001)
did find that genetic influences on reading performance were stronger
when participants were adolescents as opposed to when they were preado-
lescents or children. This finding suggests that the genetic influences
impacting reading performance are amplified as youth mature. This result
also reinforces the concept that niche picking and gene-environment
covariation (which may increase in prevalence with age) might play a role

in the observed magnification of genetic influences over time. Similarly, Harlaar, et al. (2007) found that genetic influences on early reading achievement predicted the extent to which children sought out reading experiences, and these reading experiences, in turn, predicted children's later reading achievement through the shared environment. Although this study did not address whether such links grew stronger with age, their findings similarly suggest that niche picking might be one important factor to consider in studying genetic influences on reading. The presence of both stable and novel genetic influences on reading development suggests that reading skills mature in a complex manner which may vary across different time points. These variations can be due to genes coming "online" or going "offline" at different points in development or due to a covariation between genetic and environmental influences such as niche picking.

Environmental Influences

Studies show that the influence of shared and non-shared environmental effects are often significant, but typically account for smaller proportions of variance compared to genetic influences. Although environmental influences exert main effects on reading skills, environmental influences also *interact* with genetic influences to predict reading skills. That is, the effects of genetic propensities can change depending on the context. For example, Taylor, et al. (2010) found that how effective the instruction children receive from their teacher (i.e., quality) moderates the influence of genetics on reading achievement. The pattern of the moderation revealed that genetic influences on reading achievement were stronger when teaching quality was high, whereas genetic influences were weaker when teaching quality was low. This finding suggested that high teaching quality may allow students' full genetic potential to be reached. Similarly, Hart, Soden, Johnson, Schatschneider, and Taylor (2013) found that genetic influences on reading comprehension were greater under conditions of lower school-level SES compared to higher school-level SES. These findings suggested that low environmental quality leads to the greatest expression of genetic predispositions. Thus, environmental contexts can influence heritability through their influence on gene expression.

Interestingly, other studies examined a similar question but focused on moderation effects at *low* reading ability and *high* reading ability (Friend, DeFries, & Olson, 2008; Friend, et al., 2009; Pennington, et al., 2009). Results suggested that genetic influences on low reading ability were higher among those whose parents had a *high* level of education and lower for those whose parents had a *low* level of education (Friend, et al., 2008), whereas for above average reading ability genetic influences were the highest among those whose parents had a *low* level of education and were the lowest among those whose parents had a *high* level of education (Friend, et al., 2009;

Pennington, et al., 2009). Thus, for children with poor environmental supports, above average reading abilities reflected a resilience more strongly influenced by genes. For children with stronger environmental supports, above average reading abilities were not as strongly influenced by genes. Instead, these children's high reading abilities were more strongly influenced by the enriching environment in which they were growing up.

Taken together, these studies illustrate the dynamic synergism that takes place between genetic and environmental influences in predicting reading-related outcomes. These findings are particularly influential because they allow researchers to more thoroughly consider how variations in environmental contexts may impact the manner in which genetic potential influences the development of reading.

Molecular Genetics of Reading and Related Phenotypes

The behavioral genetics literature has enhanced our understanding of the genetic influences on reading and other reading-related skills (phenotypes). However, these studies are informative neither of the specific genetic abnormalities involved in reading skills nor of the biological mechanisms that might mediate these relations. Understanding the molecular genetic influences of reading skills can provide greater insights into etiological mechanisms and add specificity to our knowledge of how genes interact with, influence, and are influenced by the environment. Eventually, this knowledge might allow for the early detection of children at risk for reading problems and aid in the development of interventions or medications to treat these problems.

Review of Phenotypes and Genetic Terminology

In order to better understand the literature on molecular genetics, it is important to provide an overview of the diverse phenotypes (i.e., the behavior that is observed) used across studies. Much of the work to date has focused on studying the genetic variants that relate to weaker reading skills, such as developmental dyslexia (e.g., Petryshen & Pauls, 2009). Developmental dyslexia has been defined as extreme difficulties in mastering reading or spelling skills that cannot be attributed to intelligence, socio-economic factors, other neurological conditions, or head injury (Grigorenko, 2001). However, research suggests that dyslexia might actually represent the lower end of a reading ability spectrum, rather than constitute a distinct disorder (Shaywitz, Escobar, Shaywitz, Fletcher, & Makuch, 1992). In other words, reading ability falls along a continuum that captures both low and high levels of ability, and the thresholds that currently define disordered vs. non-disordered reading are more or less arbitrary. Therefore, researchers have also examined the genetic correlates of quantitative phenotypes that capture the defining difficulties of lower reading skills, such as single-word reading or spelling tests (e.g., Fisher, et al., 2002; Scerri, et al., 2011).

In addition, researchers have examined the genetic correlates of various cognitive processes thought to underlie reading skills, such as orthographic processing, phoneme awareness, rapid automatized naming, and phonological short-term memory (Bates, et al., 2011; de Kovel, et al., 2008; Raskind, et al., 2005; Scerri, et al., 2004). These skills are some of the building blocks of reading abilities and are possible *endophenotypes* associated with lower reading skills. Endophenotypes have been defined as "measureable components unseen by the unaided eye along the pathway between disease and distal genotype ... An endophenotype may be neurophysiological, biochemical, endocrinological, neuroanatomical, cognitive, or neuropsychological (including configured self-report data) in nature" (Gottesman & Gould, 2003, p. 1). Because endophenotypes might be more directly influenced by biological and genetic processes than their associated phenotype (e.g., dyslexia), genetic variants might show stronger and/or more consistent relations with endophenotypes than with phenotypes. For these reasons, studying endophenotypes might serve to clarify the genetic underpinnings of disorders such as dyslexia, and specifically for lower ends of the reading continuum.

Finally, an explanation of some of the widely used terms in the molecular genetics literature is warranted. Deoxyribonucleic acid (DNA) is composed of repeating units called nucleotides (i.e., A, T, C, or G). A single nucleotide polymorphism (SNP) occurs when individuals vary in what specific nucleotide (i.e., A, T, C, or G) they have in the same position on the DNA sequence (rather than all individuals having the exact same nucleotide, which also occurs). Because these SNPs vary between people, it is thought that the individual differences in reading skills might be due, in part, to the individual differences of these SNPs. Much of the literature discussed in the following sections has focused on identifying the SNPs, or other similar genetic markers, important to reading skills.

Linkage and Association Studies

Genetic linkage and association studies have been the most commonly used approaches for identifying genetic variants involved in reading phenotypes. Genetic linkage studies investigate whether individuals in a family who share the same disorder also share the same ancestral DNA at a given genetic location (i.e., locus). This approach operates under the assumption that, for example, two relatives who both have reading disability should have inherited the same DNA segment from a common ancestor, and this DNA segment may contain a genetic marker for reading disability.

Linkage studies have identified nine possible genetic loci involved in reading skills, called *DYX1* through *DYX9*. Among some of the phenotypes that have been found to be associated with these loci include specific language impairment (see Chapter 6), as well as weakness in regular word spelling, phonemic decoding efficiency, reading of irregular words, phonological and orthographic coding, and overall reading performance (see Carrion-Castillo, et al., 2013, for more details). Some of these loci have shown similar relations to reading skills across studies (e.g., *DYX1–3*) but not all have been well studied, and more research is needed (e.g., *DYX4–9*). (For a comprehensive review of the genetic linkage literature, refer to Carrion-Castillo, et al. (2013) and Petryshen & Pauls (2009).)

Genetic association studies examine whether genetic markers occur at different frequencies across differing levels of a phenotype, such as along the continuum of reading skills. The SNPs that are located within the reading disability susceptibility 1 candidate gene 1 (*DYX1C1*) are some of the most studied genetic markers for reading disability using association study methods. The gene was first identified through the study of a Finnish family in which many of the members had reading problems (Nopola-Hemmi, et al., 2000). However, findings are mixed. Some studies reported associations between the SNPs of this gene and reading disability, orthographic choice tasks, and quantitative measures of reading-related traits (e.g. Bates, et al, 2010; Brkanac, et al., 2007; Paracchini, et al., 2011; Scerri, et al., 2004; Taipale, et al., 2003; Wigg, et al., 2004). Conversely, other studies found no association between these SNPs and low reading skills (Bellini, et al., 2005; Cope, et al., 2004; Marino, et al., 2005; Meng, et al., 2005). Moreover, two meta-analyses concluded that there was little or no evidence that these SNPs were associated with low reading skills (Tran, et al., 2013; Zou, et al., 2012).

The doublecortin domain-containing protein 2 (*DCDC2*) gene is located in the *DYX2* region. Similar to the *DYX1C1* gene, some studies have found that *DCDC2* SNPs including rs807724, rs793862, rs807701, and other genetic markers, such as BV677278, are associated with lower levels of reading skills, a homonym choice task, quantitative measures of reading, reading fluency, and nonsense word repetition (Marino, et al., 2012; Meng, et al., 2005; Newbury, et al., 2011; Scerri, et al., 2011; Schumacher, et al., 2006). However, other studies found no association between variants in this gene and low reading skills (Brkanac, et al., 2007; Venkatesh, et al., 2013; Zuo, et al., 2012). A recent meta-analysis which investigated the roles of rs807724, rs793862, rs807701, rs1087266, and BV677278 on low reading skills found that rs807701 was the only marker significantly associated with deficits in reading.

The *KIAA0319* gene is located on the same chromosome as *DCDC2*. Several studies have also shown an association between SNPs within this gene and reading skills (Cope, et al., 2005; Francks, et al., 2004; Newbury, et al., 2011; Paracchini, et al., 2008; Rice, Smith, & Gayán, 2009). However, others did not find an association between variants in this gene and low reading skills (Brkanac, et al., 2007; Ludwig, et al., 2008; Schumacher, et al., 2006). Despite the mixed findings in the literature, a meta-analysis demonstrated that the *KIAA0319* SNP, rs4504469, was significantly associated with low reading skills (Zou, et al., 2012).

Other genes have also been implicated in reading-related phenotypes, but will not be discussed in the current review (for a comprehensive review of some of the other genes and of the genes reviewed earlier, refer to Carrion-Castillo, et al. 2013; Petryshen & Pauls, 2009; and Scerri & Schulte-Körne, 2010). As is evident by the brief review of the candidate gene literature, the replication of findings across studies has been difficult. This may be due to the fact that reading is a complex trait that is not influenced by one genetic variant with large effects (e.g., phenylketonuria, PKU) but instead is influenced by many genetic variants with very small effects, called polygenic inheritance (Hulme & Snowling, 2009). Interestingly, this finding supports the view that reading disability might simply represent the lower tail of reading ability as a whole, and, therefore, may be a quantitative, or continuous, trait rather than a categorical disorder. This is because traits that are influenced by polygenic inheritance tend to be continuous and normally distributed (e.g., Wahlsten, 2012). Reading skills do indeed follow a normal distribution. Despite the difficulty in finding specific genes related to reading skills, the molecular genetic literature has proven useful in understanding the biological underpinnings associated with low reading skills. For example, Poelmans, Buitelaar, Pauls, and Franke (2011) found that 10 of 14 reading candidate genes fit into a theoretical molecular network. Specifically, they found that these 10 genes (i.e., *DCDC2, DYX1C1, KIAA0319, KIAA0319L, ROBO1, S100B, DOCK4, FMR1, DIP2A, GTF2I*) all encode proteins that are directly or indirectly involved in neuronal migration and/or the directed outgrowth of axons. Therefore, this theoretical molecular network is consistent with the idea that the biological underpinnings associated with reading deficits are also associated with neuronal migration (Galaburda, 2005).

In addition to the effects of SNPs on reading-related outcomes, whose effect sizes are very small, other molecular genetic variations and processes effect biological functioning and, therefore, likely have an influence over reading levels. However, many of these other methods are in their infancy and have not yet been rigorously applied in the study of reading phenotypes. Some future avenues of research that may prove fruitful in the study of reading include examining the effects of functional conserved noncoding sequences, functional human nonprotein-coding RNAs, and epigenetic mechanisms on reading skills (see Grigorenko, 2013).

Many candidate genes studies have focused on discovering genetic variation whose influence is specific to weaker reading skills. However, it is also likely that genetic variation contributing to other cognitive functional processes such as attention, working memory, and intelligence, play a role in the variation in reading ability. As an example, the *COMT Val158met* genetic marker is functionally tied to dopamine functioning and has been associated with executive functioning (Giakoumaki, Roussos, & Bitsios, 2008). Grigorenko, et al. (2007) found that this genetic marker had a significant main effect on reading comprehension, which likely reflects the fact that executive functioning influences reading comprehension (see Chapter 5). Furthermore, this genetic marker interacted with maternal rejection to predict reading comprehension. The *COMT* genetic marker had a stronger influence on reading comprehension for individuals with higher levels of maternal rejection compared to individuals with lower levels of maternal rejection. Results from this study suggest that examining genetic markers involved in the development of reading-related cognitive abilities might be important in enhancing our understanding of the genetic basis of reading. Furthermore, genetic influences on reading might be stronger or only present under certain environmental conditions, and, therefore, must be considered within a broader environmental context.

Conclusion

The important contributions that reading skills lend to lifelong success make the development of reading a crucial process to understand. Behavior genetic studies are able to provide insights into the etiology of reading through several methods, which have been highlighted in this chapter. Conclusions from behavior genetics literature support the importance of genetic contributions to reading, but also provide a more in-depth understanding of how genetic influences may vary due to different developmental time periods or different environmental contexts. Additionally, molecular genetic studies are able to further explain the genetic mechanisms that influence reading by identifying and assessing the frequency of genetic correlates of reading skills across reading levels. In general, while these findings need to be interpreted carefully and cautiously, outcomes from behavior and molecular genetic research provide information that researchers and practitioners can use to think about the ways in which instruction, home, school, and neighborhood environments can influence or be influenced by our genetic makeup and how these influences impact reading development and related skills.

References

Alfassi, M. (2004). Reading to learn: Effects of combined strategy instruction on high school students. *Journal of Educational Research*, *97*(4), 171–185.

August, G. J., & Garfinkel, B. D. (1990). Comorbidity of ADHD and reading disability among clinic-referred children. *Journal of Abnormal Child Psychology*, *18*(1), 29–45.

Badian, N. (1983). Dyscalculia and nonverbal disorders of learning. In H. Myklebust (Ed.), *Progress in Learning Disabilities*. New York: Grune & Stratton.

Bates, T. C., Lind, P. A., Luciano, M., Montgomery, G. W., Martin, N. G., & Wright, M. J. (2010). Dyslexia and DYX1C1: deficits in reading and spelling associated with a missense mutation. *Molecular Psychiatry, 15*(12), 1190–1196.

Bates, T. C., Luciano, M., Medland, S. E., Montgomery, G. W., Wright, M. J., & Martin, N. G. (2011). Genetic variance in a component of the language acquisition device: ROBO1 polymorphisms associated with phonological buffer deficits. *Behavior Genetics, 41*(1), 50–57.

Beck, I. L., Perfetti, C. A., & McKeown, M. G. (1982). Effects of long-term vocabulary instruction on lexical access and reading comprehension. *Journal of Educational Psychology, 74*, 506–521.

Bellini, G., Bravaccio, C., Calamoneri, F., Cocuzza, M. D., Fiorillo, P., Gagliano, A., et al. (2005). No evidence for association between dyslexia and DYX1C1 functional variants in a group of children and adolescents from Southern Italy. *Journal of Molecular Neuroscience, 27*(3), 311–314.

Betjemann, R. S., Willcutt, E. G., Olson, R. K., Keenan, J. M., DeFries, J. C., & Wadsworth, S. J. (2008). Word reading and reading comprehension: stability, overlap and independence. *Reading and Writing, 21*(5), 539–558.

Brkanac, Z., Chapman, N. H., Matsushita, M. M., Chun, L., Nielsen, K., Cochrane, E., et al. (2007). Evaluation of candidate genes for DYX1 and DYX2 in families with dyslexia. *American Journal of Medical Genetics Part B: Neuropsychiatric Genetics, 144*(4), 556–560.

Byrne, B., Coventry, W. L., Olson, R. K., Hulslander, J., Wadsworth, S., DeFries, J. C., et al. (2008). A behaviour-genetic analysis of orthographic learning, spelling and decoding. *Journal of Research in Reading, 31*(1), 8–21.

Byrne, B., Coventry, W. L., Olson, R. K., Samuelsson, S., Corley, R., Willcutt, E. G., et al. (2009). Genetic and environmental influences on aspects of literacy and language in early childhood: Continuity and change from preschool to Grade 2. *Journal of Neurolinguistics, 22*(3), 219–236.

Byrne, B., Coventry, W. L., Olson, R. K., Wadsworth, S. J., Samuelsson, S., Petrill, S. A., et al. (2010). "Teacher effects" in early literacy development: Evidence from a study of twins. *Journal of Educational Psychology, 102*(1), 32.

Byrne, B., Delaland, C., Fielding-Barnsley, R., Quain, P., Samuelsson, S., Hoien, T., et al. (2002). Longitudinal twin study of early reading development in three countries: Preliminary results. *Annals of Dyslexia, 52*, 49–73.

Byrne, B., Samuelsson, S., Wadsworth, S., Hulslander, J., Corley, R., Defries, J. C., et al. (2007). Longitudinal twin study of early literacy development: Preschool through grade 1. *Reading and Writing, 20*(1–2), 77–102.

Cain, K., & Oakhill, J. (2009). Reading comprehension development from 8 to 14 years: The contribution of component skills and processes. In R. K. Wagner, C. Schatschneider, & C. Phythian-Sence (Eds.), *Beyond Decoding. The Behavioral and Biological Foundations of Reading Comprehension.* New York: Guilford Press.

Carrion-Castillo, A., Franke, B., & Fisher, S. E. (2013). Molecular genetics of dyslexia: An overview. *Dyslexia, 19*(4), 214–240.

Christopher, M. E., Hulslander, J., Byrne, B., Samuelsson, S., Keenan, J. M., Pennington, B., et al. (2013a). Modeling the etiology of individual differences in early reading development: Evidence for strong genetic influences. *Scientific Studies of Reading, 17*(5), 350–368.

Cope, N. A., Hill, G., Van Den Bree, M., Harold, D., Moskvina, V., Green, E. K., et al. (2004). No support for association between dyslexia susceptibility 1 candidate 1 and developmental dyslexia. *Molecular Psychiatry, 10*(3), 237–238.

Cope, N., Harold, D., Hill, G., Moskvina, V., Stevenson, J., Holmans, P., et al. (2005). Strong evidence that *KIAA0319* on chromosome 6p is a susceptibility gene for developmental dyslexia. *American Journal of Human Genetics, 76*(4), 581–591.

Cutting, L. E., Materek, A., Cole, C. A., Levine, T. M., & Mahone, E. M. (2009). Effects of fluency, oral language, and executive function on reading comprehension performance. *Annals of Dyslexia, 59*(1), 34–54.

Darki, F., Peyrard-Janvid, M., Matsson, H., Kere, J., & Klingberg, T. (2012). Three dyslexia susceptibility genes, *DYX1C1, DCDC2,* and *KIAA0319,* affect temporo-parietal white matter structure. *Biological Psychiatry, 72*(8), 671–676.

DeFries, J. C., & Gillis, J. J. (1993) Genetics of reading disability. In R. Plomin & G. E. McClearn (Eds.), *Nature Nurture and Psychology.* Washington, DC: American Psychological Association.

DeFries, J. C., & Light, J. G. (1996). Twin studies of reading disability. In J. H. Beitchman, N. J. Cohen, M. M. Konstantareas, & R. Tannock (Eds.), *Language, Learning, and Behavior Disorders: Developmental, Biological, and Clinical Perspectives.* New York: Cambridge University Press.

de Jong, P. F., & van der Leij, A. (2002). Effects of phonological abilities and linguistic comprehension on the development of reading. *Scientific Studies of Reading, 6*(1), 51–77.

de Kovel, C. G., Franke, B., Hol, F. A., Lebrec, J. J., Maassen, B., Brunner, H., et al. (2008). Confirmation of dyslexia susceptibility loci on chromosomes 1p and 2p, but not 6p in a Dutch sib-pair collection. *American Journal of Medical Genetics Part B: Neuropsychiatric Genetics, 147*(3), 294–300.

Dick, D. M., Pagan, J. L., Viken, R., Purcell, S., Kaprio, J., Pulkkinen, L., et al. (2007). Changing environmental influences on substance use across adolescence. *Twin Research and Human Genetics, 10,* 315–326.

Fisher, S. E., Francks, C., Marlow, A. J., MacPhie, I. L., Newbury, D. F., Cardon, L. R., et al. (2002). Independent genome-wide scans identify a chromosome 18 quantitative-trait locus influencing dyslexia. *Nature Genetics, 30*(1), 86–91.

Francks, C., Paracchini, S., Smith, S. D., Richardson, A. J., Scerri, T. S., Cardon, L. R., et al. (2004). A 77-kilobase region of chromosome 6p22. 2 is associated with dyslexia in families from the United Kingdom and from the United States. *American Journal of Human Genetics, 75*(6), 1046–1058.

Friend, A., DeFries, J. C., & Olson, R. K. (2008). Parental education moderates genetic influences on reading disability. *Psychological Science, 19*(11), 1124–1130.

Friend, A., DeFries, J. C., Olson, R. K., Pennington, B., Harlaar, N., Byrne, B., et al. M. (2009). Heritability of high reading ability and its interaction with parental education. *Behavior Genetics, 39*(4), 427–436.

Finucci, J. M., & Childs, B. (1981) Are there really more dyslexic boys than girls? In A. Ansara, N. Geschwind, A. Galaburda, M. Albert, & N. Gartrell (Eds.), *Sex Differences in Dyslexia.* Towson, MD: Orton Dyslexia Society.

Flynn, J. M., & Rahbar, M. H. (1994). Prevalence of reading failure in boys compared with girls. *Psychology in the Schools, 31,* 66–71.

Fowler, T., Lifford, K., Shelton, K., Rice, F., Thapar, A., Neale, M. C., et al. (2007). Exploring the relationship between genetic and environmental influences on initiation and progression of substance use. *Addiction, 102*, 413–422.

Fuchs, L. S., Fuchs, D., Hosp, M. K., & Jenkins, J. R. (2001). Oral reading fluency as an indicator of reading competence: A theoretical, empirical, and historical analysis. *Scientific Studies of Reading, 5*(3), 239–256.

Galaburda, A. M. (2005). Dyslexia—a molecular disorder of neuronal migration. *Annals of Dyslexia, 55*(2), 151–165.

Giakoumaki, S. G., Roussos, P., & Bitsios, P. (2008). Improvement of prepulse inhibition and executive function by the COMT inhibitor tolcapone depends on COMT Val158Met polymorphism. *Neuropsychopharmacology, 33*(13), 3058–3068.

Gottesman, I. I., & Gould, T. D. (2003). The endophenotype concept in psychiatry: Etymology and strategic intentions. *American Journal of Psychiatry, 160*(4), 636–645.

Grigorenko, E. L. (2001). Developmental dyslexia: An update on genes, brains, and environments. *Journal of Child Psychology and Psychiatry, 42*(1), 91–125.

Grigorenko, E. L. (2013). What we know (or do not know) about the genetics of reading comprehension and other reading-related processes. In B. Miller, L. Cutting, L., & P. McCardle (Eds.), *Unraveling Reading Comprehension*. Baltimore, MD: Paul H. Brookes.

Grigorenko, E. L., Deyoung, C. G., Getchell, M., Haeffel, G. J., Klinteberg, B. A., Koposov, R. A., et al. (2007). Exploring interactive effects of genes and environments in etiology of individual differences in reading comprehension. *Development and Psychopathology, 19*(4), 1089.

Hanna, P. R. (1965). Phoneme-grapheme correspondences as cues to spelling improvement. *Research in the Teaching of English, 1*(2), 201–223.

Harlaar, N., Cutting, L., Deater-Deckard, K., DeThorne, L. S., Justice, L. M., Schatschneider, C., et al. (2010). Predicting individual differences in reading comprehension: A twin study. *Annals of Dyslexia, 60*(2), 265–288.

Harlaar, N., Dale, P. S., & Plomin, R. (2007a). From learning to read to reading to learn: Substantial and stable genetic influence. *Child Development, 78*(1), 116–131.

Harlaar, N., Dale, P. S., & Plomin, R. (2007b). Reading exposure: A (largely) environmental risk factor with environmentally-mediated effects on reading performance in the primary school years. *Journal of Child Psychology and Psychiatry, 48*(12), 1192–1199.

Harlaar, N., Kovas, Y., Dale, P. S., Petrill, S. A., & Plomin, R. (2012). Mathematics is differentially related to reading comprehension and word decoding: Evidence from a genetically sensitive design. *Journal of Educational Psychology, 104*(3), 622.

Harlaar, N., Spinath, F. M., Dale, P. S., & Plomin, R. (2005). Genetic influences on early word recognition abilities and disabilities: A study of 7-year-old twins. *Journal of Child Psychology and Psychiatry, 46*(4), 373–384.

Hart, S. A., Logan, J. A., Soden-Hensler, B., Kershaw, S., Taylor, J., & Schatschneider, C. (2013). Exploring how nature and nurture affect the development of reading: An analysis of the Florida twin project on reading. *Developmental Psychology, 49*, 1971–1981.

Hart, S. A., Petrill, S. A., DeThorne, L. S., Deater-Deckard, K., Thompson, L. A., Schatschneider, C., et al. (2009). Environmental influences on the longitudinal covariance of expressive vocabulary: Measuring the home literacy environment in a genetically sensitive design. *Journal of Child Psychology and Psychiatry, 50,* 911–919.

Hart, S. A., Petrill, S. A., & Thompson, L. A. (2010). A factorial analysis of timed and untimed measures of mathematics and reading abilities in school aged twins. *Learning and Individual Differences, 20*(2), 63–69.

Hart, S. A., Petrill, S. A., Thompson, L. A., & Plomin, R. (2009). The ABCs of math: A genetic analysis of mathematics and its links with reading ability and general cognitive ability. *Journal of Educational Psychology, 101,* 388–405.

Hart, S. A., Soden, B., Johnson, W., Schatschneider, C., & Taylor, J. (2013). Expanding the environment: gene × school-level SES interaction on reading comprehension. *Journal of Child Psychology and Psychiatry, 54,* 1047–1055.

Haworth, C. M. A., Wright, M. J., Martin, N. W., Martin, N. G., Boomsma, D. I., Bartels, M., et al. (2009). A twin study of the genetics of high cognitive ability selected from 11,000 twin pairs in six studies from four countries. *Behavior Genetics, 39*(4), 359–370.

Hayiou-Thomas, M. E., Kovas, Y., Harlaar, N., Plomin, R., Bishop, D. V. M., & Dale, P. S. (2006). Common aetiology for diverse language skills in 4 1/2-year-old twins. *Journal of Child Language, 33*(2), 339–368.

Hulme, C., & Snowling, M. J. (2009). *Developmental Disorders of Language Learning and Cognition.* New York: John Wiley & Sons.

Keenan, J. M., Betjemann, R. S., & Olson, R. K. (2008). Reading comprehension tests vary in the skills they assess: Differential dependence on decoding and oral comprehension. *Scientific Studies of Reading, 12*(3), 281–300.

Keenan, J. M., Betjemann, R. S., Wadsworth, S. J., DeFries, J. C., & Olson, R. K. (2006). Genetic and environmental influences on reading and listening comprehension. *Special Issue: Reading and Genetics, 29*(1), 75–91.

Kendeou, P., van den Broek, P., White, M. J., & Lynch, J. S. (2009). Predicting reading comprehension in early elementary school: The independent contributions of oral language and decoding skills. *Journal of Educational Psychology, 101*(4), 765–778.

Kim, Y.-S., Petscher, Y., Schatschneider, C., & Foorman, B. (2010). Does growth rate in oral reading fluency matter in predicting reading comprehension achievement? *Journal of Educational Psychology, 102*(3), 652.

Kim, Y.-S., Wagner, R. K., & Foster, E. (2011). Relations among oral reading fluency, silent reading fluency, and reading comprehension: A latent variable study of first-grade readers. *Scientific Studies of Reading, 15*(4), 338–362.

Knopik, V. S., Alarcón, M., & DeFries, J. C. (1998). Common and specific gender influences on individual differences in reading performance: A twin study. *Personality and Individual Differences, 25*(2), 269–277.

Kovas, Y., Haworth, C. M. A., Harlaar, N., Petrill, S. A., Dale, P. S., & Plomin, R. (2007). Overlap and specificity of genetic and environmental influences on mathematics and reading disability in 10-year-old twins. *Journal of Child Psychology and Psychiatry, 48*(9), 914–922.

Light, J. G., & DeFries, J. C. (1995). Comorbidity of reading and mathematics disabilities: Genetic and environmental etiologies. *Journal of Learning Disabilities, 28*(2), 96–106.

Logan, J. A., Hart, S. A., Cutting, L., Deater-Deckard, K., Schatschneider, C., & Petrill, S. (2013). Reading development in young children: Genetic and environmental influences. *Child Development, 84*(6), 2131–2144.

Ludwig, K. U., Roeske, D., Schumacher, J., Schulte-Körne, G., König, I. R., Warnke, A., et al. (2008). Investigation of interaction between DCDC2 and KIAA0319 in a large German dyslexia sample. *Journal of Neural Transmission, 115*(11), 1587–1589.

Marino, C., Giorda, R., Lorusso, M. L., Vanzin, L., Salandi, N., Nobile, M., et al. (2005). A family-based association study does not support DYX1C1 on 15q21. 3 as a candidate gene in developmental dyslexia. *European Journal of Human Genetics, 13*(4), 491–499.

Marino, C., Meng, H., Mascheretti, S., Rusconi, M., Cope, N., Giorda, R., et al. (2012). DCDC2 genetic variants and susceptibility to developmental dyslexia. *Psychiatric Genetics, 22*(1), 25.

Meaburn, E. L., Harlaar, N., Craig, I. W., Schalkwyk, L. C., & Plomin, R. (2007). Quantitative trait locus association scan of early reading disability and ability using pooled DNA and 100K SNP microarrays in a sample of 5760 children. *Molecular Psychiatry, 13*(7), 729–740.

Meng, H., Hager, K., Held, M., Page, G. P., Olson, R. K., Pennington, B. F., et al. (2005). TDT-association analysis of EKN1 and dyslexia in a Colorado twin cohort. *Human Genetics, 118*(1), 87–90.

Meyers, J. S., & Dick, D. M. (2010). Genetic and environmental risk factors for adolescent-onset substance use disorders. *Child and Adolescent Psychiatric Clinics of North America, 19*, 465–477.

Miller, B., Cutting, L., & McCardle, P. (Eds.). (2013) *Unraveling Reading Comprehension.* Baltimore, MD: Paul H. Brookes.

Naiden, N. (1976). Ratio of boys to girls among disabled readers. *Reading Teacher, 92*, 432–442.

Nass, R. (1993). Sex differences in learning abilities and disabilities. *Annals of Dyslexia, 43*, 61–77.

Neale, M., & Cardon, L. (1992). *Methodology for Genetic Studies of Twins and Families.* Dordrecht: Kluwer Academic.

Newbury, D. F., Paracchini, S., Scerri, T. S., Winchester, L., Addis, L., Richardson, A. J., et al. (2011). Investigation of dyslexia and SLI risk variants in reading- and language-impaired subjects. *Behavior Genetics, 41*(1), 90–104.

Nopola-Hemmi, J., Taipale, M., Haltia, T., Lehesjoki, A. E., Voutilainen, A., & Kere, J. (2000). Two translocations of chromosome 15q associated with dyslexia. *Journal of Medical Genetics, 37*(10), 771–775.

Oakhill, J., & Cain, K. (2003). The development of comprehension skills. In T. Nunes & P. Bryant (Eds.), *Handbook of Children's Literacy.* Dordrecht: Kluwer Academic.

Oliver, B. R., & Plomin, R. (2007). Twins' early development study (TEDS): A multivariate, longitudinal genetic investigation of language, cognition and behavior problems from childhood through adolescence. *Twin Research and Human Genetics, 10*(1), 96–105.

Olson, R. K., Datta, H., Gayan, J., & DeFries, J. C. (in press). A behavioral-genetic analysis of reading disabilities and component processes. In R. M. Klein & R. A. McMullen (Eds.), *Converging Methods for Understanding Reading and Dyslexia.* Cambridge, MA: MIT Press.

Olson, R. K., Keenan, J. M., Byrne, B., Samuelsson, S., Coventry, W. L., Corley, R., et al. (2011). Genetic and environmental influences on vocabulary and reading development. *Scientific Studies of Reading, 15*(1), 26–46.

Olson, R. K., Rack, J. P., Conners, F. A., DeFries, J. C., & Fulker, D. W. (1991). Genetic etiology of individual differences in reading disability. In L. V. Feagans, E. J. Short, & L. J. Meltzer (Eds.), *Subtypes of Learning Disabilities: Theoretical Perspectives and Research*. Hillsdale, NJ: Erlbaum.

Paracchini, S., Ang, Q. W., Stanley, F. J., Monaco, A. P., Pennell, C. E., & Whitehouse, A. J. O. (2011). Analysis of dyslexia candidate genes in the Raine cohort representing the general Australian population. *Genes, Brain and Behavior*, *10*(2), 158–165.

Paracchini, S., Steer, C., Buckingham, L. L., Morris, A., Ring, S., Scerri, T., et al. (2008). Association of the KIAA0319 dyslexia susceptibility gene with reading skills in the general population. *American Journal of Psychiatry*, *165*(12), 1576–1584.

Paracchini, S., Thomas, A., Castro, S., Lai, C., Paramasivam, M., Wang, Y., et al. (2006). The chromosome 6p22 haplotype associated with dyslexia reduces the expression of KIAA0319, a novel gene involved in neuronal migration. *Human Molecular Genetics*, *15*(10), 1659–1666.

Pennington, B. F., & Bishop, D. V. (2009). Relations among speech, language, and reading disorders. *Annual Review of Psychology*, *60*, 283–306.

Pennington, B. F., McGrath, L. M., Rosenberg, J., Barnard, H., Smith, S. D., Willcutt, E. G., et al. (2009). Gene × environment interactions in reading disability and attention-deficit/hyperactivity disorder. *Developmental Psychology*, *45*(1), 77.

Petrill, S. A. (2013). Related reading comprehension to language and broader reading skills: A behavioral genetics approach. In B. Miller, L. Cutting, & P. McCardle (Eds.), *Unraveling Reading Comprehension*. Baltimore, MD: Paul H. Brookes.

Petrill, S. A., Deater-Deckard, K., Schatschneider, C., & Davis, C. (2005). Measured environmental influences on early reading: Evidence from an adoption study. *Scientific Studies of Reading*, *9*(3), 237–259.

Petrill, S. A., Deater-Deckard, K., Thompson, L. A., DeThorne, L. S., & Schatschneider, C. (2006). Reading skills in early readers: Genetic and shared environmental influences. *Journal of Learning Disabilities*, *39*(1), 48–55.

Petrill, S. A., Deater-Deckard, K., Thompson, L. A., Schatschneider, C., DeThorne, L. S., & Vandenbergh, D. J. (2007). Longitudinal genetic analysis of early reading: The Western Reserve reading project. *Reading and Writing*, *20*(1–2), 127–146.

Petrill, S. A., Hart, S. A., Harlaar, N., Logan, J., Justice, L. M., Schatschneider, C., et al. (2010a). Genetic and environmental influences on the growth of early reading skills. *Journal of Child Psychology and Psychiatry*, *51*(6), 660–667.

Petryshen, T. L., & Pauls, D. L. (2009). The genetics of reading disability. *Current Psychiatry Reports*, *11*(2), 149–155.

Plomin, R., & Kovas, Y. (2005). Generalist genes and learning disabilities. *Psychological Bulletin*, *131*(4), 592.

Poelmans, G., Buitelaar, J. K., Pauls, D. L., & Franke, B. (2011). A theoretical molecular network for dyslexia: integrating available genetic findings. *Molecular Psychiatry*, *16*(4), 365–382.

Priya, K. (2009). The roles of fluent decoding and vocabulary in the development of reading comprehension. In R. K. Wagner, C. Schatschneider, & C. Phythian-Sence (Eds.), *Beyond Decoding. The Behavioral and Biological Foundations of Reading Comprehension*. New York: Guilford Press.

Quinn, J. M., Wagner, R. K., Petscher, Y., & Lopez, D. (2014). Developmental relations between vocabulary knowledge and reading comprehension: A latent change score modeling study. *Child Development*, *86*(1), 159–175.

Raskind, W. H., Igo, R. P., Chapman, N. H., Berninger, V. W., Thomson, J. B., Matsushita, M., et al. (2005). A genome scan in multigenerational families with dyslexia: Identification of a novel locus on chromosome 2q that contributes to phonological decoding efficiency. *Molecular Psychiatry, 10*(7), 699–711.

Rice, M. L., Smith, S. D., & Gayán, J. (2009). Convergent genetic linkage and associations to language, speech and reading measures in families of probands with specific language impairment. *Journal of Neurodevelopmental Disorders, 1*(4), 264–282.

Rourke, B. P. (1993). Arithmetic disabilities, specific and otherwise: A neuropsychological perspective. *Journal of Learning Disabilities, 26*, 214–226.

Samuelsson, S., Byrne, B., Olson, R. K., Hulslander, J., Wadsworth, S., Corley, R., et al. (2008). Response to early literacy instruction in the United States, Australia, and Scandinavia: A behavioral-genetic analysis. *Learning and Individual Differences, 18*(3), 289–295.

Scerri, T. S., Fisher, S. E., Francks, C., MacPhie, I. L., Paracchini, S., Richardson, A. J., et al. (2004). Putative functional alleles of DYX1C1 are not associated with dyslexia susceptibility in a large sample of sibling pairs from the UK. *Journal of Medical Genetics, 41*(11), 853–857.

Scerri, T. S., Morris, A. P., Buckingham, L. L., Newbury, D. F., Miller, L. L., Monaco, A. P., et al. (2011). DCDC2, KIAA0319 and CMIP are associated with reading-related traits. *Biological Psychiatry, 70*(3), 237–245.

Scerri, T. S., & Schulte-Körne, G. (2010). Genetics of developmental dyslexia. *European Child & Adolescent Psychiatry, 19*(3), 179–197.

Schumacher, J., Anthoni, H., Dahdouh, F., König, I. R., Hillmer, A. M., Kluck, N., et al. (2006). Strong genetic evidence of DCDC2 as a susceptibility gene for dyslexia. *American Journal of Human Genetics, 78*(1), 52–62.

Sesma, H. W., Mahone, E. M., Levine, T., Eason, S. H., & Cutting, L. E. (2009). The contribution of executive skills to reading comprehension. *Child Neuropsychology, 15*(3), 232–246.

Shaywitz, S. E., Escobar, M. D., Shaywitz, B. A., Fletcher, J. M., & Makuch, R. (1992). Evidence that dyslexia may represent the lower tail of a normal distribution of reading ability. *New England Journal of Medicine, 326*(3), 145–150.

Shaywitz, S., Shaywitz, B., Fletcher, J., & Escobar, M. (1990). Prevalence of reading disability in boys and girls. *Journal of the American Medical Association, 264*, 998–1002.

Spinath, F. M., Price, T. S., Dale, P. S., & Plomin, R. (2004). The genetic and environmental origins of language disability and ability. *Child Development, 75*(2), 445–454.

Stanovich, K. (1986). Cognitive processes and the reading problems of learning disabled children: Evaluating the assumption of specificity. In J. K. Torgesen & B. Y. L. Wong (Eds.), *Psychological and Educational Perspectives on Learning Disabilities*. Orlando, FL: Academic Press.

Taipale, M., Kaminen, N., Nopola-Hemmi, J., Haltia, T., Myllyluoma, B., Lyytinen, H., et al. (2003). A candidate gene for developmental dyslexia encodes a nuclear tetratricopeptide repeat domain protein dynamically regulated in brain. *Proceedings of the National Academy of Sciences, 100*(20), 11553–11558.

Tapia-Páez, I., Tammimies, K., Massinen, S., Roy, A. L., & Kere, J. (2008). The complex of TFII-I, PARP1, and SFPQ proteins regulates the DYX1C1 gene implicated in neuronal migration and dyslexia. *FASEB Journal, 22*(8), 3001–3009.

Taylor, J., Roehrig, A. D., Hensler, B. S., Connor, C. M., & Schatschneider, C. (2010). Teacher quality moderates the genetic effects on early reading. *Science, 328*(5977), 512–514.

Tran, C., Gagnon, F., Wigg, K. G., Feng, Y., Gomez, L., Cate-Carter, T. D., et al. (2013). A family-based association analysis and meta-analysis of the reading disabilities candidate gene DYX1C1. *American Journal of Medical Genetics Part B: Neuropsychiatric Genetics, 162*(2), 146–156.

Venkatesh, S. K., Siddaiah, A., Padakannaya, P., & Ramachandra, N. B. (2013). Analysis of genetic variants of dyslexia candidate genes KIAA0319 and DCDC2 in Indian population. *Journal of Human Genetics, 58*(8), 531–538.

Wadsworth, S. J., Corley, R. P., Hewitt, J. K., & DeFries, J. C. (2001). Stability of genetic and environmental influences on reading performance at 7, 12, and 16 years of age in the Colorado Adoption Project. *Behavior Genetics, 31*(4), 353–359.

Wadsworth, S. J., Olson, R. K., Pennington, B. F., & DeFries, J. C. (2000). Differential genetic etiology of reading disability as a function of IQ. *Journal of Learning Disabilities, 33*(2), 192–199.

Wahlsten, D. (2012). The hunt for gene effects pertinent to behavioral traits and psychiatric disorders: From mouse to human. *Developmental Psychobiology, 54*(5), 475–492.

Wigg, K. G., Couto, J. M., Feng, Y., Anderson, B., Cate-Carter, T. D., Macciardi, F., et al. (2004) Support for EKN1 as the susceptibility locus for dyslexia on 15q21. *Molecular Psychiatry, 9*, 1111–1121.

Zou, L., Chen, W., Shao, S., Sun, Z., Zhong, R., Shi, J., et al. (2012). Genetic variant in KIAA0319, but not in DYX1C1, is associated with risk of dyslexia: An integrated meta-analysis. *American Journal of Medical Genetics Part B: Neuropsychiatric Genetics, 159*(8), 970–976.

Chapter 3

Perception, Reading, and Digital Media

Kristy Roschke and Ralph Radach

The need for sound reading skills has never been greater as young people prepare to meet the demands of the twenty-first-century workplace, especially those related to digital technologies (National Research Council, 2012). The current generation of students, often referred to as Generation Z or "Digital Natives" (Zimmerman, 2011), is more connected than any group in history. One study showed the average American household with children aged 4–14 owns an average of 10 devices, with kids using an average of five of them (Freeman, 2012). Tablet devices are also playing an increasing role in children's first learning experiences (Maragioglio, 2012). Schools have recognized the importance of incorporating technology into the classroom in even the earliest grades because, as Thoman and Jolls (2004) note, "to ignore the media-rich environment [students] bring with them to school is to shortchange them for life" (p. 20). Additionally, students are motivated by learning with technology and the Internet promotes self-learning habits, facts that further underscore the utility of technology in the classroom (Davidson & Goldberg, 2010).

Although research is accumulating on how best to incorporate technology into the classroom (see Cheung & Dubey, 2010; Clarke & Zagarell, 2012; Deng & Zhang, 2007; Okojie & Olinzock, 2006), little information exists on how students process information using these technological tools (see Castek, 2008; Coiro & Dobler, 2007). Zimmerman (2011) notes that digital natives may assume that they are proficient in digital technologies, but they often require additional training to maximize their digital literacy skills. As young people's daily screen time increases, so does the amount of reading they do on digital devices; however, the question remains whether technology affects how young people learn to read. This chapter will provide a brief overview of the perception literature related to traditional, linear texts and will then discuss how existing research methodologies can be utilized and expanded to include new technologies in order to better understand the development of reading comprehension skills in a digital environment.

Cognitive Development and Perception

Literacy is vital to success in our society. Strong reading comprehension skills are fundamental to all facets of learning because most content-area knowledge is accessed through reading (Miller & O'Donnell, 2013). The underlying cognitive processes involved in reading are of special interest to perception researchers and cognitive psychologists; particularly as national data show young students are struggling to read at a basic level even as the efforts for intervention have increased (Miller & O'Donnell, 2013). Perception, together with memory and learning, is one of the core domains of information processing that researchers need to study in order to better understand the development of reading comprehension skills.

In terms of cognitive development, the act of perception begins with bottom-up processing as infants move from instinctive reflexive actions toward symbolic thought (Piaget, 1960). At this early stage, perception involves taking in the shapes, colors, and movements of their surroundings to make sense of whole systems. As children's cognitive development progresses, they increasingly activate top-down processing by bringing in prior experience and understanding of the world in order to make meaning of sensory messages. This more complex practice includes using knowledge and inferences to provide context for those messages (Bernstein, 2010). The development of perceptual skills takes a similar trajectory relative to reading fluency and comprehension, as young readers move from bottom-up, code-focused processing to top-down, meaning-focused processing.

Looking at the level of letter perception, processing begins with the visual analysis of features (strokes, angles, and curves) and their spatially ordered combinations that determine the informational content of alphabetic characters (see Balota, Yap & Cortese, 2006; Grainger, Rey & Dufau, 2008, for detailed discussions). The basic contribution of low-level visual processing routines is to transform this raw material into an abstract orthographic code so that letter information can be maintained and integrated across successive eye fixations (McConkie and Zola, 1979; see later for more information on eye movements). Further processing then uses the orthographic code to form letter clusters that act as word candidates, which are then recognized as known words via comparison with representations in a specific compartment of long-term memory, referred to as the mental lexicon. The perceptual and cognitive routines involved in this cascade of processing up to word recognition are referred to as decoding. The development, especially in terms of becoming more and more automatic, of such processing routines is the foundation of skilled reading and a precondition for more successful reading comprehension.

Rapp and van den Broek (2005) describe reading comprehension as "an ongoing process involving fluctuations in the activation of concepts as the reader proceeds through the text, resulting in a gradually emerging

interpretation of the material" (p. 276). As such, underlying cognitive processes such as attention, memory, perception, and reasoning are continually
activated during reading. The ways in which the reader engages in the text
through these and other cognitive tasks impact comprehension.

Toffler (1971) pointed out more than 40 years ago that curriculum
should be based on the skills needed for the future. The push to prepare
students for the twenty-first-century workplace has never been more
prevalent than in today's American school system. The Common Core
Standards adopted across the U.S. address these new competencies.
Included in the language arts standards are the ability to "integrate and
evaluate content presented in diverse media and formats, including visually
and quantitatively, as well as in words" and to "gather relevant information
from multiple print and digital sources, assess the credibility and accuracy
of each source, and integrate the information while avoiding plagiarism"
(Common Core Standards, 2012).

The Internet has become a dominant source of information (Castek,
2008), one that researchers argue requires a new set of reading skills and
strategies for reading online texts (Castek, 2008; Coiro & Dobler, 2007; Leu,
et al., 2011; Margolin, et al., 2013). Following Coiro (2011), we will define
online texts as texts displayed in a digital environment that may include
interactive elements such as hyperlinks and images, and that may be displayed in an open networked system like the Internet or in a more restricted
environment such as an e-reader. Online reading is not to be confused with
online measures of reading comprehension, such as eye movement studies,
that monitor comprehension during the act of reading. Up to now, little
research exists on perception and online reading comprehension.

Perception and Reading Comprehension

The study of perceptual processes in reading comprehension is plagued by
the same challenges facing reading research in general: the complexity of the
issue has created a broad but disjointed collection of literature that favors
specific methodologies or "mini-theories" (Rapp & van den Broek, 2005)
and does only begin to work together in creating a more complete picture
of the reading process (see Kennedy, Radach, Heller, & Pynte, 2000, for work
on reading as a perceptual process). As is the case in the greater reading comprehension literature, information processing research is somewhat divided
by studies concerned with the process of reading, or the online, moment-by-
moment actions, versus those that examine the products, or offline measures.

Eye Movement Research

Eye movement studies spanning more than 30 years have offered important
insight into the underlying perceptual and cognitive processes involved in

reading (for a detailed overview of the eye movement literature, see Radach & Kennedy, 2004, 2013; Rayner, 2009). As will become apparent in this section, eye movements are part and parcel of the reading process, as they constitute the only observable behavior in silent reading. At the same time the oculomotor measures derived from eye movement data provide a valid and relatively unobtrusive record of moment-to-moment perceptual and cognitive processing during continuous reading.

Contrary to our subjective impression that written text steadily streams into our consciousness, the acquisition of visual information during reading begins in a strictly discontinuous fashion. Our eyes travel in fast movements, referred to as saccades (from the French word for "to jerk") across a line of text. Saccades are actually the fastest movements executed by the human body, with durations starting around 20 ms and getting about 2 or 2.5 ms longer per degree of visual angle (Becker, 1989). An eye movement recording situation with state-of-the-art equipment is depicted in Figure 3.1 a and b and Figure 3.2 shows a typical movement pattern (scan path) as commonly seen in text reading.

As it is apparent in Figure 3.2, most saccades move from left to right, with some landing in the same word and some moving on to the next word or other words, to the right. This proportion of "progressive saccades" can include between 70 and 95 percent, depending on various dimensions of text difficulty and reader ability. However, there are also saccades moving in the opposite direction, again either within the same word or going further back to the left. The distinction between eye movements within or across word boundaries is important, as patterns of fixations on specific words reflect the mental effort invested in letter and word processing (see McConkie, et al., 1991, for work pioneering this approach in research on reading development).

Figure 3.1a

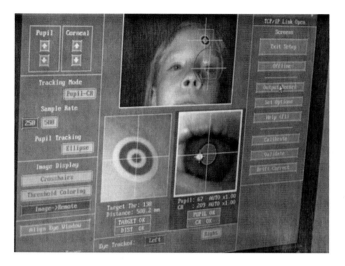

Figure 3.1b

The extent (or amplitude) of progressive saccades is in the order of one to 20 letters, with means for good readers ranging from about six to nine letters, and substantially less for developing and struggling readers. Regressive saccades back to the left extend only about half these distances. There are several reasons why regressions occur, including corrective movements when a word has been skipped accidentally, completion or revision of word processing, or search for information needed to integrate meaning on the sentence and text level (Inhoff, Weger, & Radach, 2005).

Saccades are interrupted by periods of relative stability, referred to as fixations. These pauses last between 60 and over 500 ms, with means in the order of 200 to 250 ms. Only during fixations is letter and word information being acquired, so that the perceptual front end of reading involves the integration of information packages acquired in successive visual snapshots.[1] The region around the current fixation position within which information is acquired within one visual snapshot is generally referred to as the perceptual span. The extent of the span can be determined using the so-called moving window technique, where text outside a pre-specified region around the fixation is masked, e.g., with meaningless letter strings. As the

---

1 The functional visual field in reading is often divided into a foveal region with a radius of one degree around the current fixation, a parafoveal region up to five degrees to the left and right and a more distant peripheral region. It is important to note that in much of the eye movement literature the term *foveal* is used for the currently fixated word (or word N), while neighboring words are referred to as *parafoveal*, or as word N − 1, N + 1, N + 2 etc., depending on their location relative to the current fixation.

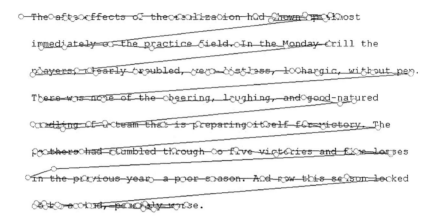

Figure 3.2

name suggests, the window moves with the eye and therefore restricts the area within which letters are visible. When the window gets too small, it slows down and impedes reading, providing an elegant way to determine the extent of the perceptual span (McConkie & Rayner, 1975; see Schotter, Angele, & Rayner, 2012, for a review). A number of studies using this methodology found that the perceptual span for word-length information extends about 15 letters to the right, while the rightward span for letter discrimination includes only eight to 10 letters. The size of the perceptual span is considerably smaller to the left of fixation, suggesting that it is not just a function of visual acuity, which is basically symmetric. Interestingly, this asymmetry in the perceptual span is also a function of reading direction. It extends further to the left when bilingual participants read in Hebrew or Arabic, indicating that it is codetermined by the dynamic allocation of attentional resources (Pollatsek, Bolozky, Well, & Rayner, 1981).

The duration and number of fixations made on a particular word is strongly related to the mental workload associated with processing this word on several levels, beginning with the extraction of letter features and extending well into the integration of meaning on the sentence and text level. The selection of words for fixation is word based, with visual-spatial and cognitive factors working together so that, as an example, longer and more difficult words have a higher probability of fixation. When a word has been selected for fixation, a saccade is programmed that, in most cases, appears to be directed towards the word center. The reason for this is that fixation positions at or slightly left of the word's center maximize letter visibility and are generally optimal for word recognition (Vitu, O'Regan, & Mittau, 1990; Stevens & Grainger, 2003). Due to visual and visuomotor constraints, many of these saccades undershoot this optimal viewing position, so that most incoming progressive saccades land about halfway between word beginning and word center, a phenomenon referred to as the "preferred viewing position" (McConkie, Kerr, Reddix, & Zola, 1988; Rayner, 1979).

Based on the obvious connection between visual perception, eye movements, and linguistic processing, there is some debate on the nature of this so-called "eye-mind relation." Some researchers claim that basically every saccade is initiated when lexical processing has reached a certain level. This is related to the assumption that reading progresses in a sequential word-to-word fashion (see the extensive literature on the E-Z reader model, e.g., Reichle, Rayner, & Pollatsek, 2003). Other researchers assume that the relation between eye and mind is more indirect so that oculomotor control is more autonomous. This is also related to the idea that two or even three words may be processed in parallel within the perceptual span (Engbert, Nuthmann, Richter, & Kliegl, 2005). One model of this type combines spatially graded letter processing within a virtual perceptual span with an interactive activation mechanism of word processing, creating an explicit connection between the perceptual front end of reading and the linguistic dynamics of word processing (Reilly & Radach, 2006).

Perceptual and Visuomotor Aspects of Reading Development

The research just described has helped develop a picture of the developmental end goal: the skilled adult reader (Blythe & Joseph, 2011). However, much less is known about the path toward successful reading comprehension because relatively little research exists on children's eye movements and the development of visual and cognitive processing. Eye movement studies involving children are less common for several reasons. The biggest constraint to date has been the technology. Until recently, the devices used to track eye movements were not conducive to use on children because they were expensive, complicated to handle, and required subjects to sit very still. As the technology has become more sophisticated, however, it is more adept at recording eye movements in an ecologically valid fashion, opening the door for more extensive use with children. The study of children's eye movements is also complicated by the fact that changes in eye movements over time may be related to both chronological development and the development of literacy skills. The large degree of variance in studies of children show that variables of chronological age, reading age, and IQ are influential in the development of oculomotor control during reading. These issues can pose methodological challenges, as it is difficult to create control groups that account for both cognitive development due to age and due to increased literacy skills (Blythe & Joseph, 2011).

The existing eye movement literature on reading development can be divided into two periods. Studies conducted before 1990 basically indicated that, as development progresses, reading becomes more efficient such that shorter and less fixations per line of text are being made. It also became clear that on the individual level both global text difficulty and reader ability strongly influence eye movements (e.g., Buswell, 1922; Taylor, 1965). Rayner (1986) found that children at the end of second grade had a smaller perceptual span than fourth and sixth graders, but that the fourth and sixth graders had the same perceptual span as adults. Research also showed that children have an asymmetrical perceptual span that is larger to the right, just as described earlier for adults. This can be taken to indicate that the dynamic allocation of visual attention develops quite early within the constraints afforded by perceptual span size and letter decoding skills. Interestingly, the perceptual span appears to be larger for faster readers, suggesting that struggling readers focus most of their visual processing resources on the currently fixated word (Häikiö, Bertram, Hyönä, & Niemi, 2009).

Beginning in the early 1990s, developmental eye movement research began to focus on local fixation patterns on individual words. This research indicated that, as known for adults, word processing effort as indexed by variables such as word length and word frequency has a profound influence on word viewing durations. The first large-scale longitudinal study was published by McConkie, Zola, Grimes, Kerr, Bryant, and Wolff (1991), who reported data from first to fifth grade students reading age-appropriate materials. They showed that, in addition to the trends mentioned earlier, the variability of fixation durations and saccade amplitudes decreased, suggesting a more regular pattern of oculomotor behavior. Another important result was a reduction in the proportion of very small progressive saccades, reflecting a trend towards less sequential (letter by letter) and more holistic word processing. Interestingly, the basic mechanisms of eye movement control such as saccade landing positions appeared to be in place very early for most children, suggesting that the visuomotor apparatus is sufficiently mature to support reading.

These results were supplemented by work comparing students reading identical sentences at grades two and four (Huestegge, Radach, Corbic, & Huestegge, 2009). It was found that a large proportion of the total difference in word viewing time was due to the frequent rereading of words in grade two. This result indicates that in addition to the acquisition of more efficient decoding skills, the integration of meaning at the sentence level constitutes a major arena for early reading development. This makes perfect sense, given the fact that reading fluency and comprehension need to share a common pool of cognitive resources (see Blythe & Joseph, 2011, for a comprehensive review of developmental eye tracking research).

More recently work, this line of work has been continued with much larger sample sizes, allowing for more fine-grain word-level analyses. As an example, Figure 3.3 summarizes results reported by Vorstius, Radach, and

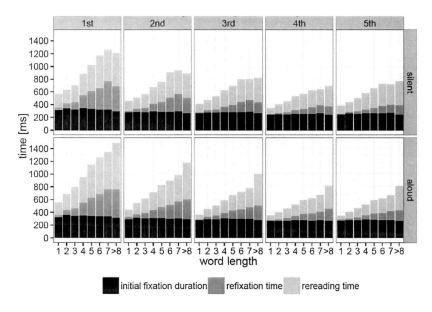

Figure 3.3

Lonigan (2014), who also provided the first detailed developmental comparison of silent and oral reading. The figure presents a comparison of the time spent fixating words as a function of their length for grades one to five. Viewing times are divided into three bins, representing the duration of the first fixation on the current word, the time spent with additional fixations before leaving (refixation time) and the time it took to come back to the word for additional fixations (rereading time).

It is generally assumed that the initial fixation duration mainly reflects orthographic and early lexical processing, while additional mental effort until the achievement of word recognition (lexical access) is associated with refixation time. Both measures are often summed up as gaze duration or first pass reading time. Finally, rereading time is thought to be strongly related to processing beyond the word level, e.g., when a word has been misinterpreted in the given context or a semantic relation within the sentence is not clear (see Inhoff & Radach, 1998, for a discussion of measures). The figure summarizes the extent of development over grades and indicates the proportion of progress made both on the lexical and post-lexical level. It is also interesting to compare silent and oral reading on this detailed level of analysis. Not only does oral reading take substantially longer, it also shows a more pronounced word length effect, reflecting more sequential, step-by-step reading with more uniform local fixation patterns. Another important constraint of eye movement control in oral reading is the coordination of visual word processing and concurrent oral language production (Inhoff, Solomon, Radach, & Seymour, 2011; Laubrock & Kliegl, 2015).

A Case Study of Perception in Non-Linear Digital Reading

Since 2014 an app called "spritz" has been causing an enormous amount of media interest around the globe. It uses a technique called rapid serial visual presentation (RSVP) to present text one word at a time on a small one-line screen. The second ingredient of the app is the centering of fixation using small bars above and below the line and red ink on the central letter to keep the eyes at a location left of the word center. The RSVP technique has been used by reading researchers over decades and is widely considered a useful methodological tool (Aaronson, 1984). The centering on an "optimal recognition point" not only resembles the optimal viewing position we have already mentioned, but is actually very similar to methods used to study visibility effects in research on single-word reading (O'Regan, 1990). The innovation of spritz is to combine these pieces of knowledge and turn them into a commercial reading device (e.g., for use with smart watches and cell phones), where each user can adjust the speed of word-by-word presentation.

Apparently, in response to criticism, the authors of the website have removed several extravagant claims on the advantages of their app, but the current website (http://www.spritzinc.com) still argues that the "technology is based on the science of how people read, how they learned to read when they were young, and what your eyes expect when you are reading." The site also claims that several test subjects "spritzed new content at over 900 words per minute and then consistently aced their non-multiple choice test afterwards." The website does not recommend a limit on the use of their method to quick checks on a smart watch, but instead asserts that two-hour sessions of continued single-word presentation are fine.

How should the science on perceptual processing in reading respond to this challenge? Equipped with some of the findings discussed in prior sections of this chapter, we can approach this question with confidence. First, the letter presentation window in the app is confined to 13 spaces, limiting parafoveal vision and thus precluding parallel word processing and the formation of meaning units. Second, the rate of word presentation is fixed, except for a small adjustment related to word length. There is no scope to adjust fixation times to accommodate the requirements of linguistic processing, so that the processing of difficult words can "spill over" when the next word is already being presented. This may limit the lexical quality (Perfetti, 2007) of word representations, especially for unfamiliar and complex words. Furthermore, there is no extra time to rest when meaning needs to be integrated at the sentence or passage level. Third, and most problematic, as we have discussed earlier, the execution of regressive sac-cades and the rereading of words is an integral part of normal reading for comprehension. We have also emphasized that this is an important focus of reading development at the elementary school level (e.g., Huestegge, et al., 2009). Consequently, it is rather straightforward to predict that reading text in any word-by-word format should be detrimental to comprehension in general and the development of optimal reading strategies in particular.

Testing this prediction, Schotter, Tran, and Rayner (2014) used an ele-gant method to examine line-by-line reading without information acquisi-tion from regressions. They masked every word with a string of "xxxxx" after the eye had moved on further to the right, effectively rendering any regressive saccade useless. Their data indicate that this manipulation had a substantial negative effect on sentence comprehension, and that regressions directly contributed to comprehension performance. Benedetto, et al. (2015) directly compared extended sessions of normal line-by-line reading with a spritz-like RSVP format. They found that the word-for-word pres-entation mode impaired literal comprehension and they attributed this result to the suppression of parafoveal processing and regressions. Interest-ingly, as spritz reading minimized eye blinks and saccadic eye movements, it also led to the increased occurrence of visual fatigue, causing symptoms referred to as the "dry eye syndrome."

In conclusion, both general findings in perception-related reading research and data from direct comparisons with normal text presentation suggest that fixation-centered word-by-word reading, as cool it may look, is not suitable to educational application. This case example also demon-strates the utility of visuomotor research methodology in the evaluation of technologically innovative modes of digital reading.

Situation Models in Reading Comprehension

Whereas eye movement studies can provide a picture of what occurs dur-ing reading, other methods are needed to determine how readers compre-hend a text. Researchers have described language as a "set of processing instructions on how to construct a mental representation of the described situation" (Zwaan & Radvansky, 1998). These mental representations, also known as situation models (van Dijk & Kintsch, 1983), are constructed through a combination of a reader's linguistic skill, prior knowledge, and interaction with the text (Magliano & Schleich, 2000). The situation model is continually updated throughout a text as the reader encounters new information (Braasch, et al., 2012). Models are constructed in a cyclical pattern in which the information presented in the text is first integrated into the model at a surface level. As the reader continues through the text, the model includes not only the lexical information, but also inferences drawn from prior knowledge (Margolin, et al., 2013). As the model becomes more complete, aspects of the reading process become more automatic, allowing the reader to focus less on individual words and more on critical thinking. Thus, situation models are closely tied with working memory, as they are representations of readers' understanding of the world (see Chapter 4 in this book for a more detailed explanation of how memory affects reading comprehension). Within a situation model, some components are monitored more closely than others in order to comprehend a text. For example, changes in time within narrative texts are monitored more closely than changes in location because time is more integral to the development of the narrative (Magliano, et al., 2007).

A Combined Approach to Studying Information Processing in Reading

Online measures of reading comprehension such as eye movement studies can address the underlying behaviors present in developing readers in a way that offline, post-reading measures such as recall and comprehension questions cannot. Eye movement studies can track how developing readers engage with a text, including the amount of time they spend on certain portions of the text, what factors disturb reading fluency, and what behaviors are modified with improved fluency (Rayner, Ardoin, & Binder, 2013). Perfetti's (1985) verbal efficiency theory suggests that as readers increase their proficiency in reading words, demands on their memory and attention related to the reading process decrease, allowing readers to focus more on the meaning of text (see Chapter 4 for more information on these issues). Eye movement studies can be utilized to monitor comprehension by focusing on reading speed and automatic processes, which can also help in the development of interventions for less skilled readers. As an example, a recent study by Connor, et al. (2015) examined the dynamics of reading comprehension on the sentence level in fifth-grade students. Their results indicate that the use of contextually atypical objects or instruments in event-describing sentences leads to inflated refixation and rereading times on such words. Interestingly, analyses of individual differences suggest that this form of comprehension monitoring is strongly related to academic language skills (see also Vorstius, Radach, Mayer, & Lonigan, 2013, for a similar approach to comprehension monitoring within the same sentence).

However, eye movement studies cannot describe what the reader is thinking in each moment that is being monitored. Experiments that include offline measurements such as comprehension quizzes help determine how adept readers are at constructing situation models to comprehend the events of a text. When used together, the two methodologies can better serve developing readers, as well as those who are teaching those developing readers. A combined approach would also be useful in assessing the perceptual processes underlying online text comprehension.

The Case for Online Reading Comprehension Methodologies

As technology plays an ever increasing role in the way we communicate, researchers from a variety of disciplines are evaluating definitions of reading and literacy, especially as it relates to online reading comprehension (Castek, 2008). Comprehending printed text is not isomorphic with comprehending digital text (Hartman, et al., 2010). The non-linear, multimodal properties of digital text have the potential to impact reading comprehension (Zumbach & Mohraz, 2008). Cognitive tasks other than those traditionally associated with reading comprehension may be needed in constructing a situation model to navigate a digital text. For instance, online reading requires the ability to search for information, synthesize information across disparate websites, and critically evaluate online sources (Castek, 2008; Coiro, 2011; Margolin, et al., 2013). These additional tasks add to the cognitive load, which may result in decreased text comprehension.

Whereas some research has been conducted comparing reading printed texts to digital texts, much of that research has focused on efficacy as opposed to comprehension. Research is mixed as to whether efficiency and reading ability are affected when reading digital texts, such as e-books and computer texts, as opposed to print texts (see Margolin, et al., 2013, for a more detailed account of the research). Limited research exists on online reading comprehension involving adults or children, and much of what does exist is qualitative, using such methodologies as field observations and interviews to determine comprehension (Coiro & Dobler, 2007; Schmar-Dobler, 2003).

Jeong (2010) summarized existing research comparing "e-books," defined as "text analogous to a book that is digitally displayed" on a computer screen or other e-reader, to "p-books," or paper books. He found results across studies inconsistent; they alternately find e-books to be more and less effective than, as well as the same as, p-books in terms of comprehension, eye fatigue, and students' perception of their effectiveness. Jeong's (2010) own study of 56 sixth-year Korean public school students found that students scored higher on a reading comprehension quiz following the use of p-books, possibly because reading on a screen requires more concentration. Margolin, et al. (2013), however, found no significant differences in comprehension between printed text and e-reader text in a study conducted with skilled adult readers. These differences in findings may be because of the different populations being studied.

A good example for some methodological or perhaps even political complexities involved in this kind of work is a recent study by Mangen, Walgermo, and Brønnick (2013) that has gained remarkable media recognition as defending "reading from real books" (see various articles in media such as *Scientific American* or the *Guardian*). They basically found that a group of students reading text on paper obtained better comprehension scores compared to a group reading the same materials from a computer screen. However, a closer look at the methodology of this work indicates that the paper group had simultaneous access to multiple pages, whereas the screen group was forced to scroll up and down a single screen while searching for information. The authors discuss such navigational limitations as the most likely cause for the group differences, confirming that a technical shortcoming (that will perhaps not exist in the future of e-reading) led to the observed disadvantage for reading from an electronic device. What would have been the result if the screen group had simply been given a larger monitor with multiple windows showing the entire 1200-word passage at once?

Looking at this research from a perceptual point of view, the question of display quality should be considered. When "e-reading" was still done from flickering CTR monitors, it was relatively easy to show that information acquisition from paper was more efficient and generated less visual discomfort. However, with the recent development of paper-like self-illuminated displays it is becoming problematic to generalize any results obtained with earlier, suboptimal hardware. As an example, Benedetto, et al. (2013) recently compared the effect of different display technologies on visual fatigue during extended sessions of reading. They compared text printed on paper, with presentation on an LCD display as it is common in standard computer screens, and modern e-ink technology as used in the most up-to-date e-readers. Results from both objective (blinks per second) and subjective (visual fatigue scale) measures indicated that reading on the LCD leads to higher visual fatigue compared to both e-ink and paper.

Results like these suggest that there is no longer a perceptual disadvantage of optimal electronic displays against reading from paper. Moreover, as soon as the benefits of high resolution, adjustable self-illuminated e-reading devices under dim or otherwise suboptimal lighting condition are considered, it appears likely that paper will lose the race for the "better" medium altogether. Given this situation, the focus of research may well shift from perceptual to cognitive and educational aspects of e-reading. One of the main questions in this context will likely be related to the problem of "time on task," given that e-reading devices are often connected to the Internet, confronting students with the temptation to switch to more exciting applications.

Conclusion and Discussion

The study of online reading comprehension is still in its early stages. But rapid advancements in technology and adoption rates, especially among young people, and the increased emphasis on technology in education make this an area of research that deserves increased attention. But while

97 percent of U.S. K-12 classrooms have access to the Internet (Coiro, 2011), skills for effectively using the Internet are rarely taught in the classroom (Castek, 2008). In fact, Internet skills are often taught separately as technology skills as opposed to new reading comprehension skills (Coiro, 2011). Other research suggests that the "simple view of reading" is not sufficient for online reading comprehension (Hartman, et al., 2010). The process of reading is now deictic (Leu, et al., 2008) and likely requires new instructional practices and interventions to assist developing readers.

The small amount of current research that exists is mixed as to whether reading in an online environment affects comprehension in different ways from controlled print reading environments. This research has been conducted mostly by literacy and education scholars with an emphasis on implications for classroom technology use. Cognitive psychologists have yet to delve into this topic to look at potential differences in the underlying processes involved in online reading comprehension, particularly with regard to the role of perception across media. Whereas eye movement studies have traditionally been conducted using technology connected to a computer screen, the controlled, unidirectional experience typically only includes a few lines of text, as opposed to an open reading experience. An exception to this norm is a study by Radach, Huestegge, and Reilly (2008), who looked at an important form factor by comparing sentence-based and corpus-based reading. A comparison of identical sentences presented in isolation vs. as part of a novel showed that a variety of factors affected low-level cognitive processes when reading in an "ecologically plausible context". The authors concluded that the perceptual and cognitive processes involved in reading are dynamically interactive, with "high-level factors routinely and directly affect[ing] low-level processes" (Radach, et al., 2008, p. 687). This study underscores the importance of evaluating the implications of multidirectional online reading environments on the comprehension of developing readers.

For decades perception researchers have studied the cognitive processes involved in reading, but various challenges have limited the research related to young readers. This is changing, however, in large part due to advancements in eye-tracking technology. There are now several initiatives where groups of researchers especially in the U.S. and in the European Union conduct large-scale longitudinal studies of reading developments that combine education science- and cognitive science-based theories and methods. Eye movement research with developing readers can be beneficial in bridging the gap between basic research and educational applications (Radach & Kennedy, 2013). In this context, researchers should also seize the opportunity to expand existing approaches to include new technologies to better understand the development of reading comprehension skills in a digital environment.

Perception research can help identify where and how readers struggle in a moment-by-moment analysis and help determine where lapses in comprehension take place; this information can have great implications in the development of curriculum and interventions that can help struggling readers and improve reading comprehension across skill levels. Integrating perception research more closely with other reading comprehension research can create a more complete picture of the cognitive development of young readers. Furthermore, because digital technology is playing an increasing role in learning—from the earliest home learning experiences to implementation of technology tools in schools across the U.S.—a great opportunity exists for perception researchers to study if young people read multifaceted digital texts the same way they read traditional linear texts. Online methods of studying perceptual processes during reading can help determine what happens at a cognitive level as children navigate the Internet and other digital text sources. Although the multifaceted nature of online reading is difficult to control and thus presents many challenges for perception researchers, some tools exist to help overcome such challenges. One possibility to accommodate for the open environment is to employ data-harvesting tools that track online behaviors such as mouse clicks and page views in tandem with eye movement studies to help track reader comprehension (Hartman, et al., 2010).

Current U.S. educational policy stresses the importance of twenty-first-century workplace skills, in which technology plays an integral role. Not only does an increasing majority of the reading and communicating we do involve digital technology, but the Internet has also been found to be a motivator for reading (Castek, 2008). If performance differences are found to exist in online reading comprehension, and if such differences can be traced to the underlying perceptual and cognitive component processes, this could have important implications for classroom practices and interventions.

References

Aaronson, D. (1984). Computer methods and ecological validity in reading research. *Behavior Research Methods, Instruments & Computers, 16*, 102–108.

Balota, D., Yap, M., & Cortese, M. (2006). Visual word recognition: The journey from features to meaning. In J. Traxler & M. A. Gernsbacher (Eds.), *Handbook of Psycholinguistics* (6th ed.). Amsterdam: Elsevier.

Becker, W. (1989) Metrics. In R. H. Wurtz & M. E. Goldberg (Eds.), *The Neurobiology of Saccadic Eye Movements*. Amsterdam: Elsevier.

Benedetto, S., Carbone, A., Pedrotti, M., Le Fevre, K., Yahia Bey, L., & Baccino, T. (2015). Rapid serial visual presentation in reading: The case of Spritz. *Computers in Human Behavior, 45*, 352–358.

Benedetto, S., Drai-Zerbib, V., Pedrotti, M., Tissier, G., & Baccino, T. (2013) E-readers and visual fatigue. *PLOS ONE, 8*(12), e83676.

Bernstein, D. A. (2010). *Essentials of Psychology* (5th ed.). London: Cengage Learning.

Blythe, H. I., & Joseph, H. S. S. L. (2011). Children's eye movements during reading. In S. P. Liversedge, L. D. Gilchrist, & S. Everling (Eds.), *Oxford Handbook on Eye Movements*. Oxford: Oxford University Press.

Braasch, J. L. G., Rouet, J. F., Vibert, N., & Britt, M. A. (2012). Readers' use of source information in text comprehension. *Memory and Cognition, (40)*3, 450–465.

Buswell, G. T. (1922). *Fundamental Reading Habits: A Study of Their Development.* Chicago, IL: Chicago University Press.

Castek, J. (2008). How do 4th and 5th grade students acquire the new literacies of online reading comprehension? Exploring the contexts that facilitate learning. (Doctoral dissertation.) University of Connecticut.

Cheung, C. K., & Dubey, A. (2010). Enhancement and expansion of language education in the Internet era role of Web 2.0 technologies. *Journal of Current Issues in Media and Telecommunications, 2*(4), 387–403.

Clarke, Sr. G., and Zagarell, J. (2012). Technology in the classroom: Teachers and technology: A technological divide. *Childhood Education, 88*(2), 136–139.

Coiro, J. (2011). Predicting reading comprehension on the Internet: Contributions of offline reading skills, online reading skills, and prior knowledge. *Journal of Literacy Research, 43*(4), 352–392.

Coiro, J., & Dobler, E. (2007). Exploring the online reading comprehension strategies used by sixth-grade skilled readers to search for and locate information on the Internet. *Reading Research Quarterly, 42*(4), 214–257.

Common Core State Standards Initiative (2012). Common Core State Standards for English Language Arts and Literacy in History/Social Studies, Science, and technical subjects. Washington, DC: National Governors Association Center for Best Practices and the Council of Chief State School Officers. Retrieved from http://www.corestandards.org/

Connor, C., Radach, R., Vorstius, C., Morrison, F., McLean, L., & Day, S. (2015). Individual differences in fifth-graders' literacy and academic language predicts comprehension monitoring development: An eye-movement study. *Scientific Studies of Reading, 19*, 114–134.

Davidson, C. N., & Goldberg, D. T. (2010), *The Future of Thinking: Learning Institutions in a Digital Age.* Cambridge, MA: MIT Press.

Deng, H., & Zhang, S. (2007). What is the effectiveness of a multimedia classroom? *International Journal of Instructional Media, 34*(3), 311–322.

Engbert, R., Nuthmann, A., Richter, E. M., & Kliegl, R. (2005). SWIFT: A dynamical model of saccade generation during reading. *Psychological Review, 112*, 777–813.

Freeman, K. (2012). Popularity of tablets rising with kids [study]. *Mashable.* Retrieved from http://mashable.com/2012/08/15/popularity-of-tablets-rising/

Grainger, J., Rey, J., & Dufau, S. (2008). Letter perception: From pixels to pandemonium. *Trends in Cognitive Sciences, 12*, 381–387.

Häikiö, T., Bertram, R., Hyönä, J., & Niemi, P. (2009). Development of the letter identity span in reading: Evidence from the eye movement moving window paradigm. *Journal of Experimental Child Psychology, 102*, 167–181.

Hartman, D. K., Morsink, P. M., & Zheng, J. (2010). From print to pixels: The evolution of cognitive conceptions of reading comprehension. In E. A. Baker (Ed.), *The New Literacies: Multiple perspectives on research and practice.* New York: Guilford Press.

Huestegge, L., Radach, R., Corbic, D., & Huestegge, S. M. (2009). Oculomotor and linguistic determinants of reading development: A longitudinal study. *Vision Research*, *49*, 2948–2959.

Inhoff, A. W., & Radach, R. (1998). Definition and computation of oculomotor measures in the study of cognitive processes. In G. Underwood (Ed.), *Eye Guidance in Reading and Scene Perception*. Oxford: Elsevier.

Inhoff, A. W., Solomon, M., Radach, R., & Seymour, B. (2011). Temporal dynamics of the eye voice span and eye movement control during oral reading. *Journal of Cognitive Psychology*, *23*, 543–558.

Inhoff, A. W., Weger, U. W., & Radach, R. (2005). Sources of information for the programming of short- and long-range regressions during reading. In G. Underwood (Ed.), *Cognitive Processes in Eye Guidance*. Oxford: Oxford University Press.

Jeong, H. (2010). A comparison of the influence of electronic books and paper books on reading comprehension, eye fatigue, and perception. *Electronic Library*, *30*(3), 390–408.

Kennedy, A., Radach, R., Heller, D., & Pynte, J. (Eds). (2000). *Reading as a Perceptual Process*. Oxford: Elsevier Science.

Laubrock, J., & Kliegl, R. (2015). The eye-voice span during reading aloud. *Frontiers in Psychology*, *6*, 1432.

Leu, D. J., Coiro, J., Castek, J., Hartman, D. K., Henry, L. A., & Reinking, D. (2008). Research on instruction and assessment in the new literacies of online reading comprehension. In C. C. Block & S. R. Parris (Eds.), *Comprehension Instruction: Research-Based Best Practices*. New York: Guilford Press.

Leu, D. J., McVerry, J. G., O'Byrne, W. I., Kiili, C., Zawilinksi, L., Everett-Cacopardo, H., et al. (2011). Commentary: The new literacies of online reading comprehension: Expanding the literacy and learning curriculum. *Journal of Adolescent & Adult Literacy*, *55*(1), 5–14.

McConkie, G. W., Kerr, P. W., Reddix, M. D., & Zola, D. (1988). Eye movement control during reading: I. The location of initial eye fixation on words. *Vision Research*, *28*, 1107–1118.

McConkie, G. W., & Rayner, K. (1975). The span of the effective stimulus during a fixation in reading. *Perception & Psychophysics*, *17*, 578–587.

McConkie, G. W., & Zola, D. (1979). Is visual information integrated across successive fixations in reading? *Perception & Psychophysics*, *25*, 221–224.

McConkie, G. W., Zola, D., Grimes, J., Kerr, P. W., Bryant, N. R., & Wolff, P. M. (1991). Children's eye movements during reading. In J. F. Stein (Ed.), *Vision and Visual Dyslexia*. London: Macmillan.

Magliano, J. P., Radvansky, G. A., & Copeland, D. E. (2007). Beyond language comprehension: Situation models as a form of autobiographical memory. In F. Schmalhofer & C. A. Perfetti (Eds.), *Higher Level Language Processes in the Brain: Inference and Comprehension Processes*. Mahwah, NJ: Erlbaum.

Magliano, J. P., & Schleich, M. C. (2000). Verb aspect and situation models. *Discourse Processes*, *29*(2), 83–112.

Mangen, A., Walgermo, B. R., & Brønnick, K. (2013). Reading linear texts on paper versus computer screen: Effects on reading comprehension. *International Journal of Educational Research*, *58*, 61–68.

Maragioglio, J. (2012). iPads Boost Math Scores, Benefit Education, mobiledia.com, January 31.

Margolin, S. J., Driscoll, C., Toland, M. J., & Kegler, J. L. (2013). E-readers, computer screens, or paper: Does reading comprehension change across media platforms? *Applied Cognitive Psychology, 27*(4), 512–519.

Miller, B., & O'Donnell, C. (2013). Opening a window into reading development: Eye movements' role within a broader literacy research framework. *School Psychology Review, 42*(2), 123–139.

National Research Council. (2012). Education for life and work: Developing transferable knowledge and skills in the 21st century. Committee on Defining Deeper Learning and 21st Century Skills, J. W. Pellegrino & M. L. Hilton (Eds.). Board on Testing and Assessment and Board on Science Education, Division of Behavioral and Social Sciences and Education. Washington, DC: National Academies Press.

Nielsen (2012). American families see tablets as playmate, teacher and babysitter. Retrieved from http://www.nielsen.com/us/en/newswire/2012/american-families-see-tablets-as-playmate-teacher-and-babysitter.html

O'Regan, J. K. (1990). Eye movements and reading. In E. Kowler (Ed.), *Eye Movements and Their Role in Visual and Cognitive Processes.* Amsterdam: Elsevier.

Okojie, M. C. and Olinzock, A. (2006). Developing a positive mind-set toward the use of technology for classroom instruction. *International Journal of Instructional Media, 33*(1), 33–41.

Perfetti, C. A. (1985). *Reading Ability.* New York: Oxford University Press.

Perfetti, C. A. (2007). Reading ability: Lexical quality to comprehension. *Scientific Studies of Reading, 11*, 357–383.

Piaget, J. (1960). *The Psychology of Intelligence.* Paterson, NJ: Littlefield, Adams.

Pollatsek, A., Bolozky, S., Well, A. D., & Rayner, K. (1981). Asymmetries in the perceptual span for Israeli readers. *Brain and Language, 14*, 174–180.

Radach, R., Huestegge, L., & Reilly, R. (2008). The role of top down factors in local eye movement control during reading. *Psychological Research, 72*, 675–688.

Radach, R., & Kennedy, A. (2004). Theoretical perspectives on eye movements in reading: Past controversies, current issues, and an agenda for the future. *European Journal of Cognitive Psychology, 16*, 3–26.

Radach, R., & Kennedy, A. (2013). Eye movements in reading: Some theoretical context. *Quarterly Journal of Experimental Psychology, 66*(3), 429–452.

Rapp, D. N., & van den Broek, P. (2005). Dynamic text comprehension: An integrative view of reading. *Current Directions in Psychological Science, 14*(5), 276–279.

Rayner, K. (1979). Eye guidance in reading: Fixation locations within words. *Perception, 8*, 21–30.

Rayner, K. (1986). Eye movements and the perceptual span in beginning and skilled readers. *Journal of Experimental Child Psychology, 41*, 211–236.

Rayner, K. (2009). Eye movements and attention in reading, scene perception, and visual search. *Quarterly Journal of Experimental Psychology, 62*(8), 1457–1506.

Rayner, K., Ardoin, S. P., & Binder, K. S. (2013). Children's eye movements in reading: A commentary. *School Psychology Review, 42*(2), 223–233.

Reichle, E. D., Rayner, K., & Pollatsek, A. (2003). The E-Z reader model of eye-movement control in reading: Comparisons to other models. *Behavioral and Brain Sciences, 26*, 445–476.

Reilly, R., & Radach, R. (2006). Some empirical tests of an interactive activation model of eye movement control in reading. *Cognitive Systems Research, 7*, 34–55.

Schmar-Dobler, E. (2003). Reading on the Internet: The link between literacy and technology. *Journal of Adolescent and Adult Literacy, 47*(1), 80–85.

Schotter E. R., Angele B., & Rayner K. (2012). Parafoveal processing in reading. *Attention, Perception and Psychophysics, 74*, 5–35.

Schotter, E. R., Tran, R., & Rayner, K. (2014). Don't believe what you read (only once): Comprehension is supported by regressions during reading. *Psychological Science, 25*, 1218–1226.

Stevens, M., & Grainger, J. (2003). Letter visibility and the viewing position effect in visual word recognition. *Perception & Psychophysics, 65*, 133–151.

Taylor, S. E. (1965). Eye movements in reading: facts and fallacies. *American Educational Research Journal, 2*(4), 187–202.

Thoman, E., & Jolls, T. (2004). Media literacy—a national priority for a changing world. *American Behavorial Scientist, 48*(1), 18–29.

Toffler, A. (1971). *Future Shock.* New York: Bantam.

van Dijk, T. A., & Kintsch, W. (1983). *Strategies in Discourse Comprehension.* New York: Academic Press.

Vitu, F., O'Regan, J. K., & Mittau, M. (1990). Optimal landing position in reading isolated words and continuous text. *Perception & Psychophysics, 47*, 583–600.

Vorstius, C., Radach, R., & Lonigan, C. (2014). Eye movements in developing readers: A comparison of silent and oral sentence reading. *Visual Cognition, 22*, 458–485.

Vorstius, C., Radach, R., Mayer, M., & Lonigan, C. (2013). Monitoring local comprehension monitoring in sentence reading. *School Psychology Review, 42*, 191–206.

Zimmerman, M. (2011). Digital natives, searching behavior and the library. *New Library World, 113*(3/4), 174–201.

Zumbach, J., & Mohraz, M. (2008). Cognitive load in hypermedia reading comprehension: Influence of text type and linearity. *Computers in Human Behavior, 24*(3), 875–887.

Zwaan, R. A., & Radvansky, G. A. (1998). Situation models in language comprehension and memory. *Psychological Bulletin, 123*(2), 162–185.

Chapter 4

Memory and Learning to Read

Devin Russell and Carol McDonald Connor

Memory is learning that has persisted over time and information that can be stored and retrieved (Myers, 2004). We have good reason to be thankful for our memory, for it is our memory that defines us. Without it, we would not be able to recognize our friends or family, locate our homes, or speak our language. The importance of memory to our everyday mental processes is not yet fully understood but it is clear that memory influences nearly all aspects of our cognition, and memory's component processes are heavily utilized when acquiring new skills. While considering a skill as crucial to our development as learning to read, the importance of examining how memory affects the acquisition of this skill becomes apparent. Furthering our understanding of memory and how it influences learning to read will serve to illustrate aspects of the complex cognitive processes involved in reading comprehension, and will help scientists and educators in working towards making reading instruction more effective for students.

Memory is crucial in day-to-day mental activity and reading is a skill that draws on a vast amount of a person's cognitive abilities (Ericsson & Kintsch, 1995). Targeting aspects of memory are important to the component psycholinguistic processes used during reading comprehension, and to reading as a whole, so we begin this chapter with a brief overview of memory and then discuss which aspects of memory seem to be important for reading comprehension. We then discuss how memory affects reading skill as people age, memory deficits observed in reading disabled (RD) populations, and the possibility that memory, specifically working memory, can be used to predict reading comprehension ability and the impact of learning to read on aspects of memory. We conclude with a discussion that synthesizes information from the current science literature, discusses the implications of current findings, and considers future directions for reading and memory research.

Memory

Memory is a mental storage system where information is encoded and retained (Myers, 2004). The human body is constantly receiving sensory information from the outside world and it is the job of our senses to relay this information to the brain. Our brain can process aspects of time, space, frequency, and familiar material automatically, but some information requires effort to encode and process (Myers, 2004). Information can be encoded in acoustic, visual, and semantic forms, and there are three primary processes that lead to the formation of memories. Sensory memory is a very brief recording of the sensory stimuli present when perceiving an item. From sensory memory, information is sent to short-term or working memory (WM), where it can be actively processed and integrated with prior knowledge. Because there is simply too much information for our brains to encode at once, working memory helps determine what stimuli should be attended to and associates the stimuli with information retrieved from long-term memory (Baddeley, 2000; Engle, 2002). Finally, through a process called consolidation, information passes to long-term memory for retrieval where it can be stored indefinitely.

This description of memory briefly explains the component processes involved when a memory is being created. But which of these processes are important to developing reading comprehension skills? In order to answer this question, we must first know which abilities are necessary for text comprehension. According to Baddeley (1986), in order to comprehend text, readers must be able to build "integrated mental representations," and, in order to build an integrated mental representation, several component skills are required. First, readers must be able to simultaneously store and process information in order to integrate that information within a text. This helps the individual combine information from previous paragraphs or sentences with what is currently being read to create a coherent mental model. Readers must also be able to integrate prior knowledge with a text when generating inferences, monitoring their comprehension to ensure they understand the material, and structuring a causal and temporal sequence of events (Cain, Oakhill, & Bryant, 2004). All of these skills require the processing and storage functions of working memory, which helps to explain why working memory in particular is of such great interest to reading and memory researchers.

Working memory is conceptualized as a workspace in which integration and inference take place. Originally thought of as a sort of "black box" that could hold information until full, it is now believed that working memory is more than just a simple temporary memory store. In fact, working memory has been called the interface between perception and memory, attention, and action (Baddeley, 2000). According to Baddeley's (2000) multicomponent model of working memory, working memory is comprised of four component systems. The "central executive" is responsible for the integration of information and the coordination of its three slave systems, the phonological loop, the visuospatial sketchpad, and the episodic buffer. The phonological loop holds verbal and acoustic information in a temporary store through the use of an articulatory rehearsal system. The visuospatial sketchpad holds visuospatial information. The episodic buffer acts as a temporary interface between the loop and sketchpad slave systems. The buffer is assumed to be able to store information in a multidimensional code (Baddeley, 2000) and is controlled by the central executive, which creates coherent episodes through the binding of information from the slave systems.

The multicomponent model of working memory has been prominent in cognitive psychology since 1974, but several other popular models of working memory exist today. In 1995, Ericsson and Kintsch proposed their theory of long-term working memory (LTWM). Arguing that it is not possible to explain how memory is used in many cognitive tasks within the standard framework, Ericsson and Kintsch suggested that there are conditions in which working memory capacity can increase. They hold that LTWM is an expert skill, and that it manifests itself when engaged in a familiar knowledge domain. As an example, Kintsch, Patel, and Ericsson (1999) refer to the fact that master chess players show superior memory when asked to memorize chess positions. As a result of years of practice and study, they have developed superior memory in the domain of chess, however, when tested on memory tasks outside their domain of expertise, master chess players perform only as well as the average person.

The LTWM theory considers two components of working memory, short-term working memory and long-term working memory. Short-term working memory has a limited capacity, but is always available. By way of contrast, long-term working memory is only available in expert domains, but it has an infinite capacity. Ericsson and Kintsch hold that LTWM is a subset of long-term memory and the information in LTWM is retrievable through cues in short-term working memory. Any item or cue in the focus of attention which is linked by a stable memory structure to contents in long-term memory makes those contents immediately available. Because these stable memory structures arise through repetition and practice, LTWM is available only in the context of expert domains.

Kintsch, Patel, and Ericsson (1999) further argue that reading and listening skills are practiced by most people over a lifetime and that, for many, reading comprehension becomes an expert skill. The idea that reading comprehension is a domain of mental expertise may help to explain how many humans are able to engage in such a complex cognitive process without having to exert extraordinary effort. Keep in mind both the multicomponent model of working memory and LTWM theory when considering current findings from the reading and memory literature. Before reviewing the research, it would be appropriate to discuss what is already known about how the memory system is involved in text comprehension.

Text comprehension is a highly complex process. Indeed, its apparent complexity was a factor that led Ericsson and Kintsch to develop the theory of LTWM. With respect to text comprehension, working memory essentially serves as a buffer that enables the integration of information from long-term memory with the text being read. Van Dijk and Kintsch (1983) listed components of the memory system that seemed to be involved in text comprehension, including perceptual features, linguistic features, propositional structure, macrostructure, situation model, control structure, goals, lexical knowledge, frames, general knowledge, and episodic memory from prior text. Not only are there several components of memory that aid text comprehension, but memory, specifically working memory, is related to several of the psycholinguistic processes crucial to comprehension, such as inference making, comprehension monitoring, structuring narratives, and memory for facts (Cain, Oakhill, & Bryant, 2004; Daneman & Carpenter, 1980; Daneman & Green, 1986; Dixon, LeFevre, & Twilley, 1988; Just & Carpenter, 1992; Masson & Miller, 1983).

Given that working memory contributes to so many of the functions necessary for comprehension, the questions that surround current research in the field focus principally on whether or not working memory can be considered a direct predictor of reading comprehension and how individual differences in working memory might manifest themselves during reading. Research has already identified several direct predictors of reading comprehension including vocabulary knowledge, decoding skills, word recognition, and verbal intelligence; but should working memory be considered a direct predictor, or should it be viewed as a supporter of the psycholinguistic processes necessary for developing reading skills? Significant progress has been made toward answering these questions, and is most clearly evident in research examining reading during development and reading comprehension for individuals with reading disabilities and poor comprehension skills.

Memory and Reading During Development

Seigneuric, Ehrlich, Oakhill, and Yuill (2000) conducted a study examining the working memory resources and children's reading comprehension. Participants in the study were 48 fourth-grade French-speaking students. Students were given tests to assess reading comprehension, vocabulary, and decoding skills. In addition to these tests, performance was measured on five separate working memory tasks, two verbal, two numerical, and one spatial task. All measurements were taken across four sessions. Using correlational analyses, they found that all working memory measures, except the spatial measure, were highly correlated with reading comprehension, and the observed correlations were in the same range as the correlations between standard predictors of reading comprehension (vocabulary and decoding skills). Multiple regression analyses revealed vocabulary to be the strongest predictor of reading comprehension. Working memory measures involving words, sentences, and digits made significant contributions to variability in reading comprehension over and above the impact of vocabulary and decoding. Seigneuric, et al. concluded that working memory was an important predictor of reading comprehension when compared to other well-known predictors. Additional findings demonstrated that verbal and numerical working memory tasks predicted reading comprehension, showing that the task did not have to be reading related although the verbal working memory tasks were stronger predictors. Visuospatial measures of working memory were not significantly correlated with reading comprehension. The authors concluded that this might support the hypothesis that working memory is generalized for the language processes responsible for manipulation of words and number symbols.

In a 2005 study, Seigneuric and Ehrlich reported results from a longitudinal investigation, which focused on the contribution of working memory capacity to children's reading comprehension. At the beginning of the study, the sample consisted of 74 children and had decreased to 56 at the conclusion of the study three years later. Again, all children in the study were native speakers of French. Participants were measured in grades one, two, and three and received a large battery of tests including phonological coding, vocabulary, working memory, and reading comprehension. Working memory was measured with a listening span task. Using multiple regression analysis, researchers found that decoding skill was the dominant factor for predicting reading comprehension variance in grade one. In grade two, results showed that both decoding and vocabulary skill predicted significant variance in reading comprehension scores. It was not until grade three that working memory capacity emerged as a significant predictor where vocabulary made the largest contribution to reading comprehension, followed by decoding skill and working memory capacity. The authors argue that the results demonstrate an increase in the relation between working memory capacity and reading comprehension as a student advances in school. Results through grade three were consistent with the results obtained when studying students in grade four, which identified working memory as an important predictor of reading comprehension. As a student progresses through grade levels, word recognition becomes more automatic, and they are confronted with longer, more difficult texts. The authors suggest that because of the increase in text difficulty, factors related to text integration, such as working memory, exert an increasingly strong influence over reading comprehension.

Cain, Oakhill, and Bryant (2004) conducted a longitudinal study investigating whether there was a direct relation between children's working memory capacity and reading comprehension ability. In addition to working memory, the authors examined higher level component skills, including comprehension monitoring, story structure, and inference skills to investigate their relative associations with reading comprehension.

Researchers were able to determine the degree to which WM mediated these associations by examining them simultaneously. Participants in the study were 102 children who were measured during the years of their 8th, 9th, and 11th birthdays, and were given assessments measuring reading ability, vocabulary, verbal ability, inference and integration skill, comprehension monitoring, and knowledge of story structure. Two measures of working memory were used, a sentence span task and a digit working memory task. Results showed working memory was associated with reading comprehension over and above the contribution made by reading skill and verbal ability. The data also showed relations between comprehension monitoring, inference making, and reading comprehension skill, and these associations were not completely explained by the variance they each shared with working memory.

It seems as though previous research supports the notion that working memory can be used to predict reading comprehension, but recent findings may cast doubt on these results. A longitudinal study conducted by Oakhill and Cain (2012) investigated the possibility that word reading and reading comprehension may be determined by the same component skills that independently predict reading comprehension development. One hundred and two students participated in the study and were assessed once when they were between ages 7 and 8, again between the ages of 8 and 9, and finally between the ages of 10 and 11 years. Students were assessed on measures of reading ability, vocabulary, phonological awareness, working memory, grammatical knowledge, general intellectual ability, and specific components of comprehension (text integration and inferential processing, comprehension monitoring, and knowledge of story structure). Similar to the 2004 study, the two measures of working memory used were the listening span task and the digit span task. Contrary to the results of Seigneuric and Ehrlich (2005), Oakhill and Cain showed that working memory was not a predictor of reading comprehension or of specific discourse skills. The authors pointed out that working memory may still support many of the skills that underlie reading comprehension, but that processing capacity cannot solely explain the relations between component skills and reading comprehension.

The research just examined details several key findings that contribute to current understanding of working memory and its relation to reading comprehension and component processes. First, determinants of individual differences in reading comprehension appear to change with age (Seigneuric & Ehrlich, 2005). Whereas word reading and recognition, vocabulary, and decoding abilities are the strongest predictors of reading comprehension level during early years (Juel, Griffith, & Gough, 1986; Seigneuric & Ehrlich, 2005), working memory emerges as a significant predictor around the time a student is in grade three (about age 8 years). As the developing student is faced with more difficult texts, and as word recognition becomes more automatic, factors related to text integration, such as working memory, appear to exert an increasingly strong influence on reading comprehension. If working memory is not a direct predictor of reading comprehension, as suggested by Oakhill and Cain, it at least supports many of the component skills involved. Because reading requires information to be held in memory while subsequent material is being processed, working memory should be regarded as one of several factors that influence comprehension ability and its development.

Another potential explanation for the association between working memory and reading comprehension is that reading comprehension, and the knowledge gained from reading, may support the development of working memory. Connor and colleagues (Connor, et al., in press) examined reciprocal effects among reading comprehension, self-regulation using a measure with a strong working memory component, and vocabulary (i.e., semantic knowledge). Their model demonstrated that gains in reading comprehension predicted gains in working memory (see also discussion in Chapter 1 of the Lattice Model).

Memory and Individuals with Reading Disabilities

Significant progress has been made towards understanding how working memory impacts reading ability because of research examining individuals with reading disabilities (RD). Children with RD display a wide range of reading-related deficiencies, and not all reading disabilities are created equal. Many children with RD have trouble producing narratives with a coherent causal structure (Cain, 2003). They may also experience difficulty making links between individual sentences to establish a local coherence, and integrating new information into existing mental representations to establish global coherence. Children with RD are also poor at monitoring the "sense" of text as they read (Oakhill, Hartt, & Samols, 2005), meaning that if they encounter information in a text that contradicts previous information, they are less likely to recognize the inconsistency. All of these skills are dependent on the processing capacity of working memory because they require that information is stored in memory while other information is being processed. The following research demonstrates how weak working memory performance can affect reading comprehension ability.

A 2007 study conducted by Swanson and Jerman investigated whether children with RD differed in working memory and short-term memory growth when compared to skilled readers. Additionally, the researchers asked if growth in the executive system or the phonological storage system mediated growth in reading performance. In order to answer these questions, a longitudinal study was conducted examining 84 children between the ages of 11 and 17. Participants were divided into subgroups of children with RD, children with reading and arithmetic deficits, children with low verbal IQ, and children who were skilled readers. All participants were measured at one-year intervals for three years. Researchers used three measures of short-term memory including a forward digit span, a word span, and a pseudo-word span test, and four measures of working memory including a backward digit span task, an updating task, a digit/sentence span task, and a rhyming task. Reading comprehension and word fluency were also assessed. Results demonstrated that the estimates for working memory growth were much higher for skilled readers than for children with RD. Additionally, an HLM analysis showed that controlled attention, rather than short-term memory capacity, was related to growth in reading comprehension and reading fluency. The findings from this study are unique in that they show both working memory differences increasing with age, and that the short-term memory skills of children with RD are similar to the skills of children with typical reading skills.

Cain (2006) conducted a series of quasi-experiments in order to determine if semantic or inhibitory deficits explain the problems student with poor comprehension skills have with verbal short-term and verbal working memory. Three experiments were conducted with 26 children between the ages of 9 and 10 years. Thirteen of the children were skilled readers, and 13 had poor comprehension. All children in the study were matched for vocabulary knowledge. In experiment 1, participants were given two short-term memory tasks, a digit recall and a word recall task. Results demonstrated no differences in short-term retention and recall of digits and words between students with good and poor comprehension. These findings complement those of Swanson's 2007 study, suggesting that students with poor comprehension have intact short-term memory and can store and recall verbal material just as well as individuals without any reading disability.

The second quasi-experiment examined whether students with poor comprehension demonstrated greater impairment on word-based or number-based assessments of working memory. Children were given a working memory sentence task and a working memory counting task. Each task consisted of four trials, with each trial increasing in difficulty (i.e., increasing the storage load). The data showed significant differences between students with weak comprehension and students with good comprehension and their performance on WM tasks. Additionally, as the storage load for the task increased, the differences became more pronounced. Although good comprehenders outperformed students with weak comprehension on each task, group differences were greater for the task with high semantic content. Results from this experiment suggest that students with weak comprehension may be less able to use semantic skills to support memory.

Cain's final quasi-experiment considered the possibility that students with good and poor comprehension differ in their ability to inhibit information. This experiment used a sentence processing and memory task to compare inhibitory processing. In the first phase of the task, participants were asked to supply the experimenter with a terminal noun at the end of a sentence, i.e., fill in the blank. For example, the researcher might say "The carpenter hit the nail with a …," and the participant had to supply the final word. The participant was asked to remember the final word for a later recall test. Half of the sentences presented were experimental items for which the experimenter would produce a low-probability response. For example, if the researcher said "The carpenter hits the nail with his …," the common answer is "hammer." If the participant answered "hammer" the experimenter would disconfirm the answer, and supply a low-probability response to be remembered, in this case, "knee". In the second phase of the task, participants were again instructed to "fill in the blank" with the first word that came to mind. To test if the child had correctly remembered "knee," the experimenter would supply the sentence, "To jump high in the air, I need to bend my …" If the participant had remembered the confirmed ending they should respond with "knees." To test inhibition of the disconfirmed word "hammer," the experimenter would say "My father went to the store to buy a new …" If the participant responded with "hammer," the word had not been successfully inhibited.

Results from the final quasi-experiment showed that students with weak comprehension were more likely to provide words that should have been inhibited. In addition, Cain's study demonstrated that students with weak comprehension have the ability to store and recall verbal material, but they experienced trouble with tasks requiring the simultaneous storage and processing of verbal stimuli.

The studies outlined in this chapter, as well as others, show that individuals with weak comprehension experience difficulty with working memory tasks that require the simultaneous processing and storage of verbal materials (Cain, Oakhill, & Lemmon, 2004; Daneman & Merikle, 1996; Seigneuric, Ehrlich, Oakhill, & Yuill, 2000; Yuill, Oakhill, & Parkin, 1989). Furthermore, research demonstrates that children with weak reading comprehension skills may have weaker inhibitory mechanisms (Barnes, Faulkner, Wilkinson, & Dennis; Cain, 2006; de Beni & Palladino, 2000; Gernsbacher & Faust, 1991). This suggests that the problems experienced by individuals with RD may stem from their inability to regulate the contents of working memory, even though the storage component is intact.

A finding of particular interest is that skilled readers show age-related increases in working memory whereas children with RD exhibit minimal changes in working memory span level across ages 7 to 20 (Swanson, 2003). This discovery is intriguing, especially in conjunction with the findings of Seigneuric and Ehrlich (2005) suggesting that working memory emerges as a predictor of reading comprehension in third grade. If the working memory of children with RD fails to continue developing at age 7, and the association of working memory and reading comprehension emerges at approximately the same time, perhaps the reason working memory is not a good predictor of reading comprehension in earlier years is because the working memory capacities of young children have developed sufficiently. Furthermore, one has to wonder if working memory differences become predictive of reading comprehension in third grade because the texts are becoming more challenging, or because the working memory span of skilled readers continues to grow while the working memory of children with RD stagnates.

Contributions of Short- and Long-term Memory

What are the contributions of short-term and long-term memory to learning to read? Current reading research overwhelmingly examines working memory for good reason. The act of reading cannot take place unless one can hold information in memory while simultaneously processing information, linking it to previous knowledge and creating a coherent mental structure. This is essentially the function of working memory, but that is not to say that short-term and long-term memory do not make contributions to reading comprehension. In fact, both systems do contribute to reading comprehension despite being overshadowed by the contributions of working memory.

Short-term memory appears to support vocabulary learning and sentence parsing (Oakhill & Cain, 2012), but only weakly correlates to comprehension ability (Daneman & Merikle, 1996). No significant differences have been observed between groups of children who differ in reading comprehension and traditional measures of short-term memory (de Beni & Palladino, 2000; Oakhill & Cain, 2012; Oakhill, et al., 1986), and evidence suggests that children with RD have intact short-term memory (Cain, 2006). Long-term memory is important for reading comprehension, but not for component skills such as decoding or comprehension monitoring (Pazzaglia, Cornoldi, & Tressoldi, 1993). The integration of information with prior knowledge while reading is obviously dependent on long-term memory, because prior knowledge is contained within long-term memory. Research has shown that readers have an easier time dealing with reduced coherence in text if they have high prior knowledge about what they are reading (McNamara & Kintsch, 1996). This observation makes sense with respect to Ericsson and Kintsch's theory of long-term working memory, as a higher level of expertise would imply a more stable memory structure to long-term memory.

Synthesis, Implications, and Future Directions

The research presented strongly supports the notion that working memory plays an important role in reading comprehension. While short-term memory only weakly correlates with comprehension ability, working memory has been shown to be associated with many of the psycholinguistic processes that underlie reading comprehension ability. The effects of prior knowledge on text comprehension are unmistakably important to the reading process, but according to several models working memory allows readers to retrieve information from long-term memory and integrate it with the text currently being processed. Working memory is certainly the most influential memory process in respect to text comprehension, and research continues to reveal more about its nature and the ways in which it affects complex cognitive processes.

The research reviewed in this chapter has detailed several key observations about working memory and its relationship to reading. First, symbolic memory tasks involving the manipulation of words or numbers are far better predictors of reading comprehension than are visuospatial working memory tasks. This finding provides support for the notion that visuospatial and symbolic working memory tasks may tap separate cognitive resource pools. Second, individual differences appear to originate more from processing capacity than from storage capacity. A number of the studies reviewed in this chapter show that there exist no significant differences between the storage capacity of children with RD and children who are skilled readers. This suggests that individuals with RD have intact short-term memory (i.e., they can store just as much information as skilled readers) but they encounter problems when processing this information. Evidence from Cain's 2006 study supports this interpretation by demonstrating that children with RD had decreased ability to inhibit irrelevant information.

Finally, research seems to suggest that working memory becomes increasingly important to reading comprehension as a child develops. Evidence from Seigneuric and Ehrlich's 2005 study showed that working memory was not a predictor of reading comprehension skill until the third grade, and Swanson (2003) has observed minimal changes to the working memory capacities of children with reading disabilities from ages 7 to 20. Swanson and Jerman (2007) conjecture that children who have a large working memory capacity for language can carry out the execution of various fundamental reading processes with fewer demands on a limited resource pool than can children who have a smaller working memory capacity. As a result, children with a larger working memory capacity would have more resources available for storage while comprehending a passage. In contrast, children with a smaller working memory capacity might have fewer resources available for the maintenance of information during reading.

Returning to the Lattice Model presented in Chapter 1, it might be possible that working memory and reading comprehension are reciprocally related (Connor, et al., in review). That is, children's developing reading comprehension may strengthen working memory and developing working memory may facilitate reading comprehension. Arguably, greater background knowledge gained through reading is likely to improve working memory and so these reciprocal effects might also be indirect.

When considering the implications of these findings, the future appears to be grim for children with RD. Not only do they have the inability to regulate the contents of their working memory while reading, but their working memory capacity virtually stops increasing around the age of 7. While some may propose working memory interventions to help children with RD, Redick and colleagues (2012) assert that working memory intervention research suffers from several methodological flaws and more research is needed to determine whether working memory training can produce actual benefits for its users. Future research should focus on how to best deal with these working memory deficiencies, and how they might be prevented. Much research has already shown that teaching readers strategies such as self-explanation can greatly improve reading comprehension (McNamara, Levinstein, & Boonthum, 2004). Reading strategy training should begin early in a child's reading career in order to combat the detrimental effects of RD.

Future research examining memory and learning to read would benefit from a focus on causation—testing whether improving working memory contributes to stronger reading comprehension and vice versa. Research by Swanson and colleagues suggests that working memory is malleable (Swanson, Kehler, & Jerman, 2010; Swanson & O'Connor, 2009) but it is not clear that improved working memory actually improves reading comprehension. Quasi-experiments that compare stronger and weaker readers are biased. More often than not, children who are skilled readers with high working memory capacities come from homes where they are often read to. Is working memory improved by increased exposure to reading and literature, or do children become better readers because they have stronger working memory skills, or is there a third factor contributing to both reading comprehension and working memory? In any case, memory clearly plays a role in proficient reading comprehension but it is not clear that memory processes are malleable or good targets for reading interventions except, perhaps, as part of a multicomponent intervention. More research is needed.

References

Baddeley, A. D. (1986). *Working Memory*. Oxford: Oxford University Press.

Baddeley, A. D. (2000). The episodic buffer: A new component of working memory? *Trends in Cognitive Sciences*, 4(11), 417–423.

Barnes, M. A., Faulkner, H., Wilkinson, M., & Dennis, M. (2004). Meaning construction and integration in children with hydrocephalus. *Brain and Language*, 89(1), 47–56.

Cain, K. (2003). Text comprehension and its relation to coherence and cohesion in children's fictional narratives. *British Journal of Developmental Psychology, 21*(3), 335–351.

Cain, K. (2006). Individual differences in children's memory and reading comprehension: An investigation of semantic and inhibitory deficits. *Memory, 14,* 553–569.

Cain, K., Oakhill, J., & Bryant, P. (2004). Children's reading comprehension ability: Concurrent prediction by working memory, verbal ability, and component skills. *Journal of Educational Psychology, 96*(1), 31.

Cain, K., Oakhill, J., & Lemmon, K. (2004). Individual differences in the inference of word meanings from context: the influence of reading comprehension, vocabulary knowledge, and memory capacity. *Journal of Educational Psychology, 96*(4), 671.

Connor, C. M., Day, S. G., Phillips, B. M., Ingebrand, S., McLean, L. E., Sparapani, N., et al. (in press). Reciprocal effects of reading, vocabulary, and executive functioning in early elementary school. *Child Development.*

Daneman, M., & Carpenter, P. A. (1980). Individual differences in working memory and reading. *Journal of Verbal Learning and Verbal Behavior, 19*(4), 450–466.

Daneman, M., & Green, I. (1986). Individual differences in comprehending and producing words in context. *Journal of Memory and Language, 25*(1), 1–18.

Daneman, M., & Merikle, P. M. (1996). Working memory and language comprehension: A meta-analysis. *Psychonomic Bulletin & Review, 3*(4), 422–433.

De Beni, R., & Palladino, P. (2000). Intrusion errors in working memory tasks: Are they related to reading comprehension ability? *Learning and Individual Differences, 12*(2), 131–143.

Dixon, P., LeFevre, J. A., & Twilley, L. C. (1988). Word knowledge and working memory as predictors of reading skill. *Journal of Educational Psychology, 80*(4), 465.

Engle, R. W. (2002). Working memory capacity as executive attention. *Current Directions in Psychological Science, 11*(1), 19–23.

Ericsson, K. A., & Kintsch, W. (1995). Long-term working memory. *Psychological Review, 102*(2), 211.

Gernsbacher, M. A., & Faust, M. E. (1991). The mechanism of suppression: A component of general comprehension skill. *Journal of Experimental Psychology: Learning, Memory, and Cognition, 17*(2), 245.

Juel, C., Griffith, P. L., & Gough, P. B. (1986). Acquisition of literacy: A longitudinal study of children in first and second grade. *Journal of Educational Psychology, 78*(4), 243–255.

Just, M. A., & Carpenter, P. A. (1992). A capacity theory of comprehension: Individual differences in working memory. *Psychological Review, 99,* 122–149.

Kintsch, W., Patel, V. L., & Ericsson, K. A. (1999). The role of long-term working memory in text comprehension. *Psychologia, 42*(4), 186–198.

McNamara, D. S., & Kintsch, W. (1996). Learning from texts: Effects of prior knowledge and text coherence. *Discourse Processes, 22*(3), 247–288.

McNamara, D. S., Levinstein, I. B., & Boonthum, C. (2004). iSTART: Interactive strategy trainer for active reading and thinking. *Behavioral Research Methods, Instruments, & Computers, 36,* 222–233.

Masson, M. E., & Miller, J. A. (1983). Working memory and individual differences in comprehension and memory of text. *Journal of Educational Psychology, 75*(2), 314.

Myers, D. G. (2004). *Exploring Psychology*. Basingstoke: Macmillan.

Oakhill, J. V., & Cain, K. (2012). The precursors of reading ability in young readers: Evidence from a four-year longitudinal study. *Scientific Studies of Reading, 16*(2), 91–121.

Oakhill, J., Hartt, J., & Samols, D. (2005). Levels of comprehension monitoring and working memory in good and poor comprehenders. *Reading and Writing, 18*(7–9), 657–686.

Oakhill, J. V., Yuill, N. M., & Parkin, A. (1986). On the nature of the difference between skilled and less-skilled comprehenders. *Journal of Research in Reading, 9*, 80–91.

Pazzaglia, F., Cornoldi, C., & Tressoldi, P. E. (1993). Learning to read: Evidence on the distinction between decoding and comprehension skills. *European Journal of Psychology of Education, 8*(3), 247–258.

Redick, T. S., Shipstead, Z., Harrison, T. L., Hicks, K. L., Fried, D. E., Hambrick, D. Z., et al. (2012). No evidence of intelligence improvement after working memory training: A randomized, placebo-controlled study. *Journal of Experimental Psychology: General.* Advanced online publication.

Seigneuric, A., & Ehrlich, M. F. (2005). Contribution of working memory capacity to children's reading comprehension: A longitudinal investigation. *Reading and Writing, 18*(7–9), 617–656.

Seigneuric, A., Ehrlich, M. F., Oakhill, J. V., & Yuill, N. M. (2000). Working memory resources and children's reading comprehension. *Reading and Writing, 13*(1–2), 81–103.

Swanson, H. L. (2003). Age-related differences in learning disabled and skilled readers' working memory. *Journal of Experimental Child Psychology, 85*, 1–31.

Swanson, H. L., & Jerman, O. (2007). The influence of working memory on reading growth in subgroups of children with reading disabilities. *Journal of Experimental Child Psychology, 96*(4), 249–283.

Swanson, H. L., Kehler, P., & Jerman, O. (2010). Working memory, strategy knowledge, and strategy instruction in children with reading disabilities. *Journal of Learning Disabilities, 43*(1), 24–47.

Swanson, H. L., & O'Connor, R. (2009). The role of working memory and fluency practice on the reading comprehension of students who are dysfluent readers. *Journal of Learning Disabilities, 42*(6), 548–575.

Van Dijk, T. A., & Kintsch, W. (1983). *Strategies of Discourse Comprehension.* New York: Academic Press.

Yuill, N., Oakhill, J., & Parkin, A. (1989). Working memory, comprehension ability and the resolution of text anomaly. *British Journal of Psychology, 80*(3), 351–361.

Chapter 5

Self-Regulation and Reading Achievement

Betty Lin, Shayna S. Coburn, and Nancy Eisenberg

Understanding self-regulation has been regarded as "the single most crucial goal for advancing an understanding of development and psychopathology" (Posner & Rothbart, 2000, p. 427; Shonkoff & Phillips, 2000). Accordingly, the construct of self-regulation has garnered much interest across both developmental and educational sciences. Within the developmental sciences, a number of investigators have found associations between children's self-regulation and a range of competencies spanning emotional, behavioral, social, and academic domains (Eisenberg, Liew, & Pidada, 2004; Eisenberg et al., 2009). Similarly, studies emerging from educational sciences indicate that self-regulation appears to be a particularly important factor for predicting academic outcomes such as reading, math, etc. (Zimmerman, 2001). However, variations in semantic applications of the term "self-regulation" and different foci on socioemotional or cognitive systems have complicated efforts for integrating knowledge about the role of self-regulation in learning across disciplines. In the current chapter, we selectively review literature from cognitive, developmental, and educational sciences to provide an integrated definition of self-regulation and demonstrate the relevance of self-regulation for learning, with a specific focus on the acquisition of reading skills as an example.

What is Self-Regulation?

The term "self-regulation" was first applied to psychological literature to describe concepts of behavioral learning (Kanfer & Phillips, 1970) and has since been extended to describe the modulation of different systems (e.g., emotional, behavioral, attentional, cognitive, physiological) that influence functioning. Perhaps attributable in part to the heterogeneity in thinking about the role and function of the self in modulating each of these systems, there is some debate regarding varying distinctions of key characteristics of self-regulation. For example, although self-regulation in domains of learning often involves explicit goal behaviors (e.g., to finish reading a book), scholars who have studied self-regulation in domains of learning have often (but not always; e.g., Chartrand & Bargh, 1996) focused on self-directed and volitional processes. In contrast, self-regulation in domains of emotion modulation often involves implicit goals imposed by social norms (e.g., not showing obvious disappointment after receiving a broken gift). Thus, emotion-focused self-regulation may be more self-directed for some than others, and more purposeful for some yet more automatic for others. Another nuance that has complicated an understanding and definitions of self-regulation is that self-regulatory processes that begin purposefully and target explicit goals or goal states may, over time and practice, become automatic and implicit. For example, an early learner's initially effortful and conscious attempts to improve reading skills by sounding out phonemes for each word become automatic and less purposefully self-regulated over time as reading fluency increases.

Given the nuances in studies of self-regulation both within and across domains of functioning, scholars have diverged in their characterizations of self-regulation as volitional and/or automatic, internally and/or externally driven, and goal directed or not. To help resolve these discrepancies, some scholars have argued that it is useful to further differentiate automatic modulation that is difficult to bring under more willful control from processes that can more easily be willfully modulated and to reserve the term "self-regulation" for the latter (Eisenberg, Hofer, Sulik, & Spinrad, 2014; Eisenberg & Morris, 2002; Rothbart & Bates, 2006). These distinctions have been addressed in detail by Eisenberg and colleagues (2014).

Another important distinction regards the similarities and differences between what scholars have described as self-regulation and effortful control. Children's self-regulatory capacities are believed to have a basis in children's temperament, or biologically based proclivities for reactivity and regulation (Rothbart, 2011). Specifically, "effortful control," or the regulatory component of child temperament, is thought to serve as a foundation for the development of self-regulation across the lifespan. Rothbart and Bates (2006) defined effortful control as "the efficiency of executive attention, including the ability to inhibit a dominant response and/or to activate a subdominant response, to plan, and to detect errors" (p. 129). In other words, effortful control involves the abilities to willfully deploy attention (often called attention focusing and shifting and including cognitive distraction) and to willfully inhibit or activate behavior (inhibitory control and activational control, respectively) as needed to adapt and achieve goals. It also includes other executive functioning-related abilities such as detecting errors and planning. Effortful control provides the dispositional capacities for self-regulation, although self-regulation in a given situation may be based on learning and contextual factors. Although conceptually distinct (see Eisenberg et al., 2014, for a discussion), effortful control and self-regulation overlap in many respects and, thus, have been often used interchangeably in literature.

A final distinction regards the similarities and differences between self-regulation and executive functions. Executive functions are broader capacities, including working memory, inhibitory control, and cognitive flexibility (Rueda, Posner, & Rothbart, 2005) that support self-regulatory efforts. Cognitive mechanisms necessary for executive functions are housed primarily within the prefrontal cortex of the brain and the anterior cingulate gyrus, and together are responsible for planning, motivation, organization, problem solving, purposeful actions, and self-monitoring of progress toward goals (Baumeister & Vohs, 2012). *Working memory* involves active updating and maintaining information over a short period of time, (see Chapter 4 for a more in-depth discussion; see also Rueda et al., 2005). Although not always viewed as a component of self-regulation (Eisenberg & Zhou, 2015), working memory likely supports self-regulation (Hofmann, Schmeichel, & Baddeley, 2012). Additionally, *inhibitory control* reflect's one's capacity to resist and reduce automatic responses to unnecessary or distracting stimuli. Finally, *cognitive flexibility* is the ability to shift attention fluidly from one area of focus to another and to adjust one's behaviors to the new focus. Inhibitory control and cognitive flexibility typically are viewed as components of effortful control, as well as executive functioning (Eisenberg & Zhou, 2015). Similar to effortful control, the terms *executive functions* and *self-regulation* are conceptually distinct (see Eisenberg & Zhou, 2015, for a discussion), but are partially overlapping and have often been used interchangeably in literature, especially in studies of self-regulation and learning (e.g., Dombek & Connor, 2012).

Self-Regulation and the Acquisition of Academic Skills

Scholars have long acknowledged that different child characteristics are more or less conducive to school success. The advent of compulsory education raised interest in distinguishing children who would benefit from mainstream education from those who would require special education services (Goodwin, 2011). Although early scientific efforts were focused largely on the use of intelligence testing as a method for identifying struggling learners, even the developer of the first modern intelligence test, Alfred Binet, acknowledged the moderating influence of self-regulation (Binet & Simon, 1916). In fact, Binet cautioned that children's scholastic aptitude (i.e., ability to learn) should not be confounded with intellectual ability (Binet & Simon, 1916). He stated:

> [T]he scholastic aptitude admits of other things than intelligence; to succeed in his studies, one must have qualities which depend especially on attention, will, and character; for example a certain docility, a regularity of habits, and especially continuity of effort. A child, even if

intelligent, will learn little in class if he never listens, if he spends his time in playing tricks, in giggling, in playing truant. (p. 254)

Indeed, some studies have yielded findings supportive of the notion that children's self-regulatory capacity is an even stronger predictor of school success than is children's intelligence quotient (IQ; Blair & Razza, 2007; Duckworth, Peterson, Matthews, & Kelly, 2007; Duckworth, Tsukayama, & May, 2010; Shoda, Mischel, & Peake, 1990). Self-regulation may affect learning in two important ways. First, as much of cognitive and developmental research has highlighted, the self-regulation of basic behavioral, emotional, and attentional systems that support learning—e.g., the ability to sit still, comply with teachers' instructions, and cope with frustration when presented with challenging tasks—appears to influence the extent to which children access and benefit from formal instruction, or children's school readiness (e.g., Blair & Razza, 2007; Eisenberg, Valiente, & Eggum, 2010; Howse, Diehl, & Trivette, 2010). Second, as much of educational research has investigated, the self-regulation of higher-order cognitive systems (i.e., executive functions) that afford the capacities to set, implement, monitor, and revise learning-related goals likely directly influences children's capacity to acquire new knowledge (e.g., Duckworth et al., 2007; Duncan et al., 2007; Gollwitzer, Parks-Stamm, Jaudas, & Sheeran, 2008; Vidal-Abarca, Mañá, & Gil, 2010).

Self-Regulation and School Readiness

Even before learning can begin, children's abilities to self-regulate emotional, behavioral, and attentional systems to conform to the social and academic demands of the school environment necessarily have implications for academic success. In fact, some scholars have argued that children's self-regulatory abilities are fundamental for later academic skills (Eisenberg et al., 2010; Raver, 2002; Valiente et al., 2011). This notion has been corroborated by research indicating that self-regulation is predictive of emergent literary, vocabulary, and math skills even after controlling for pre-academic skills and other demographic contributors (Barbarin et al., 2013; Howse, Calkins, Anastopoulos, Keane, & Shelton, 2003; McClelland et al., 2007; Valiente et al., 2011). There is also evidence of reciprocal effects (Connor et al., in review). Self-regulation is believed to exert an influence on academic achievement through effects on behavioral and emotional adjustment, social competence, and positive teacher and peer relationships, and school engagement, all of which are integral to children's school readiness. In fact, Eisenberg and colleagues (2010) proposed a model in which relations between self-regulation and academic achievement are mediated by children's adjustment, social competence, and engagement. That is, observed associations between self-regulation and academic achievement are hypothesized to be attributable in part to relations between self-regulation and components of school readiness and, in turn, the relation of school readiness to academic achievement.

Children's adjustment and social competence are governed largely by children's capacities for behavioral and emotional regulation. In classroom settings, difficulties with behavioral regulation often manifest as externalizing behaviors, or "acting out" behaviors such as noncompliance (e.g., not listening to directions), defiance (e.g., talking back, arguing), hyperactivity (e.g., difficulty sitting still or staying in one's seat), impulsive responding (e.g., raising hand before questions are asked), aggression, and/or other challenging behaviors (e.g., difficulty keeping one's hands or feet to oneself, talking out of turn, vocal or motor stereotypies, etc.). Given the disruptive nature of many of these behaviors, it is not surprising that many teachers find behavioral problems to be one of the greatest barriers to children's school readiness. In a national study that surveyed nearly 3600 kindergarten teachers, more teachers reported that behavioral problems commonly impeded successful school entry more than lack of academic skills (Rimm-Kaufman, Pianta, & Cox, 2000).

Difficulties with emotion regulation may present as internalizing (i.e., inwardly directed) and/or externalizing behaviors. Internalizing forms of emotion regulation difficulties such as excessive worry, fear, sadness, and inhibition are often less disruptive, but may also interfere with children's learning readiness (Riglin, Petrides, Frederickson, & Rice, 2014). Examples of emotion regulation difficulties in classroom settings may include low frustration tolerance (e.g., as reflected in giving up easily and crying easily), difficulties concentrating secondary to disruptive emotional experiences (e.g., fixation on negative mood states or activating events instead of school work), low self-efficacy, noncompliance, defiance, and talking back.

Importantly, emotional and behavioral regulatory challenges are often interrelated. For example, children frustrated by challenging school assignments may engage in other disruptive, attention-seeking behaviors. Conversely, children who have a lot of trouble sitting still (i.e., modulating motor reactivity) may find the sedentary nature of most classroom environments to be frustrating. Both emotional and behavioral regulatory difficulties may take away from the mental and practical (e.g., time) resources children have to devote towards learning. A number of researchers have linked the amount of time children spend engaged in on-task activities with academic achievement (Curry, 1984; Taylor, Pearson, Clark, & Walpole, 2000), suggesting that the extent to which children benefit from classroom instruction is necessarily facilitated by their ability to attend to and engage in prescribed activities. Moreover, dysregulated classroom behaviors may increase the amount of time teachers spend managing behaviors and decrease the amount of time teachers are able to support learning. Skibbe and colleagues (2012) found that the class mean of students' behavioral self-regulatory skills as a whole was an even stronger predictor of growth in children's literacy skills across the academic year than children's *own* self-regulatory skills. Thus, children's difficulties with self-regulation may compromise not only their own learning readiness but also the quality of the overall learning environment.

Regulatory difficulties also have a number of social implications for children that indirectly influence children's school success. Children who have difficulty modulating emotions and behaviors are rated by teachers and parents to be less socially competent (Liew, Eisenberg, & Reiser, 2004). Moreover, the negative implications of poor social competence may be exacerbated by the co-occurrence of emotional and behavioral problems. Both lower social competence and higher behavioral problems are associated with poorer quality teacher-child and peer relationships (Newcomb, Bukowski, & Pattee, 1993; Parker & Asher, 1987), which may, in turn, decrease access to the social resources that promote learning and school engagement (Raver, 2002). Beginning as early as preschool, teachers have been found to spend less time engaged in instructional interactions, and to engage in more negative and fewer positive interactions (i.e., less praising and encouraging) with more challenging children compared to their less challenging counterparts (Arnold, McWilliams, & Arnold, 1998; Carr, Taylor, & Robinson, 1991; Raver, 2002; Shores & Wehby, 1999). Perhaps related, children who are more effective self-regulators tend to have closer relationships with their teachers, which, in turn, is related to positive school attitudes and academic performance (Eisenberg et al., 2010; Silva et al., 2011; Skibbe, Connor, Morrison, & Jewkes, 2011). Similarly, disruptive children tend to develop bad reputations with, and to be socially rejected by, their peers (Ladd & Burgess, 1999). Challenging children may be less desirable work partners, be excluded from informal class and homework assignments, and receive less classroom support and encouragement from their peers (Berndt & Keefe, 1995; Ladd & Burgess, 1999; Raver, 2002). Finally, children who engage in fewer pleasurable interactions with teachers and peers at school, receive less support with learning, and struggle to meet the demands of the classroom environment may enjoy school less and avoid school more often (Berndt & Keefe, 1995; Birch & Ladd, 1996; Murray & Greenberg, 2000; Raver, 2002).

Poor social competence appears to increase risk for school problems even in the absence of behavior problems. One study by Dombek and Connor (2012) found that among children receiving high-quality reading instruction, children who were retained at the end of the year had poorer social skills, but not more behavior problems, than their successful counterparts. It is conceivable that social skills protect against the deleterious effects of behavior problems on school achievement. Alternatively, behavior problems may be problematic only to the extent that they also compromise the child's access to social resources that promote learning and motivation.

Children's school engagement depends in large part on their abilities to effectively self-regulate their attentional systems. Unsurprisingly, children's abilities to control and sustain attention and to participate in classroom activities have been found to be related to grades and achievement test scores through the primary and secondary school years (Alexander, Entwisle, & Dauber, 1993; Mischel, Shoda, & Peake, 1988). In fact, some evidence suggests that the self-regulation of attentional systems may be an even stronger predictor of school success than the behavioral or social competencies described previously (Barriga et al., 2002; Duncan et al., 2007; Hinshaw, 1992). In a meta-analytic study that investigated contributions of various school-entry skills on achievement across six samples, Duncan and colleagues (2007) found that when controlling for pre-academic skills (i.e., math, reading, and general knowledge skills), attentional control was predictive of teacher ratings and test scores of reading and math achievement (average effect size of .10), but externalizing problems, internalizing problems, and social skills were not (average effect sizes ranged from .00 to .05). Researchers investigating differential contributions of attentional and behavioral difficulties to academic achievement in clinical samples have likewise found that attentional difficulties account for more of the variation in academic achievement than behavioral difficulties. Among children with attention deficit hyperactivity disorder (ADHD, a neurodevelopmental disorder characterized by marked difficulties with inattention, impulsivity, and/or hyperactivity), Barriga and colleagues (2002) found that the inattention component of ADHD was a stronger predictor of poor academic achievement than the hyperactivity-impulsivity component. Moreover, researchers investigating differential academic achievement in inattentive children with and without hyperactivity have failed to find across-group differences. Difficulties regulating attention may pose more risks for poor academic performance than behavioral and/or emotional problems alone, although attentional problems also appear to contribute to problem behaviors (e.g., Eisenberg et al. 2001, 2005, 2009).

Some scholars have posited that the comparatively stronger effects of attentional skills on achievement may be explained by the direct relevance of attention and the indirect relevance of behavioral and social skills for learning (Alexander et al., 1993; Cooper & Farran, 1988; Duncan et al., 2007; McClelland, Morrison, & Holmes, 2000; Searle, Miller-Lewis, Sawyer, & Baghurst, 2013). That is, whereas attentional problems directly affect children's abilities to attend to and receive instruction, behavioral and social skill deficits indirectly affect children's abilities to receive instruction by compromising attentional and social resources that, in turn, have implications for learning. If this is the case, associations between attentional difficulties and poor academic performance may explain some portion of the documented relations between behavioral/emotional problems and poor academic success (Metcalfe, Harvey, & Laws, 2013).

Hinshaw (1987) proposed that externalizing problems importantly comprise two overlapping but conceptually distinct subtypes—inattention/hyperactivity and aggression/conduct problems—both of which may have unique implications for children's academic achievement over time. In a meta-analysis that compared associations between inattention/hyperactivity and aggression/conduct problems with academic performance, Hinshaw (1992) found that inattention/hyperactivity was a stronger correlate of reading underachievement during primary school grades (i.e., approximately first through fifth grades), whereas aggression/conduct problems were stronger correlates of reading underachievement during secondary school grades (i.e., approximately sixth through twelfth grades). The salience of various regulatory difficulties for academic success may vary over time and across development.

Self-Regulated Learning

Corno and Mandinach (1983) were among the first to systematically describe the importance of the self-regulation of cognitive systems for influencing students' learning and academic achievement with self-regulated learning theory. Specifically, they defined self-regulated learning as a highly cognitively involved process in which students are actively engaged in and responsible for their own learning, and accordingly are self-reliant for problem solving through complex tasks. Importantly, Corno and Mandinach (1983) distinguished between the processes of cognitive engagement and apparent motivation/eventual task completion. They described an example in which a self-regulated learner persists in attempts to complete a challenging task by drawing from internal problem-solving resources (e.g., consulting a textbook or dictionary). In contrast, another student who also persists in attempts to complete the same task draws instead from external resources (e.g., asking a peer for help). They argued that although both students may appear equally motivated, the latter student, who draws from external resources, is actually choosing a less cognitively demanding method. Correspondingly, though both students achieve the short-term goal of completing the assignment, only the self-regulated learner acquires learning skills that afford the longer-term abilities to problem-solve and persist through difficult intellectual challenges.

Zimmerman (1986) went on to elaborate on this notion of self-regulated learning and suggested that self-regulated learners are those who are meta-cognitively, motivationally, and behaviorally active participants in their own learning. Self-regulated learners have greater capacity to plan, set goals, organize, self-monitor, and self-evaluate throughout the learning process. These capacities allow individuals to set goals about what they need to learn and what they should do to successfully learn it. These learning goals are then propelled by motivational forces including self-efficacy, self-attributions, and intrinsic task interest and, finally, are supported with behavioral efforts to select and structure learning environments that increase their likelihood for learning. Importantly, self-regulation of these higher-order, "top-down" processes is necessarily contingent first on the adequate self-regulation of those lower-order, "bottom-up" processes described previously (i.e., self-regulation of behavioral and emotional, and attentional systems). Moreover, as Blair and Diamond (2008) have underscored, self-regulation of lower and higher-order processes necessarily interact to contribute to self-regulated learning.

To better describe the ways in which each of these characteristics culminates to produce self-regulated learners, Zimmerman (2002) proposed a series of three cyclical phases describing processes that occur before, during, and after learning: forethought, performance, and self-reflection. In the *forethought* phase, students essentially weigh the costs and benefits associated with both goal attainment and self-motivation (i.e., self-efficacy, expected outcome, intrinsic interest) to decide about whether to engage in self-regulated learning. In the *performance* phase, students go on to employ strategies that facilitate goal attainment while attending to factors that may enhance or impede their learning. Finally, in the *self-reflection* phase, students evaluate their progress towards goals and their positive or negative reactions to their performance thus far, both of which then provide feedback for further cycles of learning until the desired goals are achieved or abandoned.

Notably, perhaps as a result of the focus on higher-order cognitive abilities that develop over time, this conceptualization largely mirrors those that grew out of earlier efforts to describe self-control processes in adults (Baumeister, Heatherton, & Tice, 1994; Baumeister & Vohs, 2012; Carver & Scheier, 1982). Specifically, scholars seeking to describe processes involved in self-control have broken down self-regulatory processes into three primary components: (1) establishing a goal, (2) engaging in appropriate behaviors to obtain one's goals, and (3) monitoring progress toward the goal (Baumeister et al., 1994; Baumeister & Vohs, 2012; Carver & Scheier, 1982). Although other variations and extensions of self-regulated learning have also been proposed, an exhaustive review is not within the scope of this chapter, but has been provided elsewhere (e.g., Pintrich, 2000a; Zimmerman & Schunk, 2011).

Forethought

By definition, self-regulation necessarily implies the presence of some underlying goal that one is striving towards. According to Zimmerman (2002), the forethought phase of self-regulated learning comprises two major components: task analysis and self-motivation beliefs (Zimmerman, 2002). A student's self-regulatory cycle is said to begin with *task analysis*, in which goals and strategies for goal pursuit are established. The initial goals or standards of achievement set during the forethought phase importantly provide students with criteria by which to evaluate progress in achievement situations and to decide about whether and how best to proceed with ongoing self-regulatory efforts (Wigfield, Klauda, & Cambria, 2011). A student's decision to initiate and maintain behaviors in the service of achievement-related goals is, in turn, influenced by her/his *self-motivation beliefs*, or beliefs and values about learning. Students who perceive their learning goals to be both highly desirable and highly feasible are likely to have stronger goal commitments (Gollwitzer, 1990; Heckhausen, 1977), and thus to successfully accomplish their goals (Ajzen, 1991; Webb & Sheeran, 2006). Specifically, self-motivation beliefs/values characterized by intrinsic interest in the learning goal (e.g., reading for fun versus because it is mandated; Ryan & Deci, 2001), enjoyment of the learning process (i.e., learning goal orientation; e.g., pride in becoming a better reader; Dweck, 1999; Zimmerman, 2002), perceived ability to take the steps necessary for goal attainment (i.e., self-efficacy expectations; Bandura, 1977), and perceived likelihood that the steps taken will in fact lead to goal attainment (i.e., outcome expectations; Bandura, 1977) promote successful goal attainment.

Because self-motivation beliefs play an important role in the initiation and maintenance of goal-directed behaviors, the most effective goals are ones that are also conducive to productive self-motivation beliefs. Considerable research suggests that goals predictive of successful task completion are specific (Locke & Latham, 1990), proximal in time frame (Bandura & Schunk, 1981), stated positively (i.e., promotion of positive outcomes instead of preventing negative consequences; Higgins, Shah, & Friedman, 1997), and are neither too easy nor too hard (Oettingen, 2012). For example, the goal stated "I will memorize five words on the spelling list daily" is specific (memorize five words), time-limited (daily), stated positively ("will" instead of "will not"), and reasonably attainable. In contrast, the goal stated "I will not fail the spelling test next week" is general, has no immediate time frame for enacting goal pursuit, and focuses on what *not* to do rather than what to do to promote success.

Although as previously stated, short-term (proximal) goals are more closely tied to performance on specific learning tasks than are long-term (distal) goals, long-term goals are also thought to play an important role in guiding self-regulatory efforts over time (Husman & Shell, 2008; Wigfield et al., 2011). In fact, Duckworth and colleagues (2007) have emphasized the importance of grit, defined as "perseverance and passion for long-term goals … [which] entails working strenuously toward challenges, maintaining effort and interest over years despite failure, adversity, and plateaus in progress" (p. 1087), in promoting achievement outcomes. Indeed, grit has been found to be an even stronger predictor of achievement than individual's age, IQ, or self-reported self-control (Duckworth, et al. 2007).

To clarify the interplay between short- and long-term goals in goal attainment, Zimmerman (2000) proposed that highly self-regulated individuals organize goal systems hierarchically, with short-term goals helping to regulate longer-term goal attainment. Related, Oettingen's (2012) fantasy realization theory (FRT) underscores the importance not only of setting desirable long-term future goals, but also of having a realistic appreciation for intermediate barriers to goal attainment (i.e., mental contrasting; Newell & Simon, 1972). A critical byproduct of mental contrasting is that one's goal commitment and recognition of one's need to take action (e.g., with short-term goal-setting)—both of which promote productive self-motivation beliefs—are simultaneously activated. In comparison, excessive focus on the positive feelings associated with goal attainment (i.e., indulging) or negative feelings associated with barriers to goal attainment (i.e., dwelling) are thought to breed passive inaction.

A number of studies by Oettingen and colleagues (e.g., Oettingen, 2000; Oettingen, Honig, & Gollwitzer, 2000; Oettingen, Mayer, Thorpe, Janetzke, & Lorenz, 2008; Oettingen et al., 2001) have demonstrated increased goal attainment when individuals engage in mental contrasting compared to indulging or dwelling. To provide an illustrative example, Oettingen and colleagues (2001) randomly assigned freshman students to mental contrasting, indulging, or dwelling conditions and asked them to rate expectations for excelling in mathematics. Students assigned to the mental contrasting condition were asked to list two positive aspects of the future and two aspects of reality. Those assigned to the indulging or dwelling conditions were asked instead to write four positive aspects associated with the future or four negative aspects associated with reality, respectively. Students assigned to the mental contrasting condition felt more energized about striving for excellence in math than those assigned to the indulging or dwelling conditions. Furthermore, teachers' ratings of student effort and performance during the two weeks following the experimental manipulation likewise indicated that students assigned to the mental contrasting conditions invested the most effort and received the highest grades. The combination of perseverance and realistic appraisal of barriers appears to play an important role in motivating and sustaining goal pursuit.

Performance

In the next phase of the self-regulated learning cycle, students begin to carry out actions in the service of the short- and long-term goals defined during the forethought phase and gather information about ways in which to revise goal-directed activities. According to Zimmerman (2002), this performance phase comprises two major regulatory processes: self-control and self-observation.[1] *Self-control* describes the use of various cognitive, motivational, behavioral, and/or contextual strategies to facilitate goal attainment (Pintrich, 2000b). For example, a student (Student A) who has a history of procrastinating with reading assignments due to challenges posed by reading comprehension may set a goal to read and understand 10 pages daily of a class chapter book. During the self-control phase, she may strategically plan to set aside reading time right after her afternoon snack (behavioral); sit in her room with the door closed to minimize auditory distractions (contextual); employ self-talk strategies to remind herself of the benefits of breaking the reading assignment into shorter daily reading tasks (motivational); and pause at the end of each paragraph to reflect on the key points in order to ensure reading comprehension (cognitive). The strategies chosen may vary from student to student depending on the goals, strengths, barriers, and past performance of the student.

Effective *self-observation*—the process of observing and monitoring aspects of one's own performance, conditions that improve or impede it, and its resulting effect—may facilitate the selection of more appropriate self-control strategies. For example, Student A may notice over trials that although sitting in her room helps to reduce auditory distraction, it also introduces additional visual distractions (e.g., more interesting things to do); that she experiences greater difficulty concentrating on reading after snack time; or that checking reading comprehension at the end of each paragraph is too easy and cumbersome. In contrast, Student A may also notice that breaking the reading assignment into shorter daily reading tasks effectively decreases her aversion to reading and makes the task less cumbersome than she originally anticipated.

Self-control and self-observation are interlinked regulatory processes because awareness of one's own performance informs the strategies one chooses to employ to promote goal attainment. Perhaps related, a sizeable body of research has supported the notion that the establishment of tactical "if, then" self-control strategies (i.e., implementation intentions; Gollwitzer, 1999) exerts a medium to large effect on goal attainment compared to having goals alone (Gollwitzer & Sheeran, 2006). For example, having made the aforementioned observations, Student A may employ a strategic implementation intention such as, "*If* I get distracted by things I'd rather be doing while I'm reading, *then* I will remind myself that staying focused and finishing today's reading task more efficiently will give me more time to do fun things." Notably, the ability to self-monitor and carry out various self-control strategies may depend on various self-regulatory skills and

---

1   Some scholars consider these components of Self-Control and Self-Monitoring to be distinct phases in a four-phase self-regulated learning cycle (e.g., Pintrich, 2000a and b).

executive functions discussed earlier, such as abilities to effectively monitor, plan, delay gratification, exercise inhibitory control, etc.

Self-Reflection

In the final self-reflection phase of the self-regulated learning cycle, students reflect on and evaluate their performance and progress towards goals. Distinct from the self-observation component of the performance phase in which students simply compare and contrast the effectiveness of strategies selected, students in the self-reflection phase evaluate and make attributions about their progress thus far. Students may evaluate progress by comparing self-observed performance to initial standards set during the forethought phase, to her/his own past performance, to other students' performance, and/or to parents' or teachers' standards of performance. Importantly, students' attributions of success and/or failure during the self-reflection phase (i.e., causal attribution; Graham & Williams, 2009) to controllable (e.g., effort) or uncontrollable (e.g., luck), internal (e.g., ability) or external (e.g., task difficulty), and stable (e.g., executive function deficits) or situational (e.g., mood during test day) loci have implications for subsequent self-motivation beliefs and thus persistence of goal pursuit (Weiner, 1979; Zimmerman, 2002). Students who perceive outcomes to be controllable, who attribute successes to internal and stable factors, and who attribute failures to external and unstable factors, are relatively likely to have high self-efficacy and expectancies for later success (i.e., more positive perceptions about the feasibility of related goals; Weiner, 1979).

Returning to Student A's earlier observation that she has difficulty concentrating on reading after snack time, if Student A concludes that reading will never be easy for her because of her poor reading ability (uncontrollable, internal, stable attribution for failure), she will be likely to feel that continued efforts are fruitless and may abandon her goal more quickly. In contrast, if she concludes instead that reading after snack time is difficult because she is lethargic from eating too much and not because she is unable to do the task (situational, external, unstable), she will be more likely to feel that continued efforts are warranted to revise her earlier strategy (e.g., eat less, schedule reading time before her afternoon snack) and to persist at her goal for longer.

In addition to students' outcome attributions, students' affective reactions to their performance have important implications for self-motivation beliefs. Feelings of satisfaction and positive affect are more likely to enhance, and dissatisfaction and negative affect to undermine, intrinsic interest and learning goal orientation (i.e., increased desirability of related goals; Schunk, 2001). Harking back to the earlier point about the importance of setting appropriately challenging, but attainable goals (i.e., standards of performance), poorly set goals may have implications for students' experiences of success or failure and, thus, for subsequent self-motivation beliefs and goal-striving behaviors. Finally and importantly, although studies of the self-regulation of emotionally driven processes (e.g., affect, behavior, and attention) and cognitively driven processes have tended to emerge from distinct research disciplines, they are interlinked and mutually interacting processes with emotions affecting cognitions, cognitions affecting behaviors, behaviors affecting attention, and so on (Blair & Razza, 2007).

Summary and Conclusions

In summary, research emerging from cognitive, developmental, and educational sciences has implicated the importance of self-regulation in promoting academic achievement outcomes. Insights from the cognitive and developmental sciences have emphasized the self-regulation of emotion, which affects attention and behaviors (as well as feelings) that contribute to children's socioemotional competencies and, hence, learning readiness. Poor self-regulation of emotions, behaviors, and/or attention compromises learning both directly by reducing the amount of time children spend engaged in on-task activities and indirectly by limiting children's access to social resources that support learning. In parallel, educational sciences have underscored the self-regulation of top-down (i.e., cognitive) processes in influencing children's abilities to initiate, sustain, and persist with challenging learning tasks. Although the transactional relations between the self-regulation of bottom-up and top-down processes over time remains to be well-explicated in research, the mutually interacting processes likely jointly promote student learning. Importantly, self-regulatory failures *and* successes both at and within any of the levels of functioning may have long-term effects on children's school engagement and thus school success. Academic supports that promote self-regulatory competencies both across (i.e., socioemotional and cognitive regulation) and within domains of functioning (e.g., instruction about effective goal setting) may be the most effective at improving students' achievement outcomes.

References

Ajzen, I. (1991). The theory of planned behavior. *Organizational Behavior and Human Decision Processes, 50*(2), 179–211.

Alexander, K. L., Entwisle, D. R., & Dauber, S. L. (1993). First-grade classroom behavior: Its short- and long-term consequences for school performance. *Child Development, 64*(3), 801–814.

Arnold, D. H., McWilliams, L., & Arnold, E. H. (1998). Teacher discipline and child misbehavior in day care: Untangling causality with correlational data. *Developmental Psychology, 34*(2), 276–287.

Bandura, A. (1977). *Social Learning Theory*. Englewood Cliffs, NJ: Prentice-Hall.

Bandura, A., & Schunk, D. H. (1981). Cultivating competence, self-efficacy, and intrinsic interest through proximal self-motivation. *Journal of Personality and Social Psychology, 41*(3), 586–598.

Barbarin, O., Iruka, I. U., Harradine, C., Winn, D. M. C., McKinney, M. K., & Taylor, L. C. (2013). Development of social-emotional competence in boys of color: A cross-sectional cohort analysis from pre-K to second grade. *American Journal of Orthopsychiatry, 83*(2), 145–155.

Barriga, A. Q., Doran, J. W., Newell, S. R., Morrison, E. M., Barbetti, V., & Robbins, B. D. (2002). Relationships between problem behaviors and academic achievement in adolescents: The unique role of attention problems. *Journal of Emotional and Behavioral Disorders, 10*(4), 233–240.

Baumeister, R. F., Heatherton, T. F., & Tice, D. M. (1994). *Losing Control: How and Why People Fail at Self-Regulation*: San Diego, CA: Academic Press.

Baumeister, R. F., & Vohs, K. D. (2012). *Self-Regulation and the Executive Function of the Self*. New York: Guilford Press.

Berndt, T. J., & Keefe, K. (1995). Friends' influence on adolescents' adjustment to school. *Child Development, 66*(5), 1312–1329.

Binet, A., & Simon, T. (1916). *The Development of Intelligence in Children (The Binet-Simon Scale)* Baltimore, MD: Williams & Wilkins Co.

Birch, S. H., & Ladd, G. W. (1996). Interpersonal relationships in the school environment and children's early school adjustment: The role of teachers and peers. In *Social Motivation: Understanding Children's School Adjustment*. New York: Cambridge University Press.

Blair, C., & Diamond, A. (2008). Biological processes in prevention and intervention: The promotion of self-regulation as a means of preventing school failure. *Development and Psychopathology, 20*(3), 899–911.

Blair, C., & Razza, R. P. (2007). Relating effortful control, executive function, and false belief understanding to emerging math and literacy ability in kindergarten. *Child Development, 78*(2), 647–663.

Carr, E. G., Taylor, J. C., & Robinson, S. (1991). The effects of severe behavior problems in children on the teaching behavior of adults. *Journal of Applied Behavior Analysis, 24*(3), 523–535.

Carver, C. S., & Scheier, M. F. (1982). Control theory: A useful conceptual framework for personality–social, clinical, and health psychology. *Psychological Bulletin, 92*(1), 111–135.

Chartrand, T. L., & Bargh, J. A. (1996). Automatic activation of impression formation and memorization goals: Nonconscious goal priming reproduces effects of explicit task instructions. *Journal of Personality and Social Psychology, 71*(3), 464–478.

Connor, C. M., Day, S. G., Phillips, B. M., Ingebrand, S., McLean, L. E., Sparapani, N., et al. (in press). Reciprocal effects of reading, vocabulary, and executive functioning in early elementary school. *Child Development*.

Cooper, D. H., & Farran, D. C. (1988). Behavioral risk factors in kindergarten. *Early Childhood Research Quarterly, 3*(1), 1–19.

Corno, L., & Mandinach, E. B. (1983). The role of cognitive engagement in classroom learning and motivation. *Educational Psychologist, 18*(2), 88–108.

Curry, L. (1984). Student commitment and school organization in relation to on-task behavior and achievement. *Contemporary Educational Psychology, 9*(2), 171–184.

Dombek, J. L., & Connor, C. M. (2012). Preventing retention: First grade classroom instruction and student characteristics. *Psychology in the Schools, 49*(6), 568–588.

Duckworth, A. L., Peterson, C., Matthews, M. D., & Kelly, D. R. (2007). Grit: Perseverance and passion for long-term goals. *Journal of Personality and Social Psychology, 92*(6), 1087–1101

Duckworth, A. L., Tsukayama, E., & May, H. (2010). Establishing causality using longitudinal hierarchical linear modeling: An illustration predicting achievement from self-control. *Social Psychological and Personality Science, 1*(4), 311–317.

Duncan, G. J., Dowsett, C. J., Claessens, A., Magnuson, K., Huston, A. C., Klebanov, P., et al. (2007). School readiness and later achievement. *Developmental Psychology, 43*(6), 1428–1446.

Dweck, C. S. (1999). *Self-Theories: Their Role in Motivation, Personality, and Development* New York: Psychology Press.

Eisenberg, N., Cumberland, A., Spinrad, T. L., Fabes, R. A., Shepard, S. A., Reiser, M., et al. (2001). The relations of regulation and emotionality to children's externalizing and internalizing problem behavior. *Child Development, 72*(4), 1112–1134.

Eisenberg, N., Hofer, C., Sulik, M. J., & Spinrad, T. L. (2014). Self-regulation, effortful control, and their socioemotional correlates. In *Handbook of Emotion Regulation* (2nd ed.). New York: Guilford Press.

Eisenberg, N., Liew, J., & Pidada, S. U. (2004). The longitudinal relations of regulation and emotionality to quality of Indonesian children's socioemotional functioning. *Developmental Psychology, 40*(5), 790–804.

Eisenberg, N., & Morris, A. S. (2002). Children's emotion-related regulation. In *Advances in Child Development and Behavior* (Vol. 30). San Diego, CA: Academic Press.

Eisenberg, N., Sadovsky, A., Spinrad, T. L., Fabes, R. A., Losoya, S. H., Valiente, C., et al. (2005). The relations of problem behavior status to children's negative emotionality, effortful control, and impulsivity: Concurrent relations and prediction of change. *Developmental Psychology, 41*(1), 193–211.

Eisenberg, N., Valiente, C., & Eggum, N. D. (2010). Self-regulation and school readiness. *Early Education and Development, 21*(5), 681–698.

Eisenberg, N., Valiente, C., Spinrad, T. L., Cumberland, A., Liew, J., Reiser, M., et al. (2009). Longitudinal relations of children's effortful control, impulsivity, and negative emotionality to their externalizing, internalizing, and co-occurring behavior problems. *Developmental Psychology, 45*(4), 988–1008.

Eisenberg, N., & Zhou (2015). Self-regulation: conceptual issues, and relations to developmental outcomes in childhood and adolescence. In G. Oettingen & P. M. Gollwitzer (Eds.), *Self-Regulation in Adolescence*. Cambridge: Cambridge University Press.

Gollwitzer, P. M. (1990). Action phases and mind-sets. In *Handbook of Motivation and Cognition: Foundations of Social Behavior* (Vol. 2). New York: Guilford Press.

Gollwitzer, P. M. (1999). Implementation intentions: Strong effects of simple plans. *American Psychologist, 54*(7), 493–503.

Gollwitzer, P. M., Parks-Stamm, E. J., Jaudas, A., & Sheeran, P. (2008). *Flexible Tenacity in Goal Pursuit* New York: Guilford Press.

Gollwitzer, P. M., & Sheeran, P. (2006). Implementation intentions and goal achievement: A meta-analysis of effects and processes. In *Advances in Experimental Social Psychology* (Vol. 38). San Diego, CA: Elsevier Academic.

Goodwin, C. J. (2011). *A History of Modern Psychology* (4th ed.) New York: Wiley.

Graham, S., & Williams, C. (2009). An attributional approach to motivation in school. In *Handbook of Motivation at School.* New York: Routledge.

Heckhausen, H. (1977). Achievement motivation and its constructs: A cognitive model. *Motivation and Emotion, 1*(4), 283–329.

Higgins, E. T., Shah, J., & Friedman, R. (1997). Emotional responses to goal attainment: Strength of regulatory focus as moderator. *Journal of Personality and Social Psychology, 72*(3), 515–525.

Hinshaw, S. P. (1987). On the distinction between attentional deficits/hyperactivity and conduct problems/aggression in child psychopathology. *Psychological Bulletin, 101*(3), 443–463.

Hinshaw, S. P. (1992). Externalizing behavior problems and academic underachievement in childhood and adolescence: Causal relationships and underlying mechanisms. *Psychological Bulletin, 111*(1), 127–155.

Hofmann, W., Schmeichel, B. J., & Baddeley, A. D. (2012). Executive functions and self-regulation. *Trends in Cognitive Sciences, 16*(3), 174–180.

Howse, R. B., Calkins, S. D., Anastopoulos, A. D., Keane, S. P., & Shelton, T. L. (2003). Regulatory contributors to children's kindergarten achievement. *Early Education and Development, 14*(1), 101–119.

Howse, R. B., Diehl, D. C., & Trivette, C. M. (2010). An asset-based approach to facilitating positive youth development and adoption. *Child Welfare: Journal of Policy, Practice, and Program, 89*(4), 101–116.

Husman, J., & Shell, D. F. (2008). Beliefs and perceptions about the future: A measurement of future time perspective. *Learning and Individual Differences, 18*(2), 166–175.

Kanfer, F. H., & Phillips, J. S. (1970). *Learning Foundations of Behavior Therapy.* Oxford: John Wiley & Sons.

Ladd, G. W., & Burgess, K. B. (1999). Charting the relationship trajectories of aggressive, withdrawn, and aggressive/withdrawn children during early grade school. *Child Development, 70*(4), 910–929.

Liew, J., Eisenberg, N., & Reiser, M. (2004). Preschoolers' effortful control and negative emotionality, immediate reactions to disappointment, and quality of social functioning. *Journal of Experimental Child Psychology, 89*(4), 298–313.

Locke, E. A., & Latham, G. P. (1990). *A Theory of Goal Setting & Task Performance.* Englewood Cliffs, NJ: Prentice-Hall.

McClelland, M. M., Cameron, C. E., Connor, C. M., Farris, C. L., Jewkes, A. M., & Morrison, F. J. (2007). Links between behavioral regulation and preschoolers' literacy, vocabulary, and math skills. *Developmental Psychology, 43*(4), 947–959.

McClelland, M. M., Morrison, F. J., & Holmes, D. L. (2000). Children at risk for early academic problems: The role of learning-related social skills. *Early Childhood Research Quarterly, 15*(3), 307–329.

Metcalfe, L. A., Harvey, E. A., & Laws, H. B. (2013). The longitudinal relation between academic/cognitive skills and externalizing behavior problems in preschool children. *Journal of Educational Psychology, 105*(3), 881–894.

Mischel, W., Shoda, Y., & Peake, P. K. (1988). The nature of adolescent competencies predicted by preschool delay of gratification. *Journal of Personality and Social Psychology, 54*(4), 687–696.

Murray, C., & Greenberg, M. T. (2000). Children's relationship with teachers and bonds with school. An investigation of patterns and correlates in middle childhood. *Journal of School Psychology, 38*(5), 423–445.

Newcomb, A. F., Bukowski, W. M., & Pattee, L. (1993). Children's peer relations: A meta-analytic review of popular, rejected, neglected, controversial, and average sociometric status. *Psychological Bulletin, 113*(1), 99–128.

Newell, A., & Simon, H. A. (1972). *Human Problem Solving.* Oxford: Prentice-Hall.

Oettingen, G. (2000). Expectancy effects on behavior depend on self-regulatory thought. *Social Cognition, 18*(2), 101–129.

Oettingen, G. (2012). Future thought and behaviour change. *European Review of Social Psychology, 23*(1), 1–63.

Oettingen, G., Honig, G., & Gollwitzer, P. M. (2000). Effective self-regulation of goal attainment. *International Journal of Educational Research, 33*(7), 705–732.

Oettingen, G., Mayer, D., Thorpe, J. S., Janetzke, H., & Lorenz, S. (2008). Turning fantasies about positive and negative futures into self-improvement goals. *Motivation and Emotion, 29*(4), 237–267.

Oettingen, G., Pak, H.-J., & Schnetter, K. (2001). Self-regulation of goal-setting: Turning free fantasies about the future into binding goals. *Journal of Personality and Social Psychology, 80*(5), 736–753.

Parker, J. G., & Asher, S. R. (1987). Peer relations and later personal adjustment: Are low-accepted children at risk? *Psychological Bulletin, 102*(3), 357–389.

Pintrich, P. R. (2000a). Multiple goals, multiple pathways: The role of goal orientation in learning and achievement. *Journal of Educational Psychology, 92*(3), 544–555.

Pintrich, P. R. (2000b). The role of goal orientation in self-regulated learning. In *Handbook of Self-Regulation.* San Diego, CA: Academic Press.

Posner, M. I., & Rothbart, M. K. (2000). Developing mechanisms of self-regulation. *Development and Psychopathology, 12*(3), 427–441.

Raver, C. C. (2002). Emotions matter: Making the case for the role of young children's emotional development for early school readiness. In L. Sherrod (Ed.), *Social Policy Report* (Vol. 16). London: Society for Research in Child Development.

Riglin, L., Petrides, K. V., Frederickson, N., & Rice, F. (2014). The relationship between emotional problems and subsequent school attainment: A meta-analysis. *Journal of Adolescence, 37*(4), 335–346.

Rimm-Kaufman, S. E., Pianta, R. C., & Cox, M. J. (2000). Teachers' judgments of problems in the transition to kindergarten. *Early Childhood Research Quarterly, 15*(2), 147–166.

Rothbart, M. K. (2011). *Becoming Who We Are: Temperament and Personality in Development.* New York: Guilford Press.

Rothbart, M. K., & Bates, J. E. (2006). *Temperament.* Hoboken, NJ: John Wiley & Sons Inc.

Rueda, M. R., Posner, M. I., & Rothbart, M. K. (2005). The development of executive attention: Contributions to the emergence of self-regulation. *Developmental Neuropsychology, 28*(2), 573–594

Ryan, R. M., & Deci, E. L. (2001). On happiness and human potentials: A review of research on hedonic and eudaimonic well-being. *Annual Review of Psychology, 52*, 141–166.

Schunk, D. H. (2001). Social cognitive theory and self-regulated learning. In *Self-Regulated Learning and Academic Achievement: Theoretical Perspectives* (2nd ed.). Mahwah, NJ: Erlbaum.

Searle, A. K., Miller-Lewis, L. R., Sawyer, M. G., & Baghurst, P. A. (2013). Predictors of children's kindergarten classroom engagement: Preschool adult-child relationships, self-concept, and hyperactivity/inattention. *Early Education and Development, 24*(8), 1112–1136.

Shoda, Y., Mischel, W., & Peake, P. K. (1990). Predicting adolescent cognitive and self-regulatory competencies from preschool delay of gratification: Identifying diagnostic conditions. *Developmental Psychology, 26*(6), 978–986.

Shonkoff, J. P., & Phillips, D. A. (2000). *From Neurons to Neighborhoods: The Science of Early Childhood Development.* Washington, DC: National Academies Press.

Shores, R. E., & Wehby, J. H. (1999). Analyzing the classroom social behavior of students with EBD. *Journal of Emotional and Behavioral Disorders, 7*(4), 194–199.

Silva, K. M., Spinrad, T. L., Eisenberg, N., Sulik, M. J., Valiente, C., Huerta, S., et al. (2011). Relations of children's effortful control and teacher–child relationship quality to school attitudes in a low-income sample. *Early Education and Development, 22*(3), 434–460.

Skibbe, L. E., Connor, C. M., Morrison, F. J., & Jewkes, A. M. (2011). Schooling effects on preschoolers' self-regulation, early literacy, and language growth. *Early Childhood Research Quarterly, 26*(1), 42–49.

Skibbe, L. E., Phillips, B. M., Day, S. L., Brophy-Herb, H. E., & Connor, C. M. (2012). Children's early literacy growth in relation to classmates' self-regulation. *Journal of Educational Psychology, 104*(3), 541–553.

Taylor, B. M., Pearson, P. D., Clark, K., & Walpole, S. (2000). Effective schools and accomplished teachers: Lessons about primary-grade reading instruction in low-income schools. *Elementary School Journal, 101*(2), 121–165.

Valiente, C., Eisenberg, N., Haugen, R., Spinrad, T. L., Hofer, C., Liew, J. et al. (2011). Children's effortful control and academic achievement: Mediation through social functioning. *Early Education and Development, 22*(3), 411–433.

Vidal-Abarca, E., Mañá, A., & Gil, L. (2010). Individual differences for self-regulating task-oriented reading activities. *Journal of Educational Psychology, 102*(4), 817–826.

Webb, T. L., & Sheeran, P. (2006). Does changing behavioral intentions engender behavior change? A meta-analysis of the experimental evidence. *Psychological Bulletin, 132*(2), 249–268.

Weiner, B. (1979). A theory of motivation for some classroom experiences. *Journal of Educational Psychology, 71*(1), 3–25.

Wigfield, A., Klauda, S. L., & Cambria, J. (2011). Influences on the development of academic self-regulatory processes. In *Handbook of Self-Regulation of Learning and Performance.* New York: Routledge.

Zimmerman, B. J. (1986). Becoming a self-regulated learner: Which are the key subprocesses? *Contemporary Educational Psychology, 11*(4), 307–313.

Zimmerman, B. J. (2000). Attaining self-regulation: A social cognitive perspective. In *Handbook of Self-Regulation.* San Diego, CA: Academic Press.

Zimmerman, B. J. (2001). Theories of self-regulated learning and academic achievement: An overview and analysis. In *Self-Regulated Learning and Academic Achievement: Theoretical Perspectives* (2nd ed.). Mahwah, NJ: Erlbaum.

Zimmerman, B. J. (2002). Achieving academic excellence: A self-regulatory perspective. In *The Pursuit of Excellence Through Education*. Mahwah, NJ: Erlbaum.

Zimmerman, B. J., & Schunk, D. H. (2011). Self-regulated learning and performance: An introduction and an overview. In *Handbook of Self-Regulation of Learning and Performance*. New York: Routledge.

Chapter 6

The Role of Language Development in the Successful Comprehension of Texts

Laura K. Allen and Danielle S. McNamara

One of the most important skills acquired by humans is the ability to coherently and effectively communicate complex concepts, ideas, desires, and emotions to others. Indeed, it may be this very language system that serves to separate humans from other animals (Bloom, 2000). Although many animal species have the capacity to communicate simple desires and needs through the use of sounds and gestures, no other species is comparable to humans with respect to the generativity, creativity, and complexity of their communication systems. As humans, we possess the capacity to freely manipulate various elements of our language system for the purpose of expressing complex concepts in specific and meaningful ways. Further, we can both produce and comprehend words and sentences that we have never previously been exposed to.

The development of this language system is a multifaceted process that requires understanding at several levels. Children must understand the basic units of sound (phonemes) and how these sounds are combined to create grammatical units (morphemes). Additionally, they must know how to connect these morphemes to produce meaningful information (syntax), how to determine the meaning of words and sentences (semantics), and how to remain sensitive and responsive to the context of a given language exchange (pragmatics). Given this wealth of knowledge required for successful language use, as well as the strategies needed to access and leverage this knowledge, we can assume that children with the capacity for language have developed a strong and generative system.

As human language relies on such a powerful system, it is not surprising that the animals that have developed the richest system of communication have also developed the most sophisticated set of reasoning skills and strategies (Darwin, 1874, as cited in Bloom, 2000). In fact, it has been argued that acquiring a natural language is a *necessary* prerequisite for the development of concepts and complex reasoning skills (Carruthers, 1996, 2012; Clark, 1996). The primary argument behind this claim is that reasoning is principally grounded in representational systems (that symbols stand for real things), which children learn to produce, manipulate, and comprehend as they develop their language skills. Importantly, this intricate connection between language and reasoning skills suggests that the study of language development can provide important insights into the higher level characteristics of human cognition.

One important aspect of language is literacy development—learning to comprehend and produce symbolic language (e.g., writing). Indeed, reading comprehension and writing skills are critical for success in the classroom as well as in the workplace (Powell, 2009). Additionally, as discussed in Chapter 3, the rise of online media, news stories, and electronic messaging has ensured that strong literacy skills are increasingly important for the digestion and dissemination of information. A key factor in the development of strong literacy skills is the strength of a child's language system. In order to comprehend text, for instance, a child must be able to recognize words and parse sentences, as well as have higher level skills related to the generation of inferences and the connection of textual information to prior world knowledge.

Research suggests that language skills are one of the strongest predictors of skilled reading comprehension among children (Dickinson, Golinkoff, & Hirsh-Pasek, 2010; Scarborough, 2001). This relation between language skills and reading comprehension has most commonly been investigated in terms of the direct effects of language knowledge on reading comprehension skills (e.g., correlations between vocabulary knowledge and reading skills; Allen, et al., 2014; Dickinson, et al., 2010). However, researchers have also focused on the indirect and higher level influences of language development on reading comprehension. In this chapter, we suggest that a closer inspection of the literature on cognitive language development can expand our understanding of the relation between language and reading comprehension skills. We first describe the language acquisition process and how this relates to the overall development of the cognitive system. We then discuss how the higher level properties of language development may relate to our understanding of reading comprehension processes. Finally, we offer some suggestions for future research in the areas of language development and reading comprehension, as well as avenues for educational interventions aimed to improve reading skills.

Language Acquisition and Cognitive Development

Language skills play an important role in the development of the human cognitive system (Carruthers, 2012). Not only does language provide a means to communicate basic needs and desires, it also shapes and informs our ability to understand the surrounding environment. Research suggests that learning individual words helps us to form conceptual categories and to learn how to individuate different types of object (Gentner & Boroditsky, 2001; Waxman & Markow, 1995; Xu, 2002). Because these words help us to organize concepts, they also help us direct our attention in various ways and understand how different concepts and objects may be related to each other (Diesendruck, 2003; Mandler & McDonough, 1993). Therefore, our assignment of particular words and phrases to objects, actions, and relations allows us to understand and draw attention to similarities and differences between cognitive categories across a variety of domains.

Language also influences the development of the cognitive system. Importantly, language serves as a powerful representational resource, which enables children and adults to develop analogies for more complex thoughts and comparisons (Gentner & Medina, 1998; Hermer & Spelke, 1994). Additionally, language affords us the ability to take different perspectives on the same event, as, for example, actions can take place from different points of view or referents can be identified in numerous ways. According to research, this effect of language on cognitive processing is present at a fairly early age. Young children have the ability to perceive objects (Clark & Grossman, 1998; Clark & Svaib, 1997; Deak & Maratsos, 1998; Waxman & Hatch, 1992) and events (Gleitman, 1990) from multiple perspectives. And they recognize that the structure of a given phrase or sentence is a critical component for understanding and reflects the speaker's intentions about how an object should be perceived (Bloom & Markson, 1998).

As language influences the development of the human cognitive system, and specifically on our ability to make sense of the surrounding world, it is clear that language development must play a major role in our study of comprehension. An investigation into the language development process can provide critical information about the development of complex cognitive skills, as well as provide insight into the potential sources of difficulties on these tasks. When children are born, they begin to communicate through crying (Hoff, 2004), which is associated with negative feelings, such as hunger or discomfort (Zeskind, Klein, & Marshall, 1992). Around 12 weeks old, "cooing" emerges (Hoff, 2004). This form of expression is similar to crying, except that it is associated with positive feelings. Thus, very early in life, infants are able to express both pleasure and pain with their environment. Importantly, neither crying nor cooing is learned; rather, they are simply expressions of emotions to which adults often attach meaning (Trevarthen, 1979).

At around 6 months old, children begin their first attempts at speech through "babbling." Babbles are a child's first use of phonemes and they consist of sequences of vowels and consonants (deVilliers & deVilliers, 1978). Once children reach approximately 1 year of age, they enter a holophrastic stage. In this stage of language, children begin to use single words to convey complex meanings (Hoff, 2004). For instance, a child might say the word "Dada" to represent the more complex sentence, "Daddy, give me some food." After this phase, children begin to use "duos," which are a form of telegraphic speech where only the most essential words in a sentence are used. Typically, these duos consist of one open class word (i.e., a concrete word) and a pivot word (i.e., a word that represents a phrase). For example, a child might say, "Mama go" instead of "Mama is going." Interestingly, duos follow proper grammatical structure, which means they follow the same word order that is common in the child's native language. For instance, in the previous example, "Mama go" would mean, "Mama is going," whereas "Go mama" might serve as a command for the mother to leave.

After children progress through the early language development phrases, they experience a great increase in their vocabulary knowledge and language production skills. Specifically, between the ages of approximately 2 to 3, children progress from a vocabulary of around 250 words to approximately 1000 words (Hoff, 2004). Additionally, the sentences produced by these children grow more complex, as they develop an understanding of grammatical rules, as well as the purpose of tense markers and plural forms. Around 3 years of age, children develop the ability to use pronominal and prepositional words, which allows them to represent relations among the different objects and concepts that they perceive.

This development of language skills continues throughout childhood and into adolescence as children continue to learn new words every year. First graders, for instance, know approximately 8000–14,000 words, whereas high school students typically know over 80,000 words (Owens, 2008). Along with this increase in vocabulary size, children develop the understanding that words have multiple meanings, which indirectly prompts the development of a number of other skills, such as their ability to comprehend idioms (Bloom, 1998). Similarly, children begin to understand that meaning relies on context and intentions, which allows them to move beyond literal interpretations of language (Baumann, et al., 2005; Cain, Oakhill, & Elbro, 2003). Finally, as children' understanding of syntax and grammar develops, they begin to distinguish between passive and active voice constructions (O'Grady, 1997), understand subject–verb and noun–pronoun agreement, and use articles and connectives (Vion & Colas, 2004).

Language Development and Reasoning Ability

The development of the human language system, as well as frequent exposure to language in the surrounding environment, provide key insights into our understanding of how humans develop concepts and demonstrate flexibility and adaptivity in reasoning and problem solving. Within the context of reading comprehension, this understanding has important implications for cognitive theory, as well as for educational interventions. In terms of theory, studying the interactions between the development of language and higher order thinking skills can help us develop a deeper understanding of how individuals process textual information within the context of prior knowledge, author intentions, and a number of other environmental factors. In terms of education, this research can help us understand more broadly how different language trajectories (e.g., language disabilities, first and second language acquisition, etc.) may affect children's abilities to successfully comprehend complex texts. In this section, we focus on three effects of language development that are frequently discussed in the language development literature, but rarely, if ever, a focus of the reading comprehension literature: theory of mind, meaning making (pragmatics), and relations between language exposure and thought processes.

Theory of Mind

Theory of mind (ToM) represents the human ability to attribute mental states (e.g., thoughts, knowledge, beliefs, emotions and desires) to oneself and others (Sodian & Kristen, 2010). At a young age, children begin to pay attention to, and pick up on, the contextual and social cues in their environment. This allows them to rapidly increase the size of their vocabulary, as children who are exposed to more frequent language input from older adults and siblings are able to learn concrete and abstract words more easily (Bloom, 2000). In addition to the effect on vocabulary, older adults' expressions and discussions of their own mental states (particularly during the early stages of a child's language acquisition) help children develop a ToM (Dunn, et al., 1991; Ruffman, et al., 2002; Slaughter & Peterson, 2012). Similarly, research suggests that exposure to language at an early age may be a *necessary* condition for children's development of complex reasoning skills—particularly those related to determining false beliefs in the world (Astington & Baird, 2005).

Given the strong connection between language exposure and the development of ToM, it is important to consider how differential forms of language exposure (e.g., frequency, native/non-native language, etc.) affect ToM development. Schick, de Villiers, de Villiers, and Hoffmeister (2007) explored this research area through an examination of the language and ToM skills of 176 deaf children ranging in age from 3 years, 11 months to 8 years, 3 months. These children used either American sign language (ASL) or oral English and had either hearing parents or deaf parents who were native ASL users. Their study found that deaf children with hearing parents experienced a delay on ToM tasks, compared to the deaf children with deaf parents and to hearing controls. Similarly, the results suggested that deaf children from deaf families performed identically to the hearing controls on the ToM tasks. These findings indicate that exposure to oral language is not a critical component for the development of ToM; rather, the richness of language input (regardless of its modality) is the key component. In this study, it is assumed that the deaf children who had hearing parents had much less rich and frequent communication exchanges. This may be due to the fact that they were not exposed to a comprehensive language (i.e., many hearing parents use pidgin sign language with their deaf children), which may have led them to develop a weaker ToM compared to other children.

These results have important implications for the development of reading comprehension skills among deaf children, who typically graduate from high school at approximately a fourth-grade reading level (Erting, 1992). If students struggle to develop a strong ToM, they will frequently experience difficulties with perspective taking, imagining and simulating scenarios, as well as with expressing and experiencing emotions (Carlson & Moses, 2001; Davis, 1994). These abilities are important for text comprehension because they help children make sense of the text within the context of their own environment, such as by developing a deeper understanding of the characters' motives or making connections between text and social context (Gee, 2001).

Therefore, ensuring that young children are frequently exposed to rich and complete language input that expresses the thoughts, emotions, and mental states of other people is likely to support ToM development. Unfortunately, for some students, this exposure may be more difficult to provide. As mentioned previously, deaf children who have hearing parents (or deaf parents who are not native ASL users) are not as frequently exposed to rich language input. Thus, it is important to develop interventions that will provide students with the type of language exposure that they may be missing (Wellman, 2013). Technology has the potential to offer a fruitful direction for such interventions. For example, a computer-based tutoring intervention could be developed to specifically strengthen ToM in deaf children. This computer system could use body movement detection software (e.g., the Kinect software) to process students' sign language and could employ natural language processing (NLP) techniques to engage students in conversations about their emotions and mental states. Interventions of this type could help ensure that students with language impairments experience less of a struggle in the development of ToM and may have an indirect, positive effect on complex cognitive task performance, such as reading comprehension.

Pragmatics (Learning and Meaning Making)

A second consideration regarding language development is how students make sense of the world when they are exposed to language they do not understand. Previous research suggests that children learn and develop meaning through question asking and conversations with others (Choinard & Imberi-Olivares, 2012; Zimmerman, et al., 2009). When children encounter something that they do not understand, they first ask descriptive questions to understand more about the specific features of a given concept. Once they have a basic understanding of this concept, they begin to ask causal questions that provide information about relations among objects or people. Research suggests that children are more likely to remember information that they have specifically requested compared to information that was freely given to them (Choinard & Imberi-Olivares, 2012).

This development of meaning and memory for important information can be greatly hindered for children who have difficulties with basic language skills because they are less able to engage in conversations with others. One example of this problem is found in children with autism. Children on the autism spectrum frequently experience difficulties acquiring language and have a reduced tendency to attend to different voices and language input. When these children do succeed at learning information, they still experience difficulties with generalizing the skills and information they have learned to new settings and to new people (Carr & Kologinsky, 1983; Handleman, 1979). As a result of these difficulties, children with autism tend to have weaker ToM, vocabulary knowledge, and word-learning skills (Wellman, 2002).

Recently, computer-based instruction has emerged as an effective method to train and develop vocabulary knowledge and strategies for special populations of students, such as L1 and L2 learners (Wood, 2001) and individuals with special needs (Barker, 2003; Heiman, Nelson, Tjus, & Gilberg, 1995; Moore & Calvert, 2000). Intelligent tutoring systems (ITS) can offer students numerous opportunities to engage with adaptive instruction, practice, and feedback, and they have been shown to be as effective as human tutors (VanLehn, 2011). Importantly, these tutors have the capability of presenting multiple sources of information in parallel (e.g., text, sound, images, etc.), which is an important component of word learning (Dubois & Vial, 2000). In particular, incorporating text and visual images of vocabulary words with actual definitions and sounds facilitates learning and improves memory for target vocabulary words (Bosseler & Massaro, 2003; Dubois & Vial, 2000).

Bosseler and Massaro (2003) investigated the effects of a computer-based system, Baldi, on the vocabulary development of children with autism. In the first experiment, eight children were given pretest, tutoring sessions with the Baldi system, and a posttest 30 days after they had mastered the vocabulary items. The results of this experiment revealed that all students learned a significant number of new vocabulary words and grammar constructions from pretest to posttest. In a follow-up experiment, six children were exposed to the Baldi system and compared to a control group. The results revealed that students in the Baldi condition learned more words than students in the control group. Additionally, the students were administered a posttest in a new room with a different experimenter as the pretest and the training and they were able to generalize their learned vocabulary knowledge to this new environment. Overall, these results suggest that children with autism can benefit from language interventions provided by a computer-based program, and this learned information can transfer new environments.

Effects of Language Exposure on Thought

A final consideration in this chapter regarding the relations between language development and complex cognitive tasks such as reading comprehension relates to the effects of language exposure on information processing. According to the linguistic determinism hypothesis, the language that we are exposed to determines the way that we think (Au, 2011; deVilliers & deVilliers, 2000). In the strong version of this hypothesis, it is assumed that language is the reason we are able to dissect our physical and mental world in a meaningful way; in other words, it dictates our thinking and problem-solving abilities. According to the weak version of this hypothesis, which is more widely accepted, the language that we use (i.e., our native language) influences the efficiency with which we can employ our reasoning and problem-solving skills. Research supports this notion and suggests that even memories acquired by overhearing a second language during the early childhood years can influence cognitive development and the way that information is processed as adults (Au, 2011).

Thus, language exposure may affect performance on complex cognitive tasks, such as reading comprehension. Research suggests that bilingual children display a more advanced understanding of speakers' meanings, as well as more adult-like moral reasoning patterns than monolingual children (Siegal, Tallandini, Pellizzoni, & Michelin, 2011). Further, children exposed to a second language, even for a brief amount of time, have an easier time learning that language later in their life (Au, 2011). Bilingualism is associated with a host of other cognitive benefits, such as stronger L1 expertise, better selective attention, and better problem-solving skills (Bialystok, 2011). Importantly, many of these benefits are also associated with reading comprehension skills; thus, an important consideration for researchers and educators is how to promote these benefits of bilingualism to children who are not naturally exposed to multiple languages. At the same time, many children who are bilingual struggle to achieve grade-appropriate reading comprehension and overall school success (Melby-Lervåg & Lervåg, 2014). The causes are not well understood, but are likely attributable to factors related to poverty, family mobility, and other socioeconomic factors.

Clearly, more effective ways to provide language instruction to bilingual children are needed. Classroom-based interventions might be conceptualized that integrate multiple languages into their instruction and practice. Rather than waiting until later in life to provide instruction on a second language, educators could begin to expose students to other languages at a much earlier age. Even if students are not immersed in other environments and never reach proficiency in a second language, they may still be able to experience some of the cognitive benefits associated with the early exposure to multiple languages (Au, 2011; Siegal, et al., 2011).

Conclusions and Future Directions

Research suggests that language skills are the strongest predictor of children's development of reading proficiency (Dickinson, et al., 2010). In particular, measures of vocabulary knowledge, as well as the ability to produce more complex language (e.g., syntax) predict students' reading ability later in their lives (National Early Literacy Panel, 2008). Recently however, Dickinson and colleagues (2010) suggested that the role of language might be undersold in the literature on reading comprehension skills. They argue that researchers undersell the strength of the relation between language skills and reading development because their focus is often much too narrow. Specifically, researchers tend to focus only on the direct effects of language skills on reading comprehension (as opposed to indirect effects). For example, they focus solely on vocabulary rather than acknowledging that achievement on vocabulary tests is likely a proxy for the larger language system; they frequently analyze short time frames in their studies; and they focus too heavily on the role of rapidly developing code-based factors, often missing the more slowly developing (yet, just as important) linguistic and background knowledge factors (Dickinson, et al., 2010).

In this chapter, we have argued that the development of strong language skills can affect cognitive development and reading comprehension proficiency in a number of different ways. Beyond simply offering students linguistic and background knowledge, language skills also afford individuals the ability to reason and solve complex problems, process information contextually, and understand the beliefs and thought processes of others. In this way, Dickinson and colleagues (2010) may have still undersold the role of language for the development of reading comprehension skills. Beyond the effects of language on linguistic and background knowledge (emphasized by Dickinson and colleagues), language development can play an even larger role in fostering students' higher level cognitive skills.

As a promising avenue for improving later achievement, early childhood education is beginning to increase its focus on fostering strong language skills in students and stronger interventions for students who have language impairments. This requires a more highly trained teaching force, but this expense is clearly justified by the cost/benefit with regard to both monetary and social capital (Reynolds, Temple, Robertson, & Mann, 2002). Overall, understanding the relation between the cognitive development of complex skills, such as reading, and language acquisition, provides critical information about how we can better understand the process of learning to read.

References

Allen, L. K., Snow, E. L., Crossley, S. A., Jackson, G. T., & McNamara, D. S. (2014). Reading comprehension components and their relation to the writing process. *L'année psychologique/Topics in Cognitive Psychology, 114,* 663–691.

Astington, J. W. E., & Baird, J. A. (Eds.). (2005). *Why Language Matters for Theory of Mind.* Oxford: Oxford University Press.

Au, K. H. (2011). *Literacy Achievement and Diversity: Keys to Success for Students, Teachers, and Schools.* New York: Teachers College Press.

Barker, L. J. (2003). Computer-assisted vocabulary acquisition: The CSLU vocabulary tutor in oral-deaf education. *Journal of Deaf Studies and Deaf Education, 8,* 187–198.

Baumann, J. F., Font, G., Edwards, E. C., & Boland, E. (2005). Strategies for teaching middle-grade students to use word-part and context clues to expand reading vocabulary. In E. H. Hiebert & M. L. Kamil (Eds.), *Teaching and Learning Vocabulary: Bridging Research to Practice.* Mahwah, NJ: Erlbaum.

Bialystok, E. (2011). Reshaping the mind: The benefits of bilingualism. *Canadian Journal of Experimental Psychology, 65,* 229–235.

Bloom, P. (2000). *How Children Learn the Meanings of Words.* Cambridge, MA: MIT Press.

Bloom, P., & Markson, L. (1998). Intention and analogy in children's naming of pictorial representations. *Psychological Science, 9,* 200–204.

Bosseler, A., & Massaro, D. W. (2003). Development and evaluation of a computer-animated tutor for vocabulary and language learning in children with autism. *Journal of Autism and Developmental Disorders, 33,* 653–672.

Cain, K., Oakhill, J. V., & Elbro, C. (2003). The ability to learn new word meanings from context by school-age children with and without language comprehension difficulties. *Journal of Child Language, 30,* 681–694.

Carlson, S. M., & Moses, L. J. (2001) Individual differences in inhibitory control and children's theory of mind. *Child Development, 72,* 1032–1053.

Carr, E. G., & Kologinsky, E. (1983). Acquisition of sign language by autistic children: Spontaneity and generalization effects. *Journal of Applied Behavior Analysis, 16,* 297–314.

Carruthers, P. (1996). *Language, Thought, and Consciousness: An Essay in Philosophical Psychology.* Cambridge: Cambridge University Press.

Carruthers, P. (2012). Language in cognition. In E. Margolis, R. Samuels, & S. Stich (Eds.), *The Oxford Handbook of Philosophy of Cognitive Science.* Oxford: Oxford University Press.

Chouinard, M. M., & Imberi-Olivares, K. (2012). Getting information from other people: Who do children turn to? In M. Siegal and L. Surian (Eds.), *Access to Language and Cognitive Development.* Oxford: Oxford University Press.

Clark, A. (1996). *Being There, Putting Brain, Body and World Together Again.* Cambridge, MA: MIT Press.

Clark, E. V., & Grossman, J. B. (1998). Pragmatic directions and children's word learning. *Journal of Child Language, 25,* 1–18.

Clark, E. V., & Svaib, T. A. (1997). Speaker perspective and reference in young children. *First Language*, *17*, 57–74.

Davis, M. H. (1994) *Empathy: A Social Psychological Approach*. Dubuque, IA: Brown & Benchmark.

Deak, G., & Maratsos, M. (1998). On having complex representations of things: Preschoolers use multiple words for objects and people. *Developmental Psychology*, *34*, 224–240.

deVilliers, J. G., & deVilliers, P. A. (1978). *Language Acquisition*. Cambridge, MA: Harvard University Press.

de Villiers, J. G., & de Villiers P. A. (2000). Linguistic determinism and false belief. In P. Mitchell & K. Riggs (Eds.). *Children's Reasoning and the Mind*. Hove: Psychology Press.

Dickinson, D. K., Golinkoff, R. M., & Hirsh-Pasek, K. (2010). Speaking out for language: Why language is central to reading development. *Educational Researcher*, *39*, 305–310.

Disendruck, G. (2003). Categories for names or names for categories? The interplay between domain-specific conceptual structure and language. *Language and Cognitive Processes*, *18*, 759–787.

Dubois, M., & Vial, I. (2000). Multimedia design: The effects of relating multimodal information. *Journal of Computer Assisted Learning*, *16*, 157–165.

Dunn, J., Brown, J., Slomkowski, C., Tesla, C., & Youngblade, L. (1991). Young children's understanding of other people's feelings and beliefs: Individual differences and their antecedents. *Child Development*, *62*, 1352–1366.

Erting, C. J. (1992). Deafness and literacy: Why can't Sam read? *Sign Language Studies*, *75*, 97–112.

Gee, J. P. (2001). Reading as situated language: A sociocognitive perspective. *Journal of Adolescent & Adult Literacy*, *44*, 714–725.

Gentner, D., & Boroditsky, L. (2001). Individuation, relativity, and early word learning. In M. Bowerman & S. C. Levinson (Eds.), *Language Acquisition and Conceptual Development*. Cambridge: Cambridge University Press.

Gentner, D., & Medina, J. (1998). Similarity and the development of rules. *Cognition*, *65*, 263–297.

Gleitman, L. (1990). The structural source of verb meanings. *Language Acquisition*, *1*, 3–55.

Gupta, P., & MacWhinney, B. (1997). Vocabulary acquisition and verbal short-term memory: Computational and neural bases. *Brain and Language*, *50*, 267–333.

Handleman, J. S. (1979). Generalization by autistic-type children of verbal responses across settings. *Journal of Applied Behavior Analysis*, *12*, 273–282.

Heiman, M., Nelson, K., Tjus, T., & Gilberg, C. (1995). Increasing reading and communication skills in children with autism through an interactive multimedia program. *Journal of Autism and Developmental Disorders*, *25*, 459–480.

Hermer, L., & Spelke, E. S. (1994). A geometric process for spatial reorientation in young children. *Nature*, *370*, 57–59.

Hoff, E. (2004). *Language development* (3rd ed.). Boston, MA: Wadsworth.

Mandler, J. M., & McDonough, L. (1993). Concept formation in infancy. *Cognitive Development*, *8*, 291–318.

Melby-Lervåg, M., & Lervåg, A. (2014). Reading comprehension and its underlying components in second-language learners: A meta-analysis of studies comparing first- and second-language learners. *Psychological Bulletin*, *140*(2), 409–433.

Moore, M., & Calvert, S. (2000). Brief report: Vocabulary acquisition for children with autism: Teacher or computer instruction. *Journal of Autism and Developmental Disorders, 30,* 359–362.

National Early Literacy Panel. (2008). *Developing early literacy: Report of the National Early Literacy Panel.* Washington, DC: National Institute for Literacy.

O'Grady, W. (1997). *Syntactic Development.* Chicago, IL: University of Chicago Press.

Owens, R. E., Jr. (2008). *Language Development* (7th ed.). Boston, MA: Allyn & Bacon.

Powell, B. B. (2009). *Writing: Theory and History of the Technology of Civilization.* New York: John Wiley & Sons.

Reynolds, A. J., Temple, J. A., Robertson, D. L., & Mann, E. A. (2002). Age 21 cost-benefit analysis of the Title I Chicago child–parent centers. *Educational Evaluation and Policy Analysis, 24*(4), 267–303.

Ruffman, T., Slade, L., & Crowe, E. (2002). The relation between children's and mothers' mental state language and theory-of-mind understanding. *Child Development, 73,* 734–751.

Scarborough, H. S. (2001). Connecting early language and literacy to later reading (dis)abilities: Evidence, theory, and practice. In S. B. Neuman & D. Dickenson (Eds.), *Handbook of Early Literacy Research.* New York: Guilford Press.

Schick, B., de Villiers, P., de Villiers, J., & Hoffmeister, R. (2007). Language and theory of mind: A study of deaf children. *Child Development, 78,* 375–396.

Siegal, M., Tallandini, M. A., Pellizzoni, S., & Michelin, C. (2011). Exploring the effects of bilingualism on children's conversational understanding and moral sense. In M. Siegal & L. Surian (Eds.), *Access to Language and Cognitive Development.* New York: Oxford University Press.

Slaughter, V., & Peterson, C. (2011). How conversational input shapes theory of mind development in infancy and early childhood. In M. Siegal & L. Surian (Eds.), *Access to Language and Cognitive Development.* New York: Oxford University Press.

Sodian, B., & Kristen, S. (2010). Theory of mind. In B. M. Glatzeder, V. Goel, & A. von Muller (Eds.), *Towards a Theory of Thinking.* Berlin: Springer-Verlag.

Stanovich, K. E. (1986). Matthew effects in reading: Some consequences of individual differences in the acquisition of literacy. *Reading Research Quarterly, 21,* 360–407.

Trevarthen, C. (1979). Communication and cooperation in early infancy. A description of primary intersubjectivity. In M. Bullowa (Ed.), *Before Speech: The Beginning of Human Communication.* London: Cambridge University Press.

VanLehn, K. (2011). The relative effectiveness of human tutoring, intelligent tutoring systems and other tutoring systems. *Educational Psychologist, 46,* 4, 197–221.

Vermeer, A. (2001). Breadth and depth of vocabulary in relation to L1/L2 acquisition and frequency of input. *Applied Psycholinguistics, 22,* 217–234.

Vion, M., & Colas, A. (2004). On the use of the connective "and" in oral narration: A study of French-speaking elementary school children. *Journal of Child Language, 31,* 399–419.

Waxman, S. R., & Hatch, T. (1992). Beyond the basics: Preschool children label objects flexibly at multiple hierarchical levels. *Journal of Child Language, 19,* 153–166.

Waxman, S. R., & Markow, D. B. (1995). Words as invitations to form categories: Evidence from 12- to 13-month-old infants. *Cognitive Psychology, 29,* 257–302.

Wellman, H. (2002). Understanding the psychological world: Developing a theory of mind. In U. Goswami (Ed.), *Handbook of Cognitive Development*. Oxford: Blackwell.

Wellman, H. (2013). Deafness, thought bubbles, and theory-of-mind development. *Developmental Psychology, 49*, 2357–2367.

Wood, J. (2001). Can software support children's vocabulary development? *Language, Learning and Technology, 5*, 166–201.

Xu, F. (2002). The role of language in acquiring object kind concepts in infancy. *Cognition, 85*, 223–250.

Zeskind, P. S., Klein, L., & Marshall, T. R. (1992). Adults' perceptions of experimental modifications of durations of pauses and expiratory sounds in infant crying. *Developmental Psychology, 28*, 1153–1162.

Zimmerman, F. J., Gilkerson, J., Richards, J. A., Christakis, D. A., Xu, D., Gray, S., et al. (2009). Teaching by listening: The importance of adult-child conversations to language development. *Pediatrics, 124*, 342–349.

Chapter 7

Self-Perception and Perspective Taking

How Beliefs About Oneself and Others May Influence Reading

Henry Wynne and Carol McDonald Connor

One of the focuses within cognitive development is how the mind works to process, organize, and retrieve information that is learned (Bandura, 1993; see also Chapter 1 in this volume). Understanding how people process information has helped to clarify cognitive functioning. The causal attributions individuals make of their own cognitive functioning may be one mechanism by which cognitive functioning is developed (Bandura, 1993). In other words, the beliefs individuals have about themselves may influence how they feel, think, and behave. People may avoid activities and situations they believe would be beyond their capabilities to cope. On the other hand, people may continue to endure challenging activities and situations that they believe they are capable of handling (Bandura, 1993).

Related to one of the goals of cognitive development, the purpose of this chapter is to discuss the relevant literature on self-perception abilities and its association with reading achievement for youth. The specific goals of this chapter are to address two different questions. The first question is to examine whether self-perception influences reading achievement in children. The second question is to investigate how different self-perception abilities influence reading comprehension in youth. Specifically, this chapter will provide an overview of the literature on theory of mind (ToM) and perspective taking. The organization of this chapter will address the first question by exploring how different types of self-views, especially self-perception/self-concept and self-efficacy, influence students' reading achievement and engagement in reading. The next section of the chapter will address the second question by highlighting the research regarding different types of perception skill, namely theory of mind and perspective taking, on reading comprehension.

Self-Perception

One of the theories that has been developed to explain the role of self-perception on reading abilities is social cognitive theory (Bandura, 2006, 2012). Social cognitive theory suggests that individuals are agents, which allows them to make choices of how to respond to the external forces in their environments. Within social cognitive theory, there is a causal model depicting a triadic reciprocal relation between intrapersonal influences, behaviors, and the environment (Bandura, 2012). This triadic reciprocal relation may explain how self-perception is related to the other areas described in this edited book. Part of the social cognitive theory addresses interpersonal influences, which includes self-perception. The following sections will discuss the associations between self-perception and the behavior of reading achievement.

Shavelson, Hubner, and Stanton (1976) developed a multidimensional, hierarchical model of self-concept. According to Shavelson and colleagues (1976), self-concept is broadly defined as your own perception of yourself. Self-perception is characterized as views individuals have for themselves (Chapman & Tunmer, 2003). Because self-perception is used to define self-concept, these two terms have been used interchangeably in the literature. For the purpose of this review, both studies of self-concept and self-perception will be included in this self-perception section.

Studies on self-perception and reading suggest that there is an association. However, the direction of these relations is unclear. In a 3-year longitudinal study, it was found that perceived competence in reading was related to academic reading achievement at the end of the year for elementary students (Bouffard, Marcoux, Vezeau, & Bordeleau, 2003). This is one study that supports that self-perception may precede academic achievement.

However, another review indicated that reading difficulties usually precede student's self-perception (Chapman & Tunmer, 2003). In particular, it was found that students who had weak phonological processing using text-level cues rather than using word-level information also had lower self-perception. However, it appears that there may be a reciprocal relation of reading difficulties and self-perception starting between third and sixth grade (Chapman & Tunmer, 2003).

In another study, self-perception of academic competence at the beginning of the school year was associated with academic achievement one year later for fourth- and fifth-grade students (Stringer & Heath, 2008). When further analyses were conducted, the results demonstrated that the relation between self-perception and academic achievement might not be significant in all cases. In particular, the authors found that reading self-perception was not related to changes in the students' reading performance 1 year later. The authors noted that although there appears to be a relation between reading self-perception and reading achievement, it does not seem to relate to improvement or decline in reading academic performance.

Although there are studies to suggest that there may be an association between self-perception and academic abilities in reading, there is no consistent evidence that improving students' perceptions may lead to improved academic performance. For example, there is a report that was published by the American Psychological Society Task Force on Self-Esteem (Baumeister, Campbell, Krueger, & Vohs, 2003). One of the conclusions of the report was that there is not a strong relationship between self-esteem and academic performance. The authors defined self-esteem as how much value individuals place on themselves (Baumeister, et al., 2003). It is important to note that the focus was on global self-esteem because the purpose of the review was focused on how self-esteem may influence outcomes in general (e.g., academic performance, job performance, interpersonal relations, maladaptive behaviors, psychopathology, etc.).

However, Marsh and Craven (2006) offered an opposing view to the American Psychological report and tried to distinguish self-concept from self-esteem. The authors conducted another study and found a distinction between self-concept and self-esteem, where self-concept was related to academic achievement but not self-esteem (Marsh & O'Mara, 2008). Therefore, they concluded that self-esteem and self-concept should be viewed as two separate constructs.

Another study by Swann, Chang-Schneider, and McClarty (2007) also argued against the American Psychological report and suggested that self-views and global self-esteem were important for individuals and society. The authors felt that the results from the American Psychological report were incorrect because the way self-views were measured was flawed. As a result, the authors proposed a strategy to improve the research methodology of how constructs are measured. Swann and colleagues (2007) recommended that the level of specificity of a construct should match the specificity of the outcome being measured. For example, it would be important for researchers wanting to investigate the association between self-perception and reading to investigate the specific domain of reading self-perception with reading achievement. The work by Swann and colleagues (2007) identified this limitation in the original American Psychological report by Baumeister and colleagues (2003). In a later article, some of the original authors of American Psychological Society Task Force on Self-Esteem agreed that global self-esteem might ignore other domain specific self-schemata that can influence specific behaviors (Krueger, Vohs, & Baumeister, 2008).

The study used by Marsh and O'Mara (2008) consisted of the longitudinal study called Youth in Transition (Bachman & O'Malley, 1977; Marsh, 1990). The study included measures on self-esteem, academic self-concept, and educational attainment. The authors used the specificity matching principle by Swann and colleagues (2007) to emphasize the multidimensional approach perspective of self-concept. This was to improve the criticism of the global self-esteem that was reviewed by Baumeister and colleagues (2003). As of result of this methodological approach, it was found that there was a reciprocal relationship between academic self-concept and educational attainment. These results were maintained controlling for the effects of socioeconomic status (SES), academic ability, school grades, prior educational attainment, and self-esteem. However, self-esteem was not related to educational attainment, and this is probably because self-esteem was a global measure.

It is important to note that self-beliefs have also been described using various terms in theory and research including terms such as self-concept, self-esteem, and self-efficacy. Self-concept is characterized as a person's self-perception defining their interpretations and experiences with the environment (Shavelson, et al., 1976). Self-esteem has been defined as the descriptive component of self-concept of evaluating oneself (Beane, et al., 1980). Self-efficacy is the person's belief of their capabilities to organize and execute an action needed for a situation (Bandura, 1993). The review described next is regarding self-beliefs in general, but there were some studies represented in the review that examined self-concept related to reading abilities in particular and its relation to reading achievement.

Valentine, DuBois, and Cooper (2004) conducted a meta-analytic review of various longitudinal studies on the relation between self-beliefs and academic achievement. They found a small effect size for self-beliefs and its relation to later academic achievement, even when controlling for the initial levels of achievement (Valentine, et al., 2004). The effect sizes were stronger when the specific domains of self-beliefs (e.g., reading self-beliefs) were analyzed with the corresponding domain specific area of achievement (e.g., reading achievement). The authors reported that these results provide support for why self-beliefs might be relevant concepts to consider. However, the small effects also suggest that self-beliefs may not be a strong and pervasive influence on student achievement. Moreover, results are not indicating that interventions should be focused only on improving the self-perceptions of students but that self-beliefs should be considered when trying to improve students' mastery of a subject area (Valentine, et al., 2004).

Self-Efficacy

Self-efficacy is defined as the level of confidence one has to perform a task and is defined by two components: the belief of what a person can do with the set of skills he or she possess; and the experiences from the past that provide a framework of their ability to use the skills (Jinks & Lorsbach, 2003). Bandura's theory (1993) states that academic achievement is not only dependent on having competent skills but also on one's perception of the ability to use the skills effectively. According to Bandura, self-efficacy contributes to cognitive development and functioning. In particular, perceived self-efficacy can influence four major processes: cognitive, motivational, affective, and selection process.

A review by Jinks and Lorsbach (2003) suggested that stronger self-efficacy might motivate students to persevere during difficult situations, which may, in turn, influence academic success. In particular, they were interested in the motivational aspect of self-efficacy and how it influences academic success for students who are underachieving. Other studies have found that there is an association between self-efficacy and reading abilities. For example, academic self-efficacy was related to higher achievement in both reading and math scores in a 3-year longitudinal study of first-grade to third-grade students who were identified as lower achieving in literacy (based on the median of a state-approved measure of literacy; Liew, McTigue, Barrois, & Hughes, 2008). In particular, academic self-efficacy beliefs in both first and second grade were related to higher reading achievement in first and second grade. Although, academic self-efficacy was related to a higher association of reading achievement in third grade, when other covariates were considered (e.g., age, gender, IQ, ethnicity, SES, and adaptive/effort control), there was no significant independent contribution of academic self-efficacy in second-grade to third-grade reading achievement (Liew, et al., 2008). At the same time, newer theories indicate that these associations may be reciprocal, with stronger achievement predicting greater self-efficacy (see, further, Chapter 1).

Mindset

Work by Dweck and colleagues on "mindset" is also relevant (Blackwell, Trzesniewski, & Dweck, 2007) and builds on the constructs of self-efficacy and self-perception. The idea is that students focus on improvement instead of worrying about how smart they are. Interventions in which children were taught that intelligence could be developed and was not an inherent trait revealed stronger outcomes. Specifically, students with a growth mindset had stronger motivation, persistence, and made greater achievement gains than their peers with a trait mindset (Blackwell, et al., 2007). These results suggest that moving beyond simple positive and negative conceptualizations of self and focusing on types of perception (e.g., growth mindsets) may be be more useful in understanding the association between self-perception and achievement.

Theory of Mind

Another way to consider self-perception is to examine how perceptual abilities, such as theory of mind and perspective taking, can influence reading outcomes (also see Chapter 6 on language). Theory of mind (ToM) is the ability to understand the mental states of others (e.g., beliefs, intentions, knowledge). Mental states help others not only understand the inner lives of themselves but also understand the inner lives of other people (Dyer, Shatz, & Wellman, 2000). There are some studies that suggest that exposure to reading can influence ToM abilities. For example, exposure to children's storybooks for 4- to 6-year-olds is a predictor of ToM development (Mar, Tackett, & Moore, 2010). In other studies, parent-child reading tasks in the lab was associated with ToM performance in 4- to 7-year-old children (Adrian, Clemente, Villanueva, & Rieffe, 2005; Symons, Peterson, Slaughter, Roche, & Doyle, 2005).

Dyer, et al. (2000) found an association with reading and ToM abilities in children. This study analyzed 90 children's books for youth between the ages of 3 to 6 years old to identify if the storybooks depicted mental states. They found that there was a high rate of mental states depicted throughout the text of the book, while also depicting characters in ironic situations in the books. As a result, the authors noted that storybook reading might provide an avenue to help youth learn the mental states of others.

One way the ToM performance is developed is through parent-child relations. Children have the ability to gain an early understanding of people and the internal psychological states of other people through their interactions with others, such as parent-child interactions. Besides conversations parents have with their children, parent-child book reading is one way to have a conversation that is simultaneously and in depth about the same topic (Adrian, et al., 2005).

In another study with children between the ages of 4 to 6 years old, ToM performance was related to children's exposure to children's literature (Mar, et al., 2010). This exposure was assessed by their parents recognizing the names of different popular book titles and children's authors. This type of assessment was used to improve the parents' ability to recall books in order to control socially desirable responding. The association between the youth's exposure to children's literature and ToM abilities was even significant when controlling for age, gender, child's vocabulary, and parental income (Mar, et al., 2010). The results may suggest that children from various family backgrounds and vocabulary levels can benefit from being exposed to reading, as well as engaging the children in conversations about what was read to increase their awareness about themselves and others when reading.

Perspective Taking

Another way to understand perception is to look at perspective taking and its association with reading abilities. Perspective taking is exemplified in the classical quote "Don't judge a man until you have walked a mile in his shoes" (Emery & Mihalevich, 1992). Children must do exactly this when reading in order to understand a character. Moreover, this perspective taking ability might be considered a more mature version of theory of mind.

Perspective taking skills are thought to develop when children transition to middle school. During this time, children are beginning to think about the various perspectives in their larger social context rather than just focusing on their limited individual perspective (Emery & Mihalevich, 1992). For example, in an experimental study, teachers who led sixth-grade students in a discussion about the perspectives of the characters were able to answer more complex questions during the reading about the characters' motives, thoughts, beliefs, and feelings (Emery & Mihalevich, 1992). However, these results for perspective taking skills and reading achievement were not found for fourth- and fifth-grade students. Therefore, perspective taking abilities may be something that is developed at a later age. Nevertheless, taking different perspectives of a story can bring about a different level of understanding for the characters within the story (Emery & Mihalevich, 1992).

Without the help of teachers and adults, perspective taking appears to be a difficult task for children to master. For example, readers have to distinguish what the characters in the story know and what was intended for them only as readers (Weingartner & Klin, 2005, 2009). This skill of perspective taking during reading is usually considered something that skilled readers possess so they can keep track of what characters in the story know, or what some characters know that is unknown by others (Weingartner & Klin, 2005). Overall, studies show that text comprehension may vary depending on how the story is depicted, which might influence the cognitive processes used to understand the author's perspective and/or the characters' perspectives (Brunyé, Ditman, Mahoney, Augustyn, & Taylor, 2009; Weingartner & Klin, 2005).

One reason why individuals may not accurately understand the perspective of characters' in a story may be due to the number of cognitive resources needed to remember "who knows what" in the narrative (Weingartner & Klin, 2009). The authors reported that the implications of their findings might indicate further reasons why individuals make errors in perspective taking. For example, it can be hard to remember multiple perspectives in a story. Therefore, individuals may make errors in perspective taking when reading, because it is easier for them to assume that the ambiguous perspectives of characters are similar to their own perspective. This helps to avoid always having to correct possible inaccurate character inferences as a result of using perspective taking skills. Moreover, this reduces the demands on one's memory in trying to maintain the accuracy of multiple perspectives (Weingartner & Klin, 2009). Perspective taking, which is also similar to theory of mind, illustrates the complex skill that young readers have to use when trying to develop a higher level of reading comprehension.

Who Teaches Perception?

Parents and teachers help children develop self-perception. For example, parents have been credited for developing perceptual abilities of ToM as early as preschool by engaging their children with reading storybooks (Mar, et al., 2010; Ziv, Smadja, & Aram, 2013; also see Chapter 9).

There are many ways teachers can build self-efficacy in their students. They can teach them a growth mindset (Blackwell, et al., 2007) and can model appropriate strategies for reading to increase self-efficacy (Schunk & Zimmerman, 2007). For example, a teacher might read a paragraph to the class and then give a summary before reading them the next paragraph. Schunk and Zimmerman (2007) also suggested that teachers should form small groups for their students based on their level of self-efficacy as they currently do when forming small student groups based on learning capabilities. These examples include teachers providing models of various skills/strategies that students can use to comprehend reading material, giving encouraging feedback on how students can make improvements and ensuring that students are making continued progress in their reading abilities. It may also be useful for students to see multiple models (e.g., ways) to approach an academic problem, including models from students that originally had problems but improved when effective coping methods were used. Students who are able to see their peers persevere through problems may also build their self-efficacy by seeing someone who also had difficulties and managed to use the coping strategies to make improvements (Schunk & Zimmerman, 2007).

Also, teachers have self-perceptions about themselves. Haverback and Parault (2008) reviewed literature and found evidence that a preservice teacher's self-efficacy might be increased if they have opportunities to engage in one-on-one-tutoring in reading. This experience may give the teacher a chance to increase their confidence in their abilities and beliefs about children while also having the opportunity to see each child as an individual as well as integrate the theories they have learned in their postsecondary institution. Higher self-efficacy in teachers may also create an environment that would also help motivate and encourage their students to learn in the classroom (Haverback & Parault, 2008). However, the effect of increasing self-efficacy in new teachers is an area that needs to be studied in the future. When Haverback (2009) completed a study with preservice teachers, there was no significant relation between higher teacher self-efficacy in reading and the use of different reading strategies. Moreover, the study did not examine whether the higher teacher self-efficacy rating was related to any changes in the reading achievement of the students that were tutored.

Conclusions

The current body of literature suggests there is an association between self-beliefs and academic achievement, especially between reading self-perception and reading comprehension. However, the causal nature of the association is unknown, and as such, interventions that only try to improve self-beliefs may not be effective for increasing reading comprehension. Instead, making sure students gain fundamental and advanced reading comprehension skills may be the first step (see Chapter 12 on interventions to promote literacy). At the same time, social cognitive theory would suggest that interventions that encourage students to increase their positive self-perception in their reading abilities, as well as helping them monitor their self-views about themselves and others, including theory of mind, are ways to potentially increase the chance that students can achieve the highest level of reading comprehension while also motivating them to stay invested in improving their overall achievement.

References

Adrian, J. E., Clemente, R. A., Villanueva, L., & Rieffe, C. (2005). Parent-child picture-book reading, mothers' mental state language and children's theory of mind. *Journal of Child Language, 32*, 673–686.

Bachman, J. G., & O'Malley, P. M. (1977). Self-esteem in young men: A longitudinal analysis of the impact of educational and occupational attainment. *Journal of Personality and Social Psychology, 35*, 365–380.

Bandura, A. (1993). Perceived self-efficacy in cognitive development and functioning. *Educational Psychologist, 28*, 117–148.

Bandura, A. (2006). Toward a psychology of human agency. *Perspectives on Psychological Science, 1*, 164–180.

Bandura, A. (2012). On the functional properties of perceived self-efficacy revisited. *Journal of Management, 38*, 9–44.

Baumeister, R. F., Campbell, J. D., Krueger, J. I., & Vohs, K. D. (2003). Does high self-esteem cause better performance, interpersonal success, happiness, or healthier lifestyles? *Psychological Science in the Public Interest, 4*, 1–44.

Beane, J. A., & Lipka, R. P. (1980). Self-concept and self-esteem: A construct differentiation. *Child Study Journal, 10*, 1–6. Retrieved from http://login.ezproxy1.lib.asu.edu/login?url=http://search.proquest.com.ezproxy1.lib.asu.edu/docview/616471522?accountid=4485

Blackwell, L. S., Trzesniewski, K. H., & Dweck, C. S. (2007). Implicit theories of intelligence predict achievement across an adolescent transition: A longitudinal study and an intervention. *Child Development, 78*, 246–263.

Bouffard, T., Marcoux, M., Vezeau, C., & Bordeleau, L. (2003). Changes in self-perceptions of competence and intrinsic motivation among elementary schoolchildren. *British Journal of Educational Psychology, 73*, 171–186.

Brunyé, T. T., Ditman, T., Mahoney, C. R., Augustyn, J. S., & Taylor, H. A. (2009). When you and I share perspectives pronouns modulate perspective taking during narrative comprehension. *Psychological Science, 20*, 27–32.

Chapman, J. W., & Tunmer, W. E. (2003). Reading difficulties, reading-related self-perceptions, and strategies for overcoming negative self-beliefs. *Reading & Writing Quarterly: Overcoming Learning Difficulties, 19*, 5–24.

Cone, J. K. (1994). Appearing acts: Creating readers in a high school English class. *Harvard Educational Review, 64*, 450–473.

Dyer, J. R., Shatz, M., & Wellman, H. M. (2000). Young children's storybooks as a source of mental state information. *Cognitive Development, 15*, 17–37.

Emery, D. W., & Mihalevich, C. (1992). Directed discussion of character perspectives. *Reading Research and Instruction, 31*, 51–59.

Ferrara, S. L. N. (2005). Reading fluency and self-efficacy: A case study. *International Journal of Disability, Development and Education, 52*, 215–231.

Haverback, H. R. (2009). Situating pre-service reading teachers as tutors: Implications of teacher self-efficacy on tutoring elementary students. *Mentoring & Tutoring: Partnership in Learning, 17*(3), 251–261.

Haverback, H. R., & Parault, S. J. (2008). Pre-service reading teacher efficacy and tutoring: A review. *Educational Psychology Review, 20*, 237–255.

Jinks, J., & Lorsbach, A. (2003). Introduction: Motivation and self-efficacy belief. *Reading & Writing Quarterly, 19*, 113–118.

Krueger, J. I., Vohs, K. D., & Baumeister, R. F. (2008). Is the allure of self-esteem a mirage after all? *American Psychologist, 63*, 64–65.

Liew, J., McTigue, E. M., Barrois, L., & Hughes, J. N. (2008). Adaptive and effortful control and academic self-efficacy beliefs on achievement: A longitudinal study of 1st through 3rd graders. *Early Childhood Research Quarterly, 23*, 515–526.

Mar, R. A., Tackett, J. L., & Moore, C. (2010). Exposure to media and theory-of-mind development in preschoolers. *Cognitive Development, 25*, 69–78.

Marsh, H. W. (1990). Causal ordering of academic self-concept and academic achievement: A multiwave, longitudinal panel analysis. *Journal of Educational Psychology, 82*, 646–656.

Marsh, H. W., & Craven, R. G. (2006). Reciprocal effects of self-concept and performance from a multidimensional perspective: Beyond seductive pleasure and unidimensional perspectives. *Perspectives on Psychological Science, 1*, 133–163.

Marsh, H. W., & O'Mara, A. (2008). Reciprocal effects between academic self-concept, self-esteem, achievement, and attainment over seven adolescent years: Unidimensional and multidimensional perspectives of self-concept. *Personality and Social Psychology Bulletin, 34*, 542–552.

Prat-Sala, M., & Redford, P. (2012). Writing essays: Does self-efficacy matter? The relationship between self-efficacy in reading and in writing and undergraduate students' performance in essay writing. *Educational Psychology, 32*, 9–20.

Schunk, D. H., & Zimmerman, B. J. (2007). Influencing children's self-efficacy and self-regulation of reading and writing through modeling. *Reading & Writing Quarterly: Overcoming Learning Difficulties, 23*, 7–25.

Shavelson, R. J., Hubner, J. J., & Stanton, G. C. (1976). Self-concept: Validation of construct interpretations. *Review of Educational Research, 46*, 407–441.

Stringer, R. W., & Heath, N. (2008). Academic self-perception and its relationship to academic performance. *Canadian Journal of Education, 31*, 327–345. Retrieved from http://www.csse-scee.ca/CJE/Articles/CJE31-2.html

Swann, W. B. Jr., Chang-Schneider, C., & Larsen McClarty, K. (2007). Do people's self-views matter? Self-concept and self-esteem in everyday life. *American Psychologist, 62*, 84–94.

Symons, D. K., Peterson, C. C., Slaughter, V., Roche, J., & Doyle, E. (2005). Theory of mind and mental state discourse during book reading and story-telling tasks. *British Journal of Developmental Psychology, 23*, 81–102.

Valentine, J. C., DuBois, D. L., & Cooper, H. (2004). The relation between self-beliefs and academic achievement: A meta-analytic review. *Educational Psychologist*, *39*, 111–133.

Weingartner, K. M., & Klin, C. M. (2005). Perspective taking during reading: An on-line investigation of the illusory transparency of intention. *Memory and Cognition*, *33*, 48–58.

Weingartner, K. M., & Klin, C. M. (2009). Who knows what? Maintaining multiple perspectives during reading. *Scientific Studies of Reading*, *13*, 275–294.

Ziv, M., Smadja, M., & Aram, D. (2013). Mothers' mental-state discourse with preschoolers during storybook reading and wordless storybook telling. *Early Childhood Research Quarterly*, *28*, 177–186.

Chapter 8

The Influence of Psychological and Physical Health on Reading

Laurie Dempsey Wolf

Reading comprehension in children is frequently examined in the context of developmental milestones, neurological functioning, learning abilities, and academic achievement. It is equally important to consider the influences of emotional and physical experiences on reading comprehension. For example, as seen throughout this book, a child's ability to self-regulate, understand the perspective of others, function in the presence of ecological barriers, as well as how the child is being parented, all influence his/her cognitive, language, and literacy development. Understanding a child's reading comprehension development may also be understood more comprehensively by examining factors beyond traditional academic and neurological sources of influence. For example, probing emotional and physical health and environmental concerns that may affect a child's ability to learn, focus, and understand what they are reading may also significantly contribute to their reading abilities.

The purpose of this chapter is to investigate the impact of additional stressors such as mental and physical health issues, which may have a detrimental impact on children's ability to maintain the energy, focus, and resources needed to learn to read effectively. For example, if a child is suffering from anxiety, he/she may be unable to effectively focus on the material being read because of worries or nervousness associated with a perceived stressor. This may be especially true for children exposed to trauma or who experiencing a difficult life situation (e.g., witnessing marital abuse) as abilities, such as reading, may fall to the wayside in the presence of extreme stress. For instance, being committed to focusing and understanding a book's storyline may be nearly impossible when a child's parents are fighting in the next room or when a child is plagued by thoughts or visions of a past traumatic event.

Beyond socioemotional stress, living with chronic health problems such as diabetes, especially at a young age, can make it difficult to have the energy, time, and motivation to focus on improving reading comprehension abilities. For a child who often misses school due to medical concerns or doctor's appointments or who is too sick or fatigued to fully focus on learning in the classroom or at home, reading comprehension skills may fall lower on the list of priorities in favor of maintaining health status. Therefore, although examining traditional aspects of cognitive and academic skills on reading comprehension is important, in this chapter, we consider how often overlooked factors, such as psychological and physical health, may play a role in the development of children's reading abilities.

Psychological Health and Reading

Psychological health issues such as anxiety and depression may negatively impact reading abilities, especially comprehension, which requires extensive focus. For example, a study of children aged 6 to 11 revealed that symptoms of anxiety and depression were significantly correlated with difficulties in reading ability among other numerous cognitive skills, including attention, processing speed, executive functioning, verbal learning and memory, and other basic academic skills (Lundy, Silva, Kaemingk, Goodwin, & Quan, 2010). Further, a study of 9-year-old children reported that those with chronic emotional conditions, especially those with attention or autistic issues, scored significantly lower on tests of reading and math ability than peers without such conditions (Layte & McCrory, 2013).

Why might children with anxiety or depression exhibit poorer reading comprehension skills? Numerous reasons exist including how anxiety and depressive symptoms of withdrawn behavior, low motivation, nervousness or agitation, and trouble concentrating may make it difficult for children to become engaged in reading (Lundy, et al., 2010). For a child who finds little pleasure in learning or reading stories, is often tired and cannot focus, or who feels jittery and nervous much of the time, it is understandable that being able to read and understand complex details of a story may seem like an insurmountable task. Further, the relationship between reading and emotional distress may be bidirectional in that depressive and anxiety symptoms may make reading difficult. Relatedly, trouble with reading and academic skills may also create feelings of sadness, worthlessness, or anxiety among children because they are unable to excel in this expected area of academic achievement.

Although much of existing research suggests that poor psychological health may be associated with weaker reading abilities (Lundy, et al., 2010), the results are mixed. For example, a study of children ages 6 to 16 did not find any differences in reading abilities between children with anxiety or depression and those without such emotional struggles (Mayes & Calhoun, 2007). Potential reasons for non-significance may include smaller sample sizes of children with emotional health issues as well as imperfections in measurement such that children with anxiety or depression were not adequately detected. Research moving forward might utilize more comprehensive measures of anxiety and depression to investigate how the

severity and duration of psychological symptoms may impact reading comprehension abilities. Further, longitudinal research is needed to determine
the temporal precedence of psychological distress and reading difficulties as
well as to identify potential age ranges that are more susceptible than others
to reading troubles stemming from anxiety and depression.

Trauma and Reading

In addition to the internal stressors of psychological health on reading
comprehension, such as anxiety and depression, external psychological
stressors including traumatic life events may also create problems for reading development. In a study of first-grade children exposed to violence and
trauma, trauma-related distress was associated with a significant decrease in
both reading ability and reading achievement (Delaney-Black, et al., 2002).
Similarly, a study of 6- to 9-year-olds with a history of domestic violence
demonstrated significantly poorer scores compared to controls on standardized reading and phonological processing tests and were more likely to
meet clinical criteria for a reading disability, especially for those exposed to
psychological aggression (Blackburn, 2008).

How might trauma negatively impact a child's reading ability? Potential
mechanisms include deficits in memory and other neurological functions
that may stem from distress (e.g., anxiety, depression, fear) that continuously
triggers a child's stress response, a mechanism that is adaptive temporarily
but can be detrimental during chronic stress as it creates wear and tear on
the body (Saltzman, Holden, & Holahan, 2005). Trauma is associated with
physiological and psychological distress. In fact, children exposed to marital
violence often demonstrate elevations in physiological stress indicators,
such as heart rate and cortisol, compared to children not exposed to violence (Saltzman, et al., 2005). These elevations in stress over time may create significant disruptions in the proper childhood cognitive development
of neurological functioning and academic skills as the stress response is
frequently called to action (Turley & Obrzut, 2012). In fact, stress associated
with trauma may also be one of the factors involved in producing poor
reading abilities through its effects on neurological development as well its
acute tendency to make it difficult to fully concentrate and learn (Blackburn, 2008; Samuelson, Krueger, Burnett, & Wilson, 2010). Thus, for children experiencing traumatic events or stressful life situations, stress and
psychological symptoms associated with these experiences may create
reactivity in a child's stress response leading to detrimental outcomes on
their neurological regulation and functioning.

The neurological and developmental effects of traumatic stressors can
have a profound effect on a child's ability to adequately develop cognitive
skills such as reading. For example, children with a history of trauma or
posttraumatic stress disorder (PTSD) have shown abnormal brain structure

and functioning including deficits in memory, executive functioning, attention, and verbal abilities (Graham-Bermann, Howell, Miller, Kwek, & Lilly, 2010; Turley & Obrzut, 2012), although results are mixed (Samuelson, et al., 2010). Further, many children with a history of trauma or PTSD demonstrate impairment on neuropsychological tests of general and verbal memory (Yasik, Saigh, Oberfield, & Halamandaris, 2007). As seen in Chapter 4, memory is an essential ability needed for proficient reading comprehension. Impairments in memory may result in weaknesses in learning to read and fully understanding material. Abnormalities in memory and executive functioning may lead to general reading difficulties and may affect a child's ability to learn and remember new information (Samuelson, et al., 2010; Yasik, et al., 2007), which affects their ability to comprehend ongoing themes while reading a story.

Children with PTSD may have difficulty learning and retaining new information, which may make reading comprehension a challenge if they cannot learn and remember characters, changing storylines, or main points in a story. Among children with PTSD, performance is often impaired on learning tasks, such as those measured by the ability to recall a list of words after several verbal repetitions (Yasik, et al., 2007). Further, a study of children with a history of PTSD from witnessing domestic violence showed deficits in learning on neuropsychological tests such that children with PTSD learned more slowly and less effectively, were more bothered by interference words, and did not benefit from repeated rehearsal of words (Samuelson et al., 2010). Interestingly, deficits in learning among children with PTSD from this study were related to learning words, not to retrieving them once they were learned, indicating that impairments in learning may not necessarily be due to a failure to retrieve information, but rather to a deficit in learning the information initially (Samuelson, et al., 2010). Such difficulties could create major challenges for children attempting to learn new words and understand a story if they are struggling to encode information as they encounter it.

In addition to the impact of trauma-related physiological stress on neurological functioning, other mechanisms exist that may link trauma to poor reading abilities. Potential mechanisms include concurrent psychological distress that reduces a child's capability to properly attend to and be motivated to read. In fact, the high psychological comorbidity associated with PTSD may be a major factor in reading difficulties, because children with PTSD often experience additional psychological distress such as anxiety and depression (Yasik, et al., 2007). As noted earlier, children suffering from anxiety, depression, or hypervigilance associated with PTSD may have difficulty being motivated or focusing on reading tasks (Saltzman, et al., 2005; Turley & Obrzut, 2012).

Additionally, PTSD symptoms are associated with lower intelligence scores, although the cause for this is unknown (Saltzman, Weems, and

Carrion, 2006). It may be that significant emotional distress associated with PTSD negatively affects cognitive performance or that children who had lower intelligence scores before trauma may be at greater risk for suffering from PTSD following traumatic events, because cognitive resources and abilities to effectively process trauma are low (Saltzman, et al., 2006). Taken together, trauma and PTSD can affect children's reading comprehension abilities through neurological and psychological health and functioning.

Physical Health and Reading

In addition to chronic psychological health issues stemming from anxiety, depression, and trauma, children's ability to be proficient in reading can also be hindered by their physical health. For example, type 1 diabetes has been associated with deficits in reading and cognitive performance, although results are mixed (Kucera & Sullivan, 2011). Further, a meta-analysis revealed that children and adolescents with type 1 diabetes display deficits in reading skills as well as other related abilities including attention, motor speed and writing, and visuospatial skills (Naguib, Kulinskaya, Lomax, & Garralda, 2009). One reason for these deficits in reading and executive functioning among children with diabetes may be that, like trauma, abnormalities in neurological functioning, such as glucose dysregulation, may negatively affect proper brain development among children in early stages of growth (Naguib, et al., 2009). For example, poor metabolic control has been associated with deficits in reading skills (McCarthy, Lindgren, Mengeling, Tsalikian, & Engvall, 2003). Similarly, severe hyperglycemia (i.e., high blood sugar) has been linked with deficits in short-term memory (Naguib, et al., 2009). Thus, dysregulation of glucose and metabolic functioning early in life may negatively affect proper brain development and thereby increase risk for difficulties with cognitive skills such as reading.

Another example of chronic health conditions affecting reading surrounds children with orofacial abnormalities. Like diabetes, abnormalities in neurological functioning caused by improper physical development may create difficulties in acquiring essential cognitive skills. Among children with orofacial clefts, for example, improper development of facial structures may symbolize related abnormal brain development leading to issues in cognitive skills in addition to speech problems that can make learning to read difficult (Collett, Stott-Miller, Kapp-Simon, Cunningham, & Speltz, 2010). In fact, children with orofacial clefts score significantly lower on tests of reading comprehension, basic reading, phonological memory, and reading fluency compared to controls (Collett, et al., 2010). Further, for children with cleft lip or palate as well as reading disabilities, deficits in rapid naming and verbal expression of words suggest the potential for developmental dyslexia issues and deficits in short-term memory and word-finding abilities (Richman & Ryan, 2003). Therefore, among children with orofacial abnormalities, reading development may be related to abnormal structural development in the brain.

Unlike trauma and reading abilities, the connections between physical health and reading abilities are less clear in that many studies have shown no association between chronic health conditions and reading. For example, a review of the effects of epilepsy on academic achievement suggested that many children with epilepsy have weaker reading abilities, among other low outcomes such as math, but that results are mixed such that some samples of children with epilepsy show no reading deficits (Reilly & Neville, 2011; Völkl-Kernstock, Bauch-Prater, Ponocny-Seliger, & Feucht, 2009). Further, studies of children with chronic pain have found reading and math scores to be above average compared to healthy children although small sample size was a limitation of the study (Ho, Bennett, Cox, & Poole, 2009). Further, in a sample of 9-year-old children, chronic illness did not appear to be directly related to reading difficulties (Layte & McCrory, 2013). Rather, the impact of physical health appeared to be on children's emotional difficulties, which, in turn, affected reading achievement (Layte & McCrory, 2013). Therefore, the effects of physical health issues on reading abilities may be through abnormal neurological development as well as through an increase in emotional issues associated with the distress of having a chronic illness at a young age.

Conclusions

Emotional and physical health conditions, as well as a history of trauma are important, yet often overlooked, factors that appear to affect reading comprehension skills. By not assessing physical and emotional health when identifying children who either currently have deficits in reading comprehension or are at risk for these deficits, interventions for reading may not be effective because they are overlooking these important underlying influences.

This review has implications for assessing reading comprehension difficulties in children with poor physical and emotional health or who have experienced traumatic stressors. For example, children struggling with reading or learning should be assessed for emotional issues or stressors related to trauma using tools outside of the standard batteries that only assess academic deficits (Graham-Bermann, et al., 2010; Turley & Obrzut, 2012). Further, regular neuropsychological screening for children with physical and emotional health problems should be employed to identify those at risk for falling behind their peers in school (Collett, et al., 2010). This requires the attention of both parents and schools regarding the importance of stepping outside of traditional neuropsychological testing to also include a comprehensive clinical interview assessing emotional and physical health as well as factors at home, such as marital violence, as the effects of these stressors are substantial. For example, stress and low support within a violent home may impact development and reading ability (Blackburn, 2008) and are undoubtedly associated with related emotional distress. Further, children with emotional distress living in the midst of a difficult home environment may not get sufficient study time, may miss classes, or change schools frequently, making it challenging to find a stable environment in which to learn (Blackburn, 2008). In addition, for children living in abusive homes or living in poverty, regular reading time at home with parents may be infrequent or undervalued, as discussed in Chapter 9.

Relatedly, children with physical health issues may also face challenges in their environment that hinder their reading success. For example, missing classes due to doctor's appointments and illness or being unable to fully focus in class because of fatigue, pain, or sickness may make learning a daunting challenge. Although hospitals, families, and schools may work together to help prevent a child with physical health issues from falling behind in school, these efforts may not be enough, especially for those who are already at a higher risk for academic difficulties due to neurological abnormalities. Therefore, regular neuropsychological evaluations of children with physical health conditions may be one way to ensure that they are not falling behind their peers due to either their physical illness or associated psychological distress.

Moving forward, researchers in the field as well as parents, educators, and medical staff should work together to develop both neurological and psychological assessments that can provide a comprehensive understanding of the functioning of a child with emotional, physical, or traumatic stressors. In addition, research should investigate additional mechanisms behind the development and/or exacerbation of reading difficulties among these children through the use of comprehensive neurological and psychological evaluations and longitudinal designs. By determining early signs of risk, interventions can be created that specifically target children with psychological and physical health issues that go above and beyond traditional interventions that do not currently provide tools aimed at meeting the special needs associated with these populations. Together, researchers, families, school leaders, and practitioners can provide early help for children at risk for reading difficulties due to physical and emotional health issues in order to provide these children with the greatest opportunities for academic and life success.

References

Blackburn, J. F. (2008). Reading and phonological awareness skills in children exposed to domestic violence. *Journal of Aggression, Maltreatment, & Trauma, 17,* 415–438.

Collett, B. R., Stott-Miller, M., Kapp-Simon, K. A., Cunningham, M. L., & Speltz, M. L. (2010). Reading in children with orofacial clefts versus controls. *Journal of Pediatric Psychology, 35,* 199–208.

Delaney-Black, V., Covington, C., Ondersma, S. J., Nordstrom-Klee, B., Templin, T., Ager, J., et al. (2002). Violence exposure, trauma, and IQ and/or reading deficits among urban children. *Archives of Pediatrics and Adolescent Medicine, 156,* 280–285.

Graham-Bermann, S. A., Howell, K. H., Miller, L. E., Kwek, J., & Lilly, M. M. (2010). Traumatic events and maternal education as predictors of verbal ability for preschool children exposed to intimate partner violence (IPV). *Journal of Family Violence, 25,* 383–392.

Ho, G. H. Y., Bennett, S. M., Cox, D., & Poole, G. (2009). Brief report: Cognitive functioning and academic achievement in children and adolescents with chronic pain. *Journal of Pediatric Psychology, 34,* 311–316.

Kucera, M., & Sullivan, A. L. (2011). The educational implications of type 1 diabetes mellitus: A review of research and recommendations for school psychological practice. *Psychology in the Schools, 48,* 587–603.

Layte, R., & McCrory, C. (2013). Paediatric chronic illness and educational failure: The role of emotional and behavioural problems. *Social Psychiatry and Psychiatric Epidemiology, 48,* 1307–1316.

Lundy, S. M., Silva, G. E., Kaemingk, K. L., Goodwin, J. L., & Quan, S. F. (2010). Cognitive functioning and academic performance in elementary school children with anxious/depressed and withdrawn symptoms. *Open Pediatric Medicine Journal, 14,* 1–9.

McCarthy, A. M., Lindgren, S., Mengeling, M. A., Tsalikian, E., & Engvall, J. (2003). Factors associated with academic achievement in children with type 1 diabetes. *Diabetes Care, 26,* 112–117.

Mayes, S. D., & Calhoun, S. L. (2007). Learning, attention, writing, and processing speed in typical children and children with ADHD, autism, anxiety, depression, and oppositional-defiant disorder. *Child Neuropsychology, 13,* 469–193.

Naguib, J. M., Kulinskaya, E., Lomax, C. L., Garralda, M. E. (2009). Neuro-cognitive performance in children with type 1 diabetes—A meta-analysis. *Journal of Pediatric Psychology, 34,* 271–282.

Nation, K., Cocksey, J., Taylor, J. S. H., & Bishop, D. V. M. (2010). A longitudinal investigation of early reading and language skills in children with poor reading comprehension. *Journal of Child Psychology and Psychiatry, 51,* 1031–1039.

Reilly, C., & Neville, B. G. R. (2011). Academic achievement in children with epilepsy: A review. *Epilepsy Research, 97,* 112–123.

Richman, L. C., & Ryan, S. M. (2003). Do the reading disabilities of children with cleft fit into current models of developmental dyslexia? *Cleft Palate-Craniofacial Journal, 40,* 154–157.

Saltzman, K. M., Holden, G. W., & Holahan, C. J. (2005). The psychobiology of children exposed to marital violence. *Journal of Clinical Child and Adolescent Psychology, 34,* 129–139.

Saltzman, K. M., Weems, C. F., & Carrion, V. G. (2006). IQ and posttraumatic stress symptoms in children exposed to interpersonal violence. *Child Psychiatry and Human Development, 36,* 261–272.

Samuelson, K. W., Krueger, C. E., Burnett, C., & Wilson, C. K. (2010). Neuropsychological functioning in children with posttraumatic stress disorder. *Child Neuropsychology, 16,* 119–133.

Turley, M. R., & Obrzut, J., E. (2012). Neuropsychological effects of posttraumatic stress disorder in children and adolescents. *Canadian Journal of School Psychology, 27,* 166–182.

Völkl-Kernstock, S., Bauch-Prater, S., Ponocny-Seliger, E., & Feucht, M. (2009). Speech and school performance in children with benign partial epilepsy with centro-temporal spikes (BCECTS). *Seizure, 18,* 320–326.

Yasik, A. E., Saigh, P. A., Oberfield, R. A., & Halamandaris, P. V. (2007). Posttraumatic stress disorder: Memory and learning performance in children and adolescents. *Biological Psychiatry, 61,* 382–388.

Chapter 9

Parenting Influences on Children's Cognitive Development

Zorash Montano and Annemarie Hindman

As we learned in Chapter 2, parents may impact their child's cognitive abilities genetically (i.e., children and parents share similar genes). However, genes do not account for all the differences in an individual's cognitive abilities; rather, cognitive abilities are a product of gene-environment interactions. Parents (whether biological parents, adoptive parents, or other primary caregivers) play an essential role in cognitive development, including language and literacy development, through the learning environments they provide for children. This influence is especially salient in the earliest years of life (i.e., birth through 5), before children experience structured, formal learning experiences in kindergarten. In these years, children are building essential alphabet knowledge, phonological sensitivity, and concepts of print that will help them read text, along with vocabulary and language skills that will help them make sense of what they read (Gough & Tunmer, 1986). These competencies are profoundly and directly shaped by parents' conversations with children, their reading and discussion of books, and their explicit teaching about letters and words; and recent research has illuminated what specific practices during these activities are most closely connected to language learning and the development of reading skills. Also important, largely through indirect pathways, are other factors such as the emotional climate in the home, predominantly conceptualized as responsivity and sensitivity (Chazan-Cohen, et al., 2009; Dodici, Draper, & Peterson, 2003; Landry, et al., 2012; Taylor, Aghara, Smith, & Landry, 2008).

Because children's early language and literacy learning has such enormous implications for later success in reading and other academic areas (National Early Literacy Panel, 2009), this chapter aims to describe the extant research base regarding how parents directly and indirectly support early language and literacy learning, as well as to highlight areas that demand additional research.

Parent Practices that Directly Support Early Language and Literacy

Verbal Input and Conversations

In the course of daily life, the most commonly occurring opportunity for parents to shape children's language and literacy skills is through verbal exchanges. Through these exchanges, parents model vocabulary and grammar for children, encourage and invite child talk, and provide feedback on the meaning and structure of what children have said (Hart & Risley, 1995, 1999; Rush, 1999). In general, unless parents focus these interactions specifically on identifying letters and sounds (see section on explicit teaching later), conversations generally expose children to vocabulary words and ideas, as well as to rules about how words go together (i.e., grammar), all of which have important benefits for later reading (Sénéchal, 2006). The extant body of research has examined various aspects of parent-child exchanges in something of a patchwork; in the following, we detail the primary foci of this research base.

Amount of Talk

At a fundamental level, the amount of talk that parents provide and solicit from children is important for language development. Important early discoveries in this area came from the intensive observational work of Hart and Risley (1995, 1999), who recruited 42 families of varying socioeconomic backgrounds and visited their homes beginning when children were 7 months old and continuing until children were 36 months old. For 1 hour each month, researchers recorded the language used in the household, elucidating the body of words (e.g., how many, what type) to which children had access throughout their earliest years. One striking finding was that families varied widely in the number of words they used with children, with some children hearing approximately 600 words per hour, while others heard more than 2000 words per hour. Sharp distinctions emerged along socioeconomic lines, with children from the highest income households receiving more than three times the input of low-income peers. Another remarkable finding was that approximately 90 percent of the words that children used by age 3 were drawn from their parents' vocabularies, and that their patterns of word use (i.e., length of utterance, duration of conversation) mimicked those of their parents. Taken together, findings clearly show that children have different early exposure to language and that these differences have critical implications for their later language competence. Indeed, a follow-up study revisiting 29 of the original 42 families when children were in third grade showed that early advantages in language skills translated into later success in language, vocabulary, and reading comprehension, all of which are likely to support achievement in other areas.

Function of Talk

While more talk may be linked to stronger future skills, there is also evidence that some kinds of talk are more predictive of child outcomes than others. Subsequent work, including that of Dieterich, Assel, Swank, Smith, and Landry (2006), further untangled the nature of effective parent talk to show the unique value of verbal scaffolding. This technique, broadly defined, involves providing essential knowledge to empower the child to independently engage with a new object, word, or idea. Put another way, verbal scaffolding aims to give children the information they need to participate more fully in the world. For example, parents might label something (e.g., "That's an angelfish") and then connect that label to a helpful fact that children already know (e.g., "Remember—we saw one of those at the aquarium"). Alternatively, parents might describe the function of an object (e.g., "This fish tank keeps the fish safe inside") or help children use an object (e.g., "To feed the fish, you have to unscrew this cap on the food container"). Verbal scaffolding might also explain cause and effect relations (e.g., "If we forgot to the feed the fish, they would get very hungry") or emotions ("Your brother is feeling disappointed because he has to wait for his turn to feed the fish"). Providing rich information about the world in this specific way, rather than simply labeling objects (or not talking at all), supports children's vocabulary skills in preschool, as well as both their reading fluency and comprehension skills in the elementary grades (Dietrich, et al., 2006).

Abstraction of Talk

Taking an even more refined view of the "active ingredients" in parents' verbal input, Snow, Dickinson and Tabors found unique benefits of more abstract talk in the course of their research on the Harvard Home-School Study (Dickinson & Tabors, 2001). Recruiting 74 families from low-income households when children were 3 years of age, researchers observed language exchanges at home (e.g., meal time, discussing recent events, play time) and school each year. Of greater focus than the number of words exchanged (relative to Hart and Risley's work) was whether talk focused on contextualized topics (i.e., concrete or immediate, referring to the here-and-now) or decontextualized topics (i.e., abstract, non-immediate, or going beyond what is immediately apparent) (see Snow, et al., 1991). Findings revealed that, within this low-income sample, children had varied exposure to ambient language and to conversations at home and school. As in Hart and Risley, greater exposure to talk was linked to stronger language development 1 year later, with decontextualized talk emerging as particularly important. Moreover, adults' use of sophisticated or rare vocabulary words was linked to children's use of rare vocabulary words.

Elaboration of Talk

Further untangling the value of decontextualized talk is research on parents' elaboration during the exchanges with children, and their encouragement of children to talk more about past events, including using open-ended questions to prompt children to add more new ideas or details to the emerging narrative. Elaboration also involves reinforcing children's participation through praise and through repeating parts of what they have said. Much research on elaboration has focused specifically on parent-child reminiscing, or discussing events that have transpired in the past (see Fivush & Fromhoff, 1988; Reese & Fivush, 1993; Reese, Haden, & Fivush, 1993; Reese, Leyva, Sparks, & Grolnik, 2010). Evidence, including from experimental trials, shows that more elaboration during reminiscing with young children is related to stronger vocabulary skills (Jordan, et al., 2000; Peterson, et al., 1999; Reese, et al., 2010; Reese & Newcombe, 2007; Taumoepeau & Reese, 2010) and is also linked to knowledge of letters, sounds, and letter-sound correspondence (Sparks & Reese, 2013), potentially through child engagement and interest in books.

Rare Words

Of the constellation of studies exploring the ways in which parents' talk might support children's early emergent skills, perhaps the most focused lens is apparent in work by Weizman and Snow (2001), which emphasizes the sophistication of the vocabulary words used in parent-child exchanges. Drawing on the findings from the Harvard Home-School study (described earlier), researchers determined that much parent-child discussion involved the same relatively small body of commonly used words (about 3000 words). However, the degree to which parents and children departed from this common vocabulary to employ sophisticated or rarely used words (e.g., oxygen) in preschool was uniquely predictive of children's vocabulary skills in kindergarten, as well as into second grade. Moreover, congruent with other work detailed earlier, word learning was particularly advantaged when children heard these words in supportive contexts (i.e., with scaffolding or elaboration).

Taken together, a variety of parent conversational practices support children's development of early reading-related skills, especially language and vocabulary, but common threads include providing children with models of rich language, inviting children to practice using that language, and offering children clear, constructive, and supportive feedback on what they have said.

Book Reading

Extensive evidence across a wide range of racial, ethnic, and socioeconomic groups suggests that parents regularly read books to their young, preliterate children (Duursma & Pan, 2011; Rodriguez, Hines, & Montiel, 2009), and that this shared book reading can positively impact early precursors of reading success (Bus, et al., 1995; Farrant & Zubrick, 2013; Marulis & Neuman, 2010, 2013; Mol, et al., 2008). Book reading is most reliably linked to vocabulary and other language skills, rather than to knowledge of letters and sounds (Hindman & Morrison, 2012; Sénéchal, 2006; Sénéchal, Pagan, Lever, & Oullette, 2008), likely because most text- and reading-related discussions focus primarily on character actions and story events. Thus, during book readings, children mostly hear vocabulary and language and talk relatively little about the letters or sounds of words (Hindman, et al., 2008; Yaden, Smolkin, & MacGillivray, 1993).

A number of meta-analyses have determined that shared reading typically accounts for approximately 8 percent of the variability in preschool-aged children's vocabulary skills (Bus, van IJzendoorn, & Pellegrini, 1995; Marulis & Neuman, 2010, 2013; Mol, et al., 2008; Scarborough & Dobrich, 1994). However, research clearly indicates that not all book readings have identical effects on child skills. Instead, specific features of the parent-child exchanges during reading, largely consistent with principles of parent-child conversation detailed earlier, make a difference for child learning.

Parent-Child Dialogue During Reading

Children's vocabulary learning during book readings is enhanced by opportunities to hear more talk about the book and to talk more about the book themselves. For example, dialogic reading, a method of shared reading in which parents (or other adults) ask questions to engage their child in conversation about the story, is linked to meaningful gains in vocabulary (Arnold, et al., 1994; Lonigan & Whitehurst, 1998; Mol, Bus, de Jong, & Smeets, 2008; Whitehurst, et al., 1988). Specifically, during dialogic reading, parents not only read the text of the story aloud but also involve the child in the telling of the story so that, over time, the child could assume primary responsibility for telling the story. To achieve this goal, parents ask numerous prompts and then evaluate children's responses, expand on what children have said, and repeat parts of children's remarks to validate their participation (as represented in initial research as the PEER techniques). Specific types of prompts are recommended (as represented by the CROWD techniques), including completion, recall, open-ended, wh- (i.e., who, what, where), and distancing (or inferential). Interestingly, more recent work with dialogic reading (Lonigan, Farver, Phillips & Clancy-Menchetti, 2010) has de-emphasized distinctions between prompts and focused instead on the importance of shifting over time from simpler discussions of book vocabulary to more complex descriptions of the book and finally to discussion of emotions, narrative nuances, and inferences.

A comprehensive meta-analysis by Mol and colleagues (2008) shows that dialogic reading better supports vocabulary than reading without much extra-textual commentary, and that it is most effective when delivered by parents (rather than teachers), likely because of the rich exchanges afforded by a one-on-one context, and that it may better support learning among younger children, particularly where expressive vocabulary is concerned. That said, there are mixed effects of dialogic reading on vocabulary and language skills, including null effects (Mol, et al., 2008). These discrepancies in effectiveness likely occur because the variety of dialog engendered by dialogic reading could be quite diverse, particularly with regard to the level of abstraction in the talk, the effectiveness of the scaffolding, and the sophistication of the vocabulary. For example, some wh- questions could target very basic information (e.g., "What color is the dog?") while others could be far more challenging (e.g., "What do you think will happen next?" or "If you were the main character, what would you do?"), suggesting that the "active ingredient" of questioning could be somewhat more nuanced than the presence or absence of questions (Anderson, Anderson, Lynch, Shapiro, & Kim, 2012). In the following, we examine evidence regarding how very specific facets of parent-and-child book-related discourse may matter for children's reading development.

Contextualized and Decontextualized Talk During Reading

Whether parents use contextualized or decontextualized talk during reading might make a difference in what, and how much, children learn (Dickinson & Tabors, 2001; van Kleeck, 2008). In the context of reading, contextualized talk involves information that is apparent on the page, such as labeling and describing illustrations (e.g., "Goldilocks is wearing a red dress" or "What is this big, brown wild animal called?"). Decontextualized talk involves using the book as a springboard for more advanced discussion, such as inferences about the characters' emotions, motivations, or next steps, as well as defining words, providing additional information about story ideas, recalling previous parts of the story, and linking the story events and ideas to a child's own life (e.g., "What would you do if you got lost in the woods like Goldilocks?" or "It's very rude of Goldilocks to go into someone else's house when they aren't home").

The Harvard Home-School Study (Dickinson & Tabors, 2001) showed that parents varied in the extent to which they used book reading as an opportunity for contextualized and decontextualized discussion, and there are indications from this and other work (DeTemple, 2001; Hammet, van Kleeck, & Huberty, 2003; Hindman, et al., 2008) that contextualized talk is often more prevalent. However, these studies also show that more abstract talk is often linked to greater vocabulary growth. Further, emerging work in both homes and classrooms suggests that children's prior knowledge may play a moderating role (see Hindman, Wasik, & Erhart, 2012; Justice, Meier, & Walpole, 2005; Reese & Cox, 1999). For example, contextualized input around reading might be most useful for children with very low vocabulary knowledge (i.e., those who would benefit from a focus on the illustrations), whereas decontextualized talk might be most linked to growth among those with the highest initial skills (who, perhaps, are able to leverage what they already know to learn even more). By the same token, some research suggests that decontextualized talk during parent-child reading is most predictive of vocabulary growth among those with the lowest initial skills (who, perhaps, are able to take advantage of instruction to build new information rapidly). Further study of this issue is needed.

Defining Vocabulary

One facet of decontextualized talk that merits particular attention is defining new words during book reading. Book reading offers a virtually unparalleled opportunity to introduce new words, because books feature complex vocabulary in a meaningful context, often with illustrations to support those words (Ganea, Pickard, & DeLoache, 2008). Studies suggest that efforts to define or otherwise clearly explain words during reading is linked to child word learning (Clark, 2011; Justice, Meyer, & Walpole, 2005; Marulis & Neuman, 2013). Interestingly, there are indications that parents often miss opportunities to explicitly define words that are unfamiliar to their children in the context of shared book reading (Evans, Reynolds, Shaw, & Pursoo, 2011; Hindman, et al., 2008; Tabors, et al., 2001). For example, Hindman and Skibbe (2014) examined the shared book reading experiences of more than 700 families participating in the Early Childhood Longitudinal Study—Birth cohort Reading Aloud Together Profile study and found that almost none discussed or defined vocabulary while reading together. Similarly, Evans and colleagues (2011) asked families of first graders to read a book together featuring many unfamiliar words and discovered that, at maximum, they discussed just one in 10 of those words. However, this study also revealed that parents were more likely to define words on the last page of the narrative, suggesting that parents might provide definitions when the flow of the story was unlikely to be interrupted.

Interestingly, even when parents use book reading as an opportunity to define words, they may use less-than-optimal strategies. For example, Evans, et al. (2011) found that parents' definition efforts most often involved repeating the word, which may promote pronunciation more than comprehension. Further, few families gave a synonym or linked the word's meaning to the child's own experience, both of which would be more likely to foster new understanding. However, Clark determined that, at least when reading a book that minimized narrative complexity and highlighted novel words (i.e., one picture per page, with just word—referring to the novel item in that picture—printed below the picture), parents defined words in rich ways, activating children's background knowledge and making connections to prior experiences (Clark, 2011). Not only did children pay more attention to and repeat these unfamiliar words (likely a necessary if not sufficient gateway to remembering the word), but as children got older, they used these same techniques on their own, potentially resulting in further vocabulary increases. Thus, book reading can be, but is not always, a valuable context for parents to define new words for children, in turn supporting later reading skills.

Book Reading and Letter and Sound Knowledge

As briefly indicated already, research suggests that parents rarely point out letters and sounds when reading books with young children (see Phillips, et al., 2008); instead, they generally focus on discussion of characters and story events. Perhaps not coincidentally, children rarely look at the text of books before they have begun learning about decoding (Evans & Saint-Aubin, 2005; Justice, Skibbe, Canning, & Lankford, 2005; Roy-Charland, Saint-Aubin, & Evans, 2007). At least in theory, alphabet books provide a unique opportunity to highlight the code of print, including letters and phonological sensitivity (particularly initial sounds), as they often make each letter salient, one at a time, in sequence, and link that letter to objects whose labels begin with that sound (and, when written, that letter) (Huck, Kiefer, Helper, & Hickman, 2004). Interestingly, it seems that even when parents of preschoolers read alphabet books with children, they rarely talk about letters and sounds (i.e., between 10 and 20 percent of the total talk), particularly when a compelling narrative runs through the text (Hindman, et al., 2008; Lachner, Zevenbergen, & Zevenbergen, 2008; Yaden, et al., 1993). Even so, Stadler and McEvoy (2003) showed that, relative to other kinds of texts, alphabet books sparked greater emphasis on letters and phonological sensitivity among parents as they read with their young children. Further, discussion about letters and sounds during alphabet book readings may be more prominent as children approach the start of formal reading instruction (e.g., among 5-year-olds) (Lachner, et al., 2008). For example, Davis, Evans, and Reynolds (2010) found that, when parents of 5-year-old preliterate children read an alphabet book with simple, regular text (i.e., letters, images of objects beginning with that letter, and printed words identifying those objects), they were likely to focus on letters and letter sounds.

Regardless of child age and book type, structured interventions can enhance the frequency of parent-child talk about letters and sounds during reading (Justice, Weber, Ezell, & Bakeman, 2002; Pile, Girolametto, Johnson, Chen, & Cleave, 2010), which, in turn, improves children's knowledge of letters, sounds, and how they intersect (Justice & Ezell, 2000, 2002; Justice, Kadaverek, Bowles, & Grimm, 2005). While some training focuses on completing structured alphabet or phonological sensitivity tasks after reading (Justice, et al., 2005), other models encourage parents to point to and ask questions about the letters and letter sounds in books (Justice, Skibbe, McGinty, Piasta, & Petrill, 2011). Overall, effects of this work—often conducted with children with specific language impairment or other disabilities—generally reveal significant, educationally meaningful gains on some measures; often, however, there are also some null effects in this work (see Pile, et al., 2010), perhaps because of difficulties around feasibility and fidelity for some families (Justice, et al., 2011). Thus, this is a promising avenue for future research on shared book reading.

Explicit Teaching about Letters, Sounds in Words, and Vocabulary

Beyond book reading, parents support children's skills by engaging in explicit teaching. Remarkably less research has closely examined this facet of the home learning environment, but evidence suggests that parents teach about letters, sounds, words, and other reading-related content in many ways. Letter and sound knowledge is explicitly targeted by pointing out letters and/or their sounds, for example through using alphabet flashcards or helping children decode (or sound out) words, as well as by teaching children rhymes, chants, or songs that include repeated beginning or ending sounds (Hindman & Wasik, 2011; Sénéchal, LeFevre, Hudson, & Lawson, 1996). Comprehension-related skills might be explicitly targeted by teaching new vocabulary or grammatical constructions by using word or picture flashcards or word games. These skills could be more implicitly targeted through visits to community resources that expose children to new words and ideas (e.g., museum, zoo).

A great deal of self-report and observational work has established that most parents engage children in some of these home learning activities. For example, work by Bradley and colleagues using the HOME observation tool (Bradley, Corwyn, Burchinal, McAdoo, & Garcia Coll, 2001; Chazan-Cohen, et al., 2009), arguably the most thoroughly researched and frequently used measure of families' home learning environment, suggests that most families provide at least some of these explicit instructional opportunities at home and in the community, which in turn predict stronger language and literacy.

Moreover, consistent with the specificity that emerges in book reading research, other work with a more narrow focus suggests that particular kinds of teaching may be linked to particular kinds of skills (Hindman & Morrison, 2012; Sénéchal, 2006). For example, Sénéchal (2006) evaluated how, and how often, parents of kindergarteners explicitly taught about the letters and sounds that make up words, finding that parent teaching predicted unique variance in kindergarten alphabet knowledge, which in turn predicted phonological sensitivity. Parent teaching also predicted literacy in first grade and reading fluency in fourth grade. More nuanced still, Hindman and Morrison (2011) determined that families of children in Head Start taught children about letters and sounds several times per week (on average) and that of the constellation of home involvement practices parents used, this strategy alone was uniquely predictive of children's letter-word learning over the course of the preschool year. Therefore, the link between teaching and learning is well supported, and may be quite specific or nuanced.

Parent Teaching and Outcomes Indirectly Supportive of Literacy

It is worth noting that parents' conversations with children, shared book readings, and explicit teaching practices might support other outcomes as well, which could, over time, feed into further increases in literacy. For example, Chazan-Cohen, et al. (2009) found that more frequent home teaching in the early years of preschool was linked to more optimal approaches to learning by the time children entered kindergarten. Similarly, Hindman and Morrison (2012) found that the frequency with which parents taught children about letters, letter sounds, or writing was linked not only to higher literacy skills but to higher levels of cooperation, even when accounting for parents' responsiveness and consistent management. It is likely that instructional engagement between parents and children—potentially through any of these techniques—provides opportunities for children to develop learning-related social competence. These skills are essential for later learning in literacy and other domains (McClelland, et al., 2007).

Other Parenting Practices: Affective Support

A child's cognitive development and literacy skills are also influenced by factors that go beyond explicit reading and teaching. Affective-emotional support has also been found to have a significant effect on children's cognitive development (Chazan-Cohen, et al., 2009; Dodici, et al., 2003; Landry, et al., 2012; Taylor, et al., 2008).

The affective-emotional climate during book reading and other daily activities has been largely measured as responsiveness and sensitivity.

Responsive parenting includes emotional support, support of child signals and interests, and the quality of language input (e.g., verbal scaffolding) (Landry, et al., 2006). Taylor and colleagues (2008) examined the relation between maternal responsiveness in early childhood and children's ability to read and reading comprehension at age 8 using a diverse ethnic sample of 238 children from lower middle to lower economic backgrounds. Maternal responsiveness was assessed using a home-based observation and included warm acceptance (i.e., talking in a positive way, relaxed style, positive tone and verbal praise, physical affection, close contact) and contingent responsiveness (i.e., prompt and appropriate response, sensitive and contingent to child's cues, pacing of activities, and acceptance of child's needs and interests). Results showed that high levels of maternal responsiveness across early childhood (6, 12, and 24 months and 3½ and 4½ years) were related to better reading comprehension skills at age 8, and this relation was stronger for children with lower cognitive abilities; this interaction was not significant for word identification.

Another study evaluated the relation between parent supportiveness, home learning environment, parental depressive symptoms, and parenting stress and children's school readiness over the children's first 5 years in a low-income sample (Chazan-Cohen, et al., 2009). Supportive parenting was assessed through videotaped interactions; at 12, 24, and 36 months, supportive parenting was comprised of sensitivity, cognitive stimulation, and positive regard, and at pre-kindergarten cognitive stimulation and positive regard were assessed as a single supportiveness measure. Supportive parenting during play at 14 months was positively associated not only with better emotion regulation, but also with higher vocabulary scores and better letter-word knowledge at age 5 (Chazan-Cohen, et al., 2009).

Availability of social, emotional, and cognitive support within the home, parent-child interactions, and low parental distress are generally related to children's stronger reading abilities (Burchinal, et al., 2002). Further, children experiencing these supports benefit more from the level of closeness with their teacher during preschool.

Summary and Conclusions

It is undeniable that parents have a significant influence on their children's cognitive development, and in turn on their academic achievement. It is important also to educate parents about the necessary skills children need in order to enrich their vocabulary, learn how to read, and have better reading comprehension and about the most effective ways to promote these skills. Another important finding in the literature is that literacy skills begin to develop before a child is even able to read. Often, language is the first building block to literacy. Parents have a significant role in the development of language skills as they are predominantly responsible for the language with which children enter formal schooling. The amount and type of discourse parents share with their children significantly impacts children's language skills. It was beyond the scope of this chapter to review parenting interventions, but there is emerging evidence that when parenting practices are aligned with what correlational and longitudinal studies report, children generally achieve stronger literacy skills (e.g., Dieterich, et al., 2006). Therefore, evidence strongly suggests that parents should be encouraged to speak to their children throughout daily activities to promote language skills and enrich their vocabulary. Equally important is shared book reading. When parents read to their children, they are exposing their children to written text and enriching their vocabulary. Again, language is an important building block of reading and reading comprehension, making shared book reading important for literacy overall, even though there is little or no evidence that shared book reading predicts decoding or future reading comprehension. Further, it is important that parents go beyond the text when reading by relating themes in the book to children's lives and by encouraging children to make connections and predictions from the book, what is called meaning-focused and decontextualized dialog. Parents have unique knowledge of what their children like and know; therefore they are in a unique position of being able to relate the storybook to what their children like and know. Beyond home literacy practices, research shows that when parents directly teach their children about phonetics, decoding, and gathering meaning from text, their children have better literacy skills when they enter formal schooling. Related to beliefs, it is crucial that parents value their role as educators and understand that they too can and should take an active role in their children's instruction.

It is important to note that there are some limitations to the findings reported in this chapter. First, ethnicity and socioeconomic status may play a significant role in parents' practices and beliefs (see Chapter 10). Second, many of the recommendations made are done with the assumption that the parents are literate themselves. More research is needed on how parents who do not know how to read or have limited education can help their children develop these skills.

Parents play a crucial role in a child's development of literacy skills. Furthermore, literacy development begins before a child learns how to read and write and before they enter formal schooling. Literacy begins in the home; therefore, parents must be educated about and encouraged to create a fruitful home literacy environment for their children, as these practices will impact their children over time.

References

Abu-Rabia, S., & Yaari, I. (2012). Parent's attitudes and behavior, the learning environment, and their influence on children's early reading achievement. *Open Journal of Modern Linguistics, 2*, 170–179.

Anderson, A., Anderson, J., Lynch, J., Shapiro, J., & Kim, J. (2012). Extra-textual talk in shared book reading: A focus on questioning. *Early Child Development and Care, 182*, 1139–1154.

Arnold, D. H., Lonigan, C. J., Whitehurst, G. J., & Epstein, J. N. (1994). Accelerating language development through picture book reading: Replication and extension to a videotape training format. *Journal of Educational Psychology, 86*, 235–243.

Bradley, R. H., Corwyn, R. F., Burchinal, M., McAdoo, H. P., & Garcia Coll, C. (2001). The home environments of children in the United States. Part 2: Relations with behavioral development through age 13. *Child Development, 72*, 1868–1886.

Burchinal, M. R., Peisner-Feinberg, E., Pianta, R., & Howes, C. (2002). Development of academic skills from preschool through second grade: Family and classroom predictors of developmental trajectories. *Journal of School Psychology, 40*, 415–436.

Bus, A. G., van Ijzendoorn, M. H., & Pellegrini, A. D. (1995). Joint book reading makes for success in learning to read: A meta-analysis on intergenerational transmission of literacy. *Review of Educational Research, 65*, 1–21.

Chazan-Cohen, R., Raikes, H., Brooks-Gunn, J., Ayoub, C., Pan, B. A., Kisker, E. E., et al. (2013). Low-income children's school readiness: Parent contributions over the first five years. *Early Education & Development, 20*, 958–977.

Clark, C. (2011). Setting the baseline: The National Literacy Trust's first annual survey into reading—2010. London: National Literacy Trust.

Davis, B. J., Evans, M. A., & Reynolds, K. P. (2010). Child miscues and parental feedback during shared alphabet book reading and relations with child literacy skills. *Scientific Studies of Reading, 14*, 341–364.

DeTemple, J. M. (2001). Parents and children reading books together. In D. K. Dickinson & P. O. Tabors (Eds.), *Beginning Literacy with Language*. Baltimore, MD: Paul H. Brookes.

Dickinson, D. K., & Tabors, P. O. (2001). *Beginning Literacy with Language*. Baltimore, MD: Paul H. Brookes.

Dieterich, S. E., Assel, M. A., Swank, P., Smith, K. E., & Landry, S. H. (2006). The impact of early maternal verbal scaffolding and child language abilities on later decoding and reading comprehension skills. *Journal of School Psychology, 42*, 481–494.

Dodici, B. J., Draper, D. C., & Peterson, C. A. (2003). Early parent-child interactions and early literacy development. *Topics in Early Childhood Special Education, 23*, 123–136.

Duursma, E., & Pan, B. A. (2011). Who's reading to children in low-income families? The influence of paternal, maternal and child characteristics. *Early Child Development and Care, 181*, 1163–1180.

Evans, M. A., Fox, M., Cremaso, L., & McKinnon, L. (2004). Beginning reading: the views of parents and teachers of young children. *Journal of Educational Psychology, 96*, 130–141.

Evans, M. A., Reynolds, K., Shaw, D., & Pursoo, T. (2011). Parental explanations of vocabulary during shared book reading: A missed opportunity. *First Language, 31*, 195–213.

Evans, M. A., & Saint-Aubin, J. (2005). What children are looking at during shared storybook reading: Evidence from eye movement monitoring. *Psychological Science, 16*, 913–920.

Evans, M. A., Shaw, D., & Bell, M. (2000). Home literacy activities and their influence on early literacy skills. *Canadian Journal of Experimental Psychology, 54*, 65–75.

Farrant, B. M., & Zubrick, S. R. (2013). Parent–child book reading across early childhood and child vocabulary in the early school years: Findings from the Longitudinal Study of Australian Children. *First Language, 33,* 280–293.

Fivush, R., & Fromhoff, F. A. (1988), Style and structure in mother–child conversations about the past. *Discourse Processes, 11,* 337–355.

Ganea, P. A., Pickard, M. B., and Deloache, J. S. (2008). Transfer between picture books and the real world. *Journal of Cognition and Development, 9,* 46–66.

Gest, S. D., Freeman, N. R., Domitrovich, C. E., & Welsh, J. A. (2004). Shared book reading and children's language comprehension skills: the moderating role of parental discipline practices. *Early Childhood Research Quarterly, 19,* 319–336.

Gough, P. B., & Tunmer, W. E. (1986). Decoding, reading, and reading disability. *Remedial and Special Education, 7,* 6–10.

Hammett, L. A., Van Kleeck, A., & Huberty, C. J. (2003). Patterns of parents' extra-textual interactions during book sharing with preschool children: A cluster analysis. *Reading Research Quarterly, 38,* 442–468.

Hart, B., & Risley, T. R. (1995). *Meaningful Differences in the Everyday Experience of Young American Children.* Baltimore, MD: Paul H. Brookes.

Hart, B., & Risley, T. R. (1999). *The Social World of Children: Learning to Talk.* Baltimore, MD: Paul H. Brookes.

Hindman, A. H., Connor, C. M., Jewkes, A. M., & Morrison, F. J. (2008). Untangling the effects of shared book reading: multiple factors and their associations with preschool literacy outcomes. *Early Childhood Research Quarterly, 23,* 330–350.

Hindman, A. H., & Morrison, F. J. (2012). Differential contributions of three parenting dimensions to preschool literacy and social skills in a middle-income sample. *Merrill-Palmer Quarterly, 58,* 191–223.

Hindman, A. H., Skibbe, L. E., & Foster, T. D. (2014). Exploring the variety of parental talk during shared book reading and its contributions to preschool language and literacy: evidence from the Early Childhood Longitudinal Study— Birth Cohort. *Reading and Writing, 27,* 287–313.

Hindman, A. H., & Wasik, B. A. (2011). Exploring Head Start teachers' early language and literacy knowledge: Lessons from the *ExCELL* professional development intervention. *National Head Start Association: Dialog Journal, 14*(4), 293–315.

Hindman, A. H., Wasik, B. A., & Erhart, A. C. (2012). Shared book reading and Head Start preschoolers' vocabulary learning: The role of book-related discussion and curricular connections. *Early Education & Development, 23,* 451–474.

Hood, M., Conlon, E., & Andrews, G. (2008). Preschool home literacy practices and children's literacy development: A longitudinal analysis. *Journal of Educational Psychology, 100,* 252–271.

Huck, C. S., Kiefer, B. Z., Helper, S., & Hickman, J. (2004). *Children's Literature in the Elementary School* (8th ed.). New York: McGraw-Hill.

Jordan, G. E., Snow, C. E. and Porche, M. V. (2000) Project EASE: The effect of a family literacy project on kindergarten students' early literacy skills. *Reading Research Quarterly, 35:* 524–46.

Justice, L. M., & Ezell, H. K. (2000). Enhancing children's print and word awareness through home-based parent intervention. *American Journal of Speech-Language Pathology, 9,* 257–269.

Justice, L. M., & Ezell, H. K. (2002). Use of storybook reading to increase print awareness in at-risk children. *American Journal of Speech-Language Pathology, 11,* 17–29.

Justice, L. M., Kaderavek, J., Bowles, R. P., & Grimm, K. J. (2005). Language impairment, parent-child shared reading, and phonological awareness: A feasibility study. *Topics in Early Childhood Special Education, 25*, 143–156.

Justice, L. M., Meier, J., & Walpole, S. (2005). Learning new words from storybooks: An efficacy study with at-risk kindergartners. *Language, Speech, and Hearing Services in Schools, 36*, 17–32.

Justice, L. M., Skibbe, L., Canning, A., & Lankford, S. (2005). Preschoolers, print, and storybooks: An observational study using eye-gaze analysis. *Journal of Research in Reading, 28*, 229–243.

Justice, L. M., Skibbe, L. E., McGinty, A. S., Piasta, S. B., & Petrill, S. (2011). Feasibility, efficacy, and social validity of home-based storybook reading intervention for children with language impairment. *Journal of Speech, Language, and Hearing Research, 54*, 523–538.

Justice, L. M., Weber, S. E., Ezell, H. K., & Bakeman, R. (2002). A sequential analysis of children's responsiveness to parental print references during shared book-reading interactions. *American Journal of Speech-Language Pathology, 11*, 30–40.

Lachner, W., Zevenbergen, A., & Zevenbergen, J. (2008). Parent and child references to letters during alphabet book reading: Relations to child age and letter name knowledge. *Early Education and Development, 19*, 541–559.

Landry, S. H., Smith, K. E., & Swank, P. R. (2006). Responsive parenting: establishing early foundations for social, communication, and independent problem-solving skills. *Developmental Psychology, 42*, 627–642.

Landry, S. H., Smith, K. E., Swank, P. R., Zucker, T., Crawford, A. D., & Solari, E. F. (2012). The effects of a responsive parenting intervention on parent–child interactions during shared book reading. *Developmental Psychology, 48*, 969–986.

Lonigan, C. J., Farver, J. M., Phillips, B. M., & Clancy-Menchetti, J. (2011). Promoting the development of preschool children's emergent literacy skills: A randomized evaluation of a literacy-focused curriculum and two professional development models. *Reading and Writing, 24*, 305–337.

Lonigan, C. J., & Whitehurst, G. J. (1998). Relative efficacy of parent and teacher involvement in a shared-reading intervention for preschool children from low-income backgrounds. *Early Childhood Research Quarterly, 13*, 263–290.

McClelland, M. M., Cameron, C. E., Connor, C. M., Farris, C. L., Jewkes, A. M., & Morrison, F. J. (2007). Links between behavioral regulation and preschoolers' literacy, vocabulary, and math skills. *Developmental Psychology, 43*, 947–959.

Marulis, L. M., & Neuman, S. B. (2010). The effects of vocabulary intervention on young children's word learning: A meta-analysis. *Review of Educational Research, 80*, 300–335.

Marulis, L. M., & Neuman, S. B. (2013). How vocabulary interventions affect young children at risk: A meta-analytic review. *Journal of Research on Educational Effectiveness, 6*, 223–262.

Mol, S. E., Bus, A. G., de Jong, M. T., & Smeets, D. J. H. (2008) Added value of dialogic parent-child book readings: A meta-analysis. *Early Education & Development, 19*, 7–26.

Morrison, F. J., & Cooney, R. R. (2002). Parenting and academic achievement: multiple paths to early literacy. In J. G. Borkowski, S. L. Ramey, & M. Bristol-Power (Eds.), *Parenting and the child's world: Influences on academic, intellectual, and social-emotional development*. Monographs in Parenting. Mahwah, NJ: Erlbaum.

Nation, K., & Snowling, M. J. (2004). Beyond phonological skills: Broader language skills contribute to the development of reading. *Journal of Research in Reading, 27*, 342–356.

National Early Literacy Panel (2009). *Developing Early Literacy: Report of the National Early Literacy Panel.* Jessup, MD: National Institute for Literacy.

Peterson, C., Jesso, B., & McCabe, A. (1999) Encouraging narratives in preschoolers: An intervention study. *Journal of Child Language, 26*, 49–67.

Philips, B. M., & Lonigan, C. J. (2009). Variations in the home literacy environment of preschool children: a cluster analytic approach. *Scientific Studies of Reading, 13*, 146–174.

Philips, L. M., Norris, S. P., & Anderson, J. (2008). Unlocking the door: Is parents' reading to children the key to early literacy development? *Canadian Psychology, 49*, 82–88.

Pile, E. J., Girolametto, L., Johnson, C. J., & Cleave, P. L. (2010). Shared book reading intervention for children with language impairment: Using parents-as-aides in language intervention. *Canadian Journal of Speech-Language Pathology & Audiology, 4*, 96–109. Retrieved from http://cjslpa.ca/files/2010_CJSLPA_Vol_34/No_02_81-152/Girolametto_pile_johnson_chen_cleave_CJSLPA_2010.pdf

Reese, E., & Fivush, R. (1993). Parental styles of talking about the past. *Developmental Psychology, 29*, 596–606.

Reese, E., Haden, C. A., & Fivush, R. (1993). Mother-child conversations about the past: Relationships of style and memory over time. *Cognitive Development, 8*, 403–430.

Reese, E., Leyva, D., Sparks, A., & Grolnick, W. (2010). Maternal elaborative reminiscing increases low-income children's narrative skills relative to dialogic reading. *Early Education and Development, 21*, 318–342.

Reese, E., & Newcombe, R. (2007). Training mothers in elaborative reminiscing enhances children's autobiographical memory and narrative. *Child Development, 78*, 1153–1170.

Rodriguez, B. L., Hines, R., & Montiel, M. (2009). Mexican American mothers of low and middle socioeconomic status: Communication behaviors and interactive strategies during shared book reading. *Language, Speech, and Hearing Services in Schools, 40*, 271–282.

Roy-Charland, A., Saint-Aubin, J., & Evans, M. A. (2007). Eye movements in shared book reading with children from kindergarten to grade 4. *Reading and Writing: An Interdisciplinary Journal, 20*, 909–931.

Rush, K. L. (1999). Caregiver-child interactions and early literacy development of preschool children from low-income environments. *Topics in Early Childhood Special Education, 19*, 3–14.

Scarborough, H. S., & Dobrich, W. (1994). On the efficacy of reading to preschoolers. *Developmental Review, 14*, 245–302.

Sénéchal, M. (2006). Testing the home literacy model: Parent involvement in kindergarten is differentially related to grade 4 reading comprehension, fluency, spelling, and reading for pleasure. *Scientific Studies of Reading, 10*, 59–87.

Sénéchal, M., & LeFevre, J. A. (2002). Parental involvement in the development of children's reading skill: A five-year longitudinal study. *Child Development, 73*, 445–460.

Sénéchal, M., LeFevre, J. A., Hudson, E., & Lawson, E. P. (1996). Knowledge of storybooks as a predictor of young children's vocabulary. *Journal of Educational Psychology, 88*, 520–536.

Sénéchal, M., Pagan, S., Lever, R., & Oullette, G. P. (2008). Relations among the frequency of shared reading and 4-year-old children's vocabulary, morphological and syntax comprehension, and narrative skills. *Early Education & Development*, *19*, 27–44.

Snow, C. E., Barnes, W. E., Chandler, J., Goodman, I. F., & Hemphill, L. (1991). *Unfulfilled Expectations: Home and School Influences on Literacy*. Cambridge, MA: Harvard University Press.

Sonnenschein, S., Brody, G., & Munsterman, K. (1996). The influence of family beliefs and practices on children's early reading development. In L. Baker, P. Afferbach, & D. Reinking (Eds.), *Developing Engaged Readers in School and Home Communities*. Mahwah, NJ: Erlbaum.

Sparks, A., & Reese, E. (2013). From reminiscing to reading: Home contributions to children's developing language and literacy in low-income families. *First Language*, *33*, 89–109.

Stadler, M. A., & McEvoy, M. A. (2004). The effect of text genre on parent use of joint book reading strategies to promote phonological awareness. *Early Childhood Research Quarterly*, *18*, 502–512.

Tabors, P. O., Beals, D. E., & Weizman, Z. O. (2001). You know what oxygen is: Learning new words at home. In D. K. Dickinson & P. O. Tabors (Eds.), *Beginning Literacy with Language*. Baltimore, MD: Paul H. Brookes.

Taumoepeau, M., & Reese, E. (2013). Maternal reminiscing, elaborative talk, and children's theory of mind: An intervention study. *First Language*, *33*, 388–410.

Taylor, H. B., Anthony, J. L., Aghara, R., Smith, K. E., & Landry, S. H. (2008). The interaction of early maternal responsiveness and children's cognitive abilities on later decoding and reading comprehension skills. *Early Education & Development*, *19*, 188–207.

Van Kleeck, A. (2008). Providing preschool foundations for later reading comprehension: The importance of and ideas for targeting inferencing in storybook-sharing interventions. *Psychology in the Schools*, *45*, 627–643.

Wasik, B. A., & Bond, M. A. (2001). Beyond the pages of a book: Interactive book reading and language development in preschool classrooms. *Journal of Educational Psychology*, *93*, 243–250.

Weigel, D. J., Martin, S. S., & Bennett, K. K. (2006). Mother's literacy beliefs: connections with the home literacy environment and preschool children's literacy development. *Journal of Early Childhood Literacy*, *6*, 191–211.

Weizman, Z. O., & Snow, C. E. (2001). Lexical output as related to children's vocabulary acquisition: Effects of sophisticated exposure and support for meaning. *Developmental Psychology*, *37*, 265–279.

Whitehurst, G. J., Falco, F. L., Lonigan, C. J., Fischel, J. E., DeBaryshe, B. D., Valdez-Menchaca, M. C., et al. (1988). Accelerating language development through picture book reading. *Developmental Psychology*, *24*, 552–559.

Yaden, D. B., Smolkin, L. B., & MacGillivray, L. (1993). A psychogenic perspective on children's understanding about letter associations during alphabet book readings. *Journal of Reading Behavior*, *25*, 43–68.

Chapter 10

Ecological Influences on Literacy

Amanda Chiapa and Frederick J. Morrison

Over 30 years of research has supported the utility of Bronfenbrenner's theory (1979) that there are many contextual levels, which impact an individual's development. These concentric levels include distal factors such as one's culture, socioeconomic status, and neighborhood, as well as more immediate, proximal factors such as parents and schools. This theory is empirically supported, with a clear connection between one's environment and a number of maladaptive outcomes, including psychosocial problems such as drinking (Chassin, Pitts, & Prost, 2002; Hill & Angel, 2005), adverse health outcomes (Cohen, et al., 2003; Poulton, et al., 2002), and poorer educational and developmental trajectories (Frempong, Ma, & Mensah, 2012).

One important domain to consider is the role the environment can play in children's cognitive development, because stronger cognitive functioning is related to academic success, greater likelihood of employment, and overall well-being (Langberg, Becker, & Dvorsky, 2014). Literacy is one of the primary skills required for the development and maintenance of learning and cognitive functioning, with similar relations documented between ecological risk factors and poorer outcomes related to literacy growth. For instance, children attending Head Start preschools have demonstrated significantly lower literacy skills (one standard deviation) below the national average (Hindman, et al., 2010). Similar trajectories are associated in adulthood, with poor reading skills linked to greater educational failure (Arnbak, 2004). There is a pressing need, then, to understand the extent to which ecological factors influence children's developing literacy. The purpose of this chapter is to (1) provide an overview of the current knowledge of the relation between ecological factors (e.g., neighborhoods) and literacy skills, (2) emphasize protective or buffering effects that mitigate maladaptive literacy outcomes, and (3) discuss future directions that can inform policy and interventions.

Overview of Ecological Influences on Literacy

The underlying process of learning and cognitive development, evidence reveals, is largely context dependent (although see Chapter 2 on genetics), as reflected in well-supported social and cognitive theories such as situational learning theory (Lave & Wenger, 1991) and social semiotics (Hodge & Kress, 1988; Kress, 2004). Situational learning theory posits that the acquisition of knowledge is dependent on the activity or context of the learning, such that the individual uses previous and current experiences to understand new information. Social semiotics can be used to explain how learning occurs through its description of creating "meaning" as a social process involving the communication of signs (i.e., language). Learning, then, is an interactive process operating within a broader ecological system in which meaning is created from language. In fact, the sociocultural influence on literacy is reflected in the operationalization of this complex construct. For instance, literacy has been defined as social practices that create meaning through connections people have with media objects within their culture and subcultures (Lemke, 1998, p. 1). One can reasonably expect that the degree to which children encounter contextual risks will directly impact their ability to effectively or appropriately communicate and make connections.

According to the cumulative risk theory (Sameroff, Seifer, Baldwin, & Baldwin, 1993), the more risk factors children are exposed to, the greater the likelihood that they will experience less optimal outcomes. Unfortunately, if children live in a community characterized by stress and disadvantage, it is likely that the other contextual levels surrounding the children will be marked by similar features (e.g., poorer living conditions and schools lacking in resources). This framework underscores the importance of understanding the extent to which ecological factors impact the developmental trajectory of children in order to inform early intervention and prevention research. As can be inferred from the introduction of this chapter, ecology is a fairly broad term. This section will provide a brief overview on the present status of unique relations between specific ecological factors and literacy, with a particular focus on preschool and early elementary-aged children in order to inform early intervention and prevention research.

Distal factors

There are many far-reaching sources of influence that can impact an individual, including local and national political policies. For this chapter, we narrow our focus on neighborhood and school factors in order to provide a more targeted synthesis and discussion.

Neighborhood

Literature examining the impact of neighborhood characteristics, such as neighborhood income and exposure to violence, provides mixed results, perhaps indicating the complex nature of the extent to which more distal factors influence individual children. For instance, Froiland and colleagues (2013) found that neighborhood socioeconomic well-being (e.g., neighborhood education, financial investment in neighborhood, and poverty) were linked with home literacy and indirectly linked to early school literacy through home literacy in a sample of Head Start students. These correlational findings suggest that supporting children living in neighborhoods that may lack resources necessary for preparing children's early literacy skills might improve their later achievement. Neighborhood quality status was also found to relate to language competence in pre-K children (Barbarin, et al., 2006). Interestingly, other aspects frequently associated with impoverished or poorly resourced neighborhoods, such as neighborhood violence, may not be directly related to literacy achievement (Garo, 2013), which seems counterintuitive given the evidence of the negative impact on reading skills among children exposed to domestic violence (Blackburn, 2008) as discussed in Chapters 8 and 9. It may be that children exposed to neighborhood violence are not significantly distressed until that dysfunction occurs within the home environment, with implications that in-home factors such as supportive parenting or positive family dynamics may serve as protective factors that might offset the negative influence of neighborhood risks. Despite the complex nature through which neighborhood characteristics impact literacy, research does find an overall relation between greater neighborhood risks and poorer literacy skills, although the specific mechanisms remain to be determined.

School

School systems can be likened to a political system and are influenced by national laws, specific district policies, associated community resources, teacher instruction, and, of course, the students. An extensive body of school-based literature demonstrates complex relations between several dimensions of school-based factors and literacy skills (e.g., Connor, Morrison, & Slominski, 2006; Connor, et al., 2013; Hindman, Skibbe, Miller, & Zimmerman, 2010; Koth, Bradshaw, & Leith, 2008; Stichter, Stormont, & Lewis, 2009). At a more general or structural level, teachers in Title One schools, which serve high percentages of children living in poverty, used significantly more noninstructional related talk, had more instructional down time, and a higher number of student exits during instruction compared to non-Title classrooms (Stichter, et al., 2009). Fundamentally, differences in teaching quality should not be a function of the level of resources a school or student has. Yet, findings suggest there are distinct socioeconomically based patterns associated with children at disadvantage because of poverty. This is especially problematic given the strong links between quality of teacher instruction and stronger literacy skills (Connor, et al.,

2006, 2013). Moreover, children who are at risk due to economic disadvantage are also more likely to display difficulties with self-regulation, which is linked with reading difficulties as previously discussed in Chapter 5. Thus, children attending Title One schools are less likely to receive high-quality instruction and more likely to display additional risks associated with poorer literacy skills. However, school characteristics are not necessarily a final sentence (Hindman, et al., 2010) and will be discussed later.

Proximal Influences

Home

The home environment includes structural aspects such as the number of adults living in home, demographic characteristics such as parental education, and literacy-specific parent-child behaviors such as shared reading time. Interestingly, and perhaps intuitively, all aspects of the home environment have been linked to children's literacy development (Barbarin, et al., 2006; Feiler, 2003; Huebner, 2000; Weigel, Martin, & Bennett, 2005). Structurally, children residing in homes with an unmarried parent and another adult score lower in receptive language and identifying letters than do children in married or single-parent households. Additionally, children of lower socioeconomic status (SES), including parental education and income, evidence lower frequency of shared reading with parents (Young, Davis, Schoen, & Parker, 1998), an important skill associated with increased vocabulary and preliteracy skills. However, this association seems to disappear when taking into account SES resources such as parental education and household income (Barbarin, et al., 2006). Instead, it seems that the physical availability of resources, whether it is demonstrated through shared reading time (Weigel, et al., 2005) or home visits providing academic support (Feiler, 2003), may be more predictive of literacy growth, as well as parental level of literacy and education (Weigel, et al., 2005). This can be a frustrating or hopeful message, considering approximately 13 million children in the USA (in 2007) lived in households with incomes at or below the federal poverty threshold (DeNavas–Walt, Proctor, & Smith, 2010). In summary, findings highlight the importance of building literacy skills such as vocabulary or phoneme awareness, and the use of resources that can expose children to preliteracy skills, which is in part related to the availability of financial resources and parental literacy skills (see also Chapter 9 for a more thorough discussion on the influence of parents).

Child Factors

Having discussed different neighborhood-, school-, and home-based characteristics, one might see how impossible it is to truly tease apart these factors from the child. The home environment and parental characteristics are clearly enmeshed with individual-specific characteristics. One aspect that overlaps with shared environmental factors but can be discussed in terms of the child is ethnic identity or minority status. Empirical and descriptive findings have demonstrated that African-American children are at greater risk for poor reading achievement (Fryer & Levitt, 2006; Jencks & Phillips, 1998; Washington, 2001). Indeed, although African-American children from middle-income homes perform better on reading assessments than African-American children from low-income homes, middle-income children still report more difficulty learning to read than expected. Moreover, minority students across ethnicities report lower levels of achievement motivation than their Caucasian peers, over and above classroom- and school-level factors (Koth, et al., 2008). However, ethnic differences on language stimulation and reading comprehension skills are not universally demonstrated (Mistry, Benner, Biesanz, Clark, & Howes, 2010), suggesting the importance of disentangling the sources contributing to ethnic disparities in literacy outcomes.

The role of individual child factors will be discussed within the context of home- and school-based influences, in keeping with the empirically supported conceptualization that a child is embedded within a greater environment. As previously discussed, distal influences generally exert less influence when more proximal factors are included in the model (Barbarin, et al., 2006; Hindman, et al., 2010). For instance, Hindman and colleagues (2010) were interested in distinguishing between the effects of individual factors (demographics, social skills, language skills), parent-level factors (parent involvement, years of education, income above poverty level), and teacher-level factors (teachers' qualifications, affective climate and structure, school composition and location) and found parent-level and teacher-level factors did not contribute to literacy in Head Start students when accounting for individual characteristics. Hindman, et al. (2010) reported that although females and older Head Start students entered Head Start with higher literacy skills, they advanced more slowly from Head Start to first grade, which suggests these differences may get smaller as time spent in the school setting increases. Consistent with previously reported ethnic or cultural differences, children who entered Head Start programs with Spanish as their primary language advanced slower in literacy outcomes. It appears that one of the key individual-level factors to investigate more closely is the role that ethnic minority status plays in the acquisition and maintenance of literacy skills throughout education.

Other important individual factors to consider include self-regulation and engagement, both of which are associated with the development of literacy as described in Chapter 5 (see also Guthrie, Schafer, & Huang, 2010). Additionally, engagement in reading, which is conceptually linked to motivation, has been identified as related to reading achievement.

Interestingly, Guthrie and colleagues (2010) demonstrated that students whose mother's education was low but who were at least moderately engaged readers (compared to low engaged) showed significantly higher achievement than did students whose mother's education was greater but were disengaged readers. This was despite positive associations between mother's education and achievement. This suggests that individual factors cannot only mitigate the influence of contextual risks on literacy, but may potentially nullify risks that cannot be easily remedied (e.g., parental education, neighborhood crime).

Buffering Effects

The research literature generally reports powerful ecological effects on the advancement of literacy in children and can be perceived as pessimistic in terms of the trajectory for individuals living in disadvantaged neighborhoods, attending poorly resourced schools, and/or whose parents have limited education and other demographic risks. Some of the associated risks cannot easily be changed, such as parental education or neighborhood well-being. However, there are also malleable risk factors and evidence exists to support the efforts that have already been made. In particular, observational and intervention research points to the positive gains that can be made when targeting parents and teachers.

School Based

Teachers are primary cultivators of literacy in children, partly because children spend much of their lives in school. Although the quality of teaching can be different between schools with and without resources, promising evidence shows school-based interventions can be effective regardless of ecological conditions (Connor, et al., 2013; Vera, 2011). One of the leading evidence-based interventions targeting literacy demonstrated clear gains when students, of which 45 percent were from families living in poverty, received individualized reading instruction (Connor, et al., 2013). In fact, no student receiving individualized student instruction (ISI) for three consecutive years had a third-grade reading standard score that was less than 85 (considered below reading expectations; national mean = 100), and only two students receiving ISI scored lower than 90. These findings are encouraging and suggest that disseminating information across school districts characterized by disadvantage may be useful. If teachers are given resources that can prepare them to effectively target literacy skills, trajectories that are often associated with at-risk populations may be altered. In light of potential ethnic differences on literacy, the use of culturally sensitive materials in schools characterized by disadvantaged students may increase responsivity to interventions targeting literacy skills. Vera (2011) incorporated popular culture characters that were identified as preferred characters to teach print concepts and letter recognition to a sample of pre-kindergarten children who either met the requirements of federal income guidelines (e.g., receiving subsidized lunches) or were eligible for English as a second language services. Children in the intervention group scored higher on both print concepts and alphabet recognition compared to children in the control group, indicating the effectiveness of integrating content that is familiar and interesting to the student. It appears the use of child-preferred materials that are likely to be present in various settings outside of the school setting increases the likelihood of learning literacy skills. One possible explanation to the success of this intervention may be that children in this sample did not have exposure to many toys or related materials and were more motivated as a function of novelty more so than using culturally matched materials. Future research that goes beyond intervention effects and identifies the mechanisms through which gains are observed would be useful in understanding why some interventions work and others do not. The use of motivating material touches on the potential of establishing communication between providers in the school and home to identify preferred content and to teach parents ways to build literacy skills in the home.

Home Based

As discussed in Chapter 9, parents can play an integral role in the promotion of literacy skills through shared reading and the specific interactions revolving around literary practices (Morrison, Bachman, & Connor, 2005; Sénéchal & LeFevre, 2002; Weigel, et al., 2005). While exposure to reading books is related to later reading skills through development of vocabulary and listening comprehension skills, parental involvement as an instructor in teaching children to read was related to early literacy skills, which predicted reading skills and later reading comprehension (Sénéchal & LeFevre, 2002). Additionally, parent beliefs, including the belief in their role in children's literacy and language development and belief that reading with children is important, contributes unique variance to print knowledge, receptive and expressive language, even with other parent characteristics (e.g., parent education) in the model (Weigel, et al., 2005). Parental demographics cannot be easily manipulated, but strengthening parents' value systems pertaining to the importance of shared reading and emphasizing their important role as instructors is feasible.

School-based and home-based or parental interventions have demonstrated their effectiveness and might be particularly effective by directly and indirectly targeting individual factors critical to literacy development and maintenance. For instance, an intervention that is tailored to an individual and implemented by a teacher or parent, may directly increase engagement and motivation by providing an environment in which one is expected to be actively involved in his or her learning process. Engagement may then increase or activate other individual factors such as attention and working memory, central executive functioning processes linked to successful literacy outcomes and overall cognitive development. Interventions are then able to simultaneously effect change at the individual level and at other levels surrounding the individual.

Summary and Future Directions

Overall, research suggests the deleterious effects of ecological disadvantage on literacy, but also highlights promising avenues for altering these trajectories. At the neighborhood level, the effects on literacy are less clear, despite evidence relating structural aspects such as density, and sociodemographic factors including ethnic minority status to an array of psychosocial challenges (Sampson & Raudenbush, 2004). One of the most influential theories concerning neighborhood influence, the "broken window" theory (Wilson & Kelling, 1982) posits that visual cues of neighborhood environment can attract criminals due to the belief that residents are indifferent to illicit activity that occurs in their neighborhood. This theory has been used to describe the perpetuation of urban racial inequality (Sampson & Raudenbush, 2004). However, this brief review of the literature suggests some limitations of this theory. It may be that neighborhood quality does not consistently predict positive outcomes, including literacy, because of the collective efficacy of a given neighborhood. Collective efficacy is the shared expectations a community has for how their public space is socially controlled and has been associated with lower rates of crime over and above neighborhood structural characteristics (Sampson & Raudenbush, 1999). The extent to which neighborhood risks influence individual outcomes including academic performance may be buffered by common value systems, but more research evaluating the protective effect of these values is needed.

At the school level, research identifies a strong link between schools marked by poverty or low economic resources and lower student academic achievement including literacy performance. The mechanisms explaining this relation seem to involve lower quality of instruction and organization in the classroom as well as student motivation to learn, particularly among ethnic minority students. Potential areas to target include working within existing policies, as discussed in Chapters 11 and 12, in order to allocate resources to schools that are failing to demonstrate equal academic skills as schools with higher resources. The prevention paradox—that policies have a positive influence on more people when the larger population is targeted rather than sole focus on populations at risk—suggests that broad policies, such as universal preschool interventions, are likely to help more children experience success than are programs targeting only children living in poverty or who have reading disabilities. Thus we are not suggesting that funds should be removed from schools that are performing at desired levels of achievement. Instead, stakeholders and teachers might work together to ensure that previously shown interventions or tools can be easily implemented in the classroom. For instance, individualized teacher instruction (ISI) has demonstrated improvements in literacy (Connor, et al., 2013), highlighting the importance of providing support for teachers. Also, teaching students from culturally sensitive materials can increase literacy skills (Vera, 2011), supporting the idea that teachers and parents can work together to identify child-preferred resources to motivate students.

At the home and individual level, socioeconomic resources appear to exert the most influence on literacy outcomes. For instance, lower parental education and income and child ethnic minority status have been linked to lower literacy skills in preschool and early education. Parents who face economic distress may not have the time to engage in shared reading and increase vocabulary or other literacy-related skills. Parents with lower income also are likely to have lower levels of education, which may prevent the number of skills they can feasibly impart to their children. However, research suggests the effects of disadvantage on literacy can be buffered in the presence of positive beliefs and efforts to directly increase emergent literacy skills. For example, parental belief of the importance of reading as well as intervention services provided at the home for families who cannot easily be reached are two buffering effects connected to improved literacy. Fostering parental beliefs regarding their own ability to act as teachers and increasing the availability of funding to home-based interventions may offer ways to buffer the deleterious effects of poverty.

Ethnic minority status is not something that can—or, indeed, should—be changed. However, intervention results suggest that culturally sensitive teaching that includes motivating materials and individualized instruction should promote literacy skills across ethnicities. This is a potentially important piece of information that can guide future research and the conceptualization behind ethnic disparity on literacy. Motivation is a key component to maximizing successful outcomes.

Finally, as discussed in the earlier chapters, there is a clear contribution of neurological and genetic factors to literacy development, yet there is a scarcity of available literacy research combining these micro-proximal factors with other ecological levels. In the early 1980s, literature regarding individual differences on literacy skills adamantly argued that the cause for illiteracy was due to the perpetuation of a class-based society and not due to genetics (Bickel, 1983). While this argument is no longer dominant, genetics likewise does not appear to fully account for observed disparities, suggesting the influence of genetics through gene × environment interactions and gene niche picking is malleable (see Chapter 2). Moreover, the advancement of epigenetics indicates the flexibility of genetic influence on cognitive, social, and physiological development in different environments.

It is entirely possible that efficacious school- or home-based interventions can alter the expression—and inheritance—of genetic phenotypes, but more research is needed. Taken as a whole, economic disadvantage can limit the availability of parental and academic resources such as shared reading and individualized instruction and, when uninterrupted, is likely to perpetuate the cycle of disadvantage and illiteracy. However, school- and parent-based interventions have shown potential power to disrupt this cycle and alter the trajectory of at-risk individuals such that equal opportunity to educational success can be a reality and must be the priority in future and current efforts.

References

Arnbak, E. (2004). When are poor reading skills a threat to educational achievement? *Reading and Writing, 17*(5), 459–482.

Ayoub, C., O'Connor, E., Rappolt-Schlictmann, G., Vallotton, C., Raikes, H., & Chazan-Cohen, R. (2009). Cognitive skill performance among young children living in poverty: Risk, change, and the promotive effects of Early Head Start. *Early Childhood Research Quarterly, 24*(3), 289–305.

Barbarin, O., Bryant, D., McCandies, T., Burchinal, M., Early, D., Clifford, R., ... Howes, C. (2006). Children enrolled in public pre-K: The relation of family life, neighborhood quality, and socioeconomic resources to early competence. *American Journal of Orthopsychiatry, 76*(2), 265–276.

Bickel, R. (1983). The social circumstances of illiteracy: Interpretation and exchange in a class-based society. *Urban Review, 15*(4), 203.

Blackburn, J. F. (2008). Reading and phonological awareness skills in children exposed to domestic violence. *Journal of Aggression, Maltreatment & Trauma, 17*(4), 415–438.

Bronfenbrenner, U. (1979). *The Ecology of Human Development: Experiments by Nature and Design.* Cambridge, MA: Harvard University Press.

Cavanagh, S. (2007). Poverty's effect on U.S. scores greater than for other nations. *Education Week, 27*(15), 1, 13.

Chassin, L., Pitts, S. C., & Prost, J. (2002). Binge drinking trajectories from adolescence to emerging adulthood in a high-risk sample: Predictors and substance abuse outcomes. *Journal of Consulting and Clinical Psychology, 70*(1), 67.

Cohen, D. A., Mason, K., Bedimo, A., Scribner, R., Basolo, V., & Farley, T. A. (2003). Neighborhood physical health conditions and health. *American Journal of Public Health, 93*, 467–471.

Connor, C. M., Morrison, F. J., & Slominski, L. (2006). Preschool instruction and children's emergent literacy growth. *Journal of Educational Psychology, 98*(4), 665.

Connor, C. M., Morrison, F. J., Fishman, B., Crowe, E. C., Al Otaiba, S., & Schatschneider, C. (2013). A longitudinal cluster-randomized controlled study on the accumulating effects of individualized literacy instruction on students' reading from first through third grade. *Psychological Science, 24*(8), 1408–1419.

DeNavas-Walt, C., Proctor, B. D., & Smith, J. C. (2010). Income, poverty, and health insurance coverage in the United States: 2009. Washington, DC: U.S. Department of Commerce.

Feiler, A. (2003). Early literacy and home visiting during the reception year: Supporting "difficult to reach" families. *European Journal of Special Needs Education, 18*(2), 251.

Frempong, G., Ma, X., & Mensah, J. (2012). Access to postsecondary education: can schools compensate for socioeconomic disadvantage? *Higher Education, 63*(1), 19–32.

Froiland, J. M., Powell, D. R., Diamond, K. E., & Son, S. H. C. (2013). Neighborhood socioeconomic well-being, home literacy, and early literacy skills of at-risk pre-schoolers. *Psychology in the Schools, 50*(8), 755–769.

Fryer, R. G., & Levitt, S. D. (2006). The black-white test score gap through third grade. *American Law and Economics Review, 8*(2), 249–281.

Garo, L. (2013). Children's exposure to neighborhood poverty and violence: Implications for black student middle school literacy in Charlotte, North Carolina. *Vulnerable Children and Youth Studies, 8*(1), 60.

Guthrie, J. T., Schafer, W. D., & Huang, C. W. (2010). Benefits of opportunity to read and balanced instruction on the NAEP. *Journal of Educational Research, 94*, 143–162.

Hill, T. D., & Angel, R. J. (2005). Neighborhood disorder, psychological distress, and heavy drinking. *Social Science & Medicine, 61*(5), 965–975.

Hindman, A. H., Skibbe, L. E., Miller, A., & Zimmerman, M. (2010). Ecological contexts and early learning: Contributions of child, family, and classroom factors during Head Start, to literacy and mathematics growth through first grade. *Early Childhood Research Quarterly, 25*(2), 235–250.

Hodge, B., & Kress, G. R. (1988). *Social Semiotics*. Ithaca, NY: Cornell University Press.

Huebner, C. (2000). Community-based support for preschool readiness among children in poverty. *Journal of Education for Students Placed at Risk, 5*(3), 291.

Jencks, C., & Phillips, M. (1998). The black-white test score gap. Washington, DC: Brookings Institute.

Koth, C. W., Bradshaw, C. P., & Leaf, P. J. (2008). A multilevel study of predictors of student perceptions of school climate: The effect of classroom-level factors. *Journal of Educational Psychology, 100*(1), 96.

Kress, G. (2004). Reading images: Multimodality representation and new media. *Information Design Journal, 12*, 110–119.

Langberg, J. M., Becker, S. P., & Dvorsky, M.R. (2014). The association between sluggish cognitive tempo and academic functioning in youth with attention-deficit/hyperactivity disorder (ADHD). *Journal of Abnormal Child Psychology, 42*(1), 91–103.

Lave, J., & Wenger, E. (1991). *Situated Learning: Legitimate Peripheral Participation*. Cambridge: Cambridge University Press.

Lemke, J. (1998). Metamedia literacy: Transforming meanings and media. In D. Reinking, M. C. McKenna, L. Labbo, & R. Kieffer (Eds.), *Handbook of Literacy and Technology: Transformations in a Post-Typographic World*. Mahwah, NJ: Erlbaum.

Mistry, R. R. S., Benner, A. D., Biesanz, J. A., Clark, S. L., & Howes, C. (2010). Family and social risk, and parental investments during the early childhood years as predictors of low-income children's school readiness outcomes. *Early Childhood Research Quarterly, 25*(4), 432–449.

Morrison, F. J., Bachman, H. J., & Connor, C. M. D. (2005). *Improving Literacy in America: Guidelines from Research*. New Haven, CT: Yale University Press.

Poulton, R., Caspi, A., Milne, B. J., Thomson, W. M., Taylor, A., Sears, M. R., et al. (2002). Association between children's experience of socioeconomic disadvantage and adult health: A life-course study. *The Lancet, 360*(9346), 1640–1645.

Sameroff, A. J., Seifer, R., Baldwin, A., & Baldwin, C. (1993). Stability of intelligence from preschool to adolescence: The influence of social and family risk factors. *Child Development, 64*, 80–97.

Sampson, R. J., & Raudenbush, S. W. (1999). Systematic social observation of public spaces: A new look at disorder in urban neighborhoods. *American Journal of Sociology, 105*, 603–651.

Sampson, R. J., & Raudenbush, S. W. (2004). Seeing disorder: Neighborhood stigma and the social construction of "broken windows." *Social Psychology Quarterly, 67*(4), 319–342.

Sénéchal, M., & LeFevre, J. (2002). Parental involvement in the development of children's reading skills: A five-year longitudinal study. *Child Development, 73*, 445–460.

Stichter, J., Stormont, M., & Lewis, T. J. (2009). Instructional practices and behavior during reading: A descriptive summary and comparison of practices in title one and non-title elementary schools. *Psychology in the Schools, 46*(2), 172.

Vera, D. (2011). Using popular culture print to increase emergent literacy skills in one high-poverty urban school district. *Journal of Early Childhood Literacy, 11*(3), 307.

Washington, J. (2001). Early literacy skills in African-American children: Research considerations. *Learning Disabilities Research and Practice, 16*(4), 213.

Weigel, D. J., Martin, S. S., & Bennett, K. K. (2005). Ecological influences of the home and the child-care center on preschool-age children's literacy development. *Reading Research Quarterly, 40*(2), 204–233.

Wilson, J. Q., & Kelling, G. (1982). The police and neighborhood safety: Broken windows. *Atlantic, 127*, 29–38.

Young, K. T., Davis, K., Schoen, C., & Parker, S. (1998). Listening to parents: A national survey of parents with young children. *Archives of Pediatrics & Adolescent Medicine, 152*(3), 255.

Chapter 11

Policy and Community Influences on Learning to Read

Andre D. Mansion, Carol McDonald Connor, and Greg J. Duncan

In the United States, providing public education has been held as one of the most important functions of the federal, state, and local governments (*Brown v. Board of Education*, 1954). Education is not only important for the acquisition of knowledge, but is the foundation for the performance of our public responsibilities, professional training, and good citizenship (*Brown v. Board of Education*, 1954). At the heart of the educational experience is the process of learning to read (Common Core State Standards Initiative, CCSSI, 2010).

Basic literacy is important because it provides the foundation for social communication, the achievement of goals, and cognitive growth, as well as a multitude of other important life experiences and outcomes. Fields such as cognitive and educational psychology have long been aware of the importance of teaching children to read (Stanovich, 2000). These fields are constantly developing new approaches to improve reading instruction (see, e.g., Connor, et al., 2009). However, the governments that legislate scholastic policy, as well as the educational institutions that provide children with reading instruction, have only slowly utilized the innovative approaches suggested by these fields.

Education Policy

The U.S. Supreme Court has rarely considered the issue of the individual right to education at a federal level. When the Court finally spoke directly on the issue of the right to education in *Rodriguez v. San Antonio Independent School District* (1973), it found that the Constitution makes no mention of a fundamental right to education, and relegated the creation of educational policy to local and state governments. Consequently, state and local governments have largely been responsible for education policies such as school curriculum, school quality, compulsory education laws, and, most importantly, granting education the status of a fundamental right (Salerno, 2006). The U.S. Supreme Court has often ruled on issues related to the importance of education (see, e.g., *Brown v. Board of Education*, 1954;

Lau v. Nichols, 1974; *Plyler v. Doe*, 1982), but only insofar as to say that discrimination in education for underrepresented groups is unconstitutional. Basing these decisions on inequality, the Court has been able to sidestep the issue of the "right to education" by claiming that policies that deny some children education violate the 14th Amendment's "Equal Protection Clause" (U.S. Const. Amend. XIV, *Brown v. Board of Education*, 1954; *Lau v. Nichols*, 1974; *Plyler v. Doe*, 1982).

Although the Supreme Court has not recognized a federal right to education, the legislative and executive branches of the U.S. government have a history of involvement in educational policy. Most notably, the federal government has legislated on such educational issues as providing equal education to the poor (see, e.g., Elementary and Secondary Education Act, ESEA, of 1965) and disabled (see, e.g., Individuals with Disabilities Education Act, IDEA, of 1975). However, these acts primarily addressed "who" we should be teaching, focusing on insular and discrete subpopulations of our nation's students, while neglecting the more important "what" and "how" we should be teaching (Heise, 2006).

The federal government's role in education saw its most significant expansion with the enactment of the No Child Left Behind (NCLB) Act of 2001. Prior to NCLB, federal dollars typically accounted for less than 10 percent of the average school district budget (Heise, 2006). However, the NCLB significantly increased the amount of potentially available funding to state and local governments by redirecting federal funds to maintaining standards set by the act (Bush, 2001). First, each state had to create a single statewide accountability system for monitoring each public school's performance in a number of basic skills (Bush, 2001). Second, each school had to meet adequate yearly progress (AYP) criteria, which tracked the mandated continuous and substantial academic improvement requirement of the Act (Bush, 2001). Finally, states had to ensure that all teachers within the state were "highly qualified" to teach their assigned subject (Bush, 2001).

Eleven years after the passage of NCLB, the Obama administration offered the opportunity for states to waive some of its major requirements through approval of an individualized state plan (U.S. Department of Education, 2012). This option was designed to provide greater flexibility in educational planning for a state choosing this option, while still allowing for compliance with the statute.

The Institute of Education Sciences (IES) was established shortly after the enactment of NCLB to fund more rigorous education science. Part of this effort included the development of the What Works Clearinghouse database (WWC) (What Works Clearinghouse, 2008). Although WWC has been criticized for lacking approved programs, inconsistent results, and inadequate dissemination (Ashby, 2011; Viadero, 2007), it has the potential to bring more rigorous cognitive science to education. Of course, the criticism of too few approved programs actually reflects a larger issue in the field that, all too often, curricula and other programs are rushed to market without appropriate clinical trials. The research funding arm of IES has steadily funded such trials and produced evidence on an increasing number of effective programs. For example, a recent synthesis of IES-funded research on reading demonstrates that the number of effective interventions and instructional regimens is increasing (Connor, Alberto, Compton, & O'Connor, 2014).

Critics argue that the NCLBA still suffers from unclear, inconsistent, and ambiguous criteria. For example, the Act requires that each state develop a set of "challenging academic standards" (Bush, 2001, p. 20) for every grade and content area, but does not set these standards, allowing for inconsistencies in definitions and poor measurement of academic improvement among the states (Heise, 2006). As is discussed later, the controversy surrounding the Common Core State Standards (Common Core State Standards Initiative, 2010) has exacerbated the confusion.

In another example, grades and standardized test scores are often used in conjunction as indicators of academic achievement and improvement. However, the field of cognitive psychology tells us that grades and standardized test scores measure two very different constructs (Sass, 2006). Academic grades measure behavioral abilities and accomplishments such as completing homework, classroom participation, attitude, effort, and attendance (Sass, 2006). To a substantial extent, grades reflect a student's mastery of self-control (defined as the "ability to regulate behaviors, thoughts, emotions, and attention in the service of valued long-term goals") and self-regulation (defined as the "regulation of one's own behavior without external control or monitoring"; Sass, 2006). Standardized tests, by way of contrast, measure the ability to solve novel problems in novel formats in the course of a single occasion and in a few hours in a setting designed to minimize and maximize motivation (Sass, 2006). They reflect skills and knowledge acquired both inside and outside the classroom (Sass, 2006).

Combining grades and test scores into a single construct yields a measure of academic achievement that is much less informative than each factor interpreted on its own. Unfortunately, these deficits have yet to be addressed and remain problematic for educational institutions across the country. Moreover, it is not clear that these issues will be resolved as the Elementary and Secondary Education Act is amended, a process that has just been completed.

Educational Institutions

As we have learned in previous chapters, success in reading is influenced by cognitive processes, individual characteristics, and environmental influences, as well as a multitude of other factors. Also important to reading outcomes is the educational setting in which the individual is placed. Some federal educational legislation attempts to equalize educational opportunities across settings, but the different community options have an effect on learning to read. Although there are many different types of educational settings, this chapter focuses on some of the more common, as well as the more troublesome, educational environments. These include public schools, charter schools, and juvenile correctional education. Although all these settings attempt to teach children the fundamentals of how to read, each has its own successes and challenges in providing appropriate education to this country's youths.

Charter Schools

The first law establishing charter schools as an educational institution passed in Minnesota in 1999 (U.S. Department of Education, 2013). Since then, legislation allowing for the creation of charter schools has passed in 41 states and the District of Colombia (U.S. Department of Education, 2013). Charter schools currently serve about 1.8 million students across the United States, which is about 5 percent of the public school population (U.S. Department of Education, 2013). Although charter schools still serve a minority of students in the U.S., their popularity has grown steadily since their inception. This growth of charters in the USA lends urgency to evaluating the success of reading instruction in these settings.

Charter schools are publicly funded, yet independent organizations (Hanushek, Kain, Rivkin, & Branch, 2007). They are usually established by teachers, parents, or community groups under the terms of a "charter," and report to either a local or national authority (Hanushek, et al., 2007). This charter functions as the school's educational plan and philosophy. Charter schools receive funding from state and/or local legislatures, but they operate largely independently from state and local rules and regulations (U.S. Department of Education, 2013). Although they are free from many legislative restrictions, they must be periodically reviewed by the authority that granted the charter and their charter is subject to revocation if they do not meet the general guidelines on curriculum and management (U.S. Department of Education, 2013).

The freedom granted to charter schools is meant to support innovation that many deem lacking from the current public school system. Supporters of charter schools highlight that the charter school's independence from oversight should lead to advances in school management, school curriculum, and the use of educational technology (Hoxby, 2004). This freedom should also allow for increased efficacy in the school's educational programming, and specifically in reading instruction. Advocates of charter schools believe that choice and competition force overall improvement in the public education system and should give lower performing schools incentive to be more productive because students may move from poorer performing schools to higher performing schools.

The research on the effectiveness of charter schools in improving students' reading skills has demonstrated generally positive effects on students' math and reading outcomes but with significant regional differences according to both the national and urban charter school studies conducted by the Center for Research in Educational Outcomes (CREDO, http://credo.stanford.edu/). For example, a report on Texas charter schools found that, statewide, students attending charter schools made weaker achievement gains (http://credo.stanford.edu/pdfs/TX%20Release%20July%202015.pdf) whereas, for Ohio and California, results were more mixed (http://credo.stanford.edu/pdfs/OHPressReleaseFinal.pdf; http://credo.stanford.edu/pdfs/CARelease3_20_2014Final.pdf).

Voucher programs are used to make public funds are made available to individual parents to cover expenses associated with enrolling their child in a private school of their choosing. The idea is that these programs allow for easier transition from a poorer performing school to a better performing school (Wolf, 2008).

The Special Case of Juvenile Correctional Schools

Juvenile correctional schools present a unique problem for reading instruction. Juveniles in the correctional system are to be afforded the same rights as children in any other school. They are still subject to compulsory education laws and are given the same legal protections of equality in education as any other student. In addition, these juveniles are especially in need of reading instruction. Statistics from the juvenile justice system paint an especially grim portrait of the population of students it serves. The typical juvenile inmate is the equivalent of a ninth-grade student (about 15.5 years old), yet reads at a fourth-grade level (Vacca, 2008). In addition, about 34 percent of youth are identified as disabled, with as many as 60–70 percent receiving some type of special education, significantly higher than the 12.7 percent of public school students who receive special education (Quinn, Rutherford, Leone, Osher & Poirier, 2005). Finally, juveniles 16 years of age and older have been shown to be unlikely to return to any formal schooling after their release (Vacca, 2008).

The juvenile justice system should be taking special care to properly educate their students. Reading problems and disabilities have been associated with increased rates of recidivism (Archwamety & Katsiyannia, 2000). Repeat offenders fall an average of 2 years behind their non-repeat offending peers in reading (Foley, 2001). In addition, many of the cognitive problems that may have led to these individuals finding themselves in contact with the juvenile justice system are likely related to their increased trouble with reading. Children in the juvenile justice system have been shown to be more likely to suffer from mental disorders and cognitive deficits (Grisso, 2008; Grisso, Barnum, Fletcher, Cauffman, & Peuschold, 2001; Shufelt & Cocozza, 2006; Stewart & Trupin, 2003). These problems manifest themselves in reading comprehension problems in various hypothesized ways. For example, externalizing behavioral problems such as attention deficit/hyperactivity disorder (ADHD), oppositional defiant disorder (ODD), and conduct disorder (CD) are present in these children at rates as high as 80 percent (Shufelt & Cocozza, 2006). These types of behavioral problem are thought to interfere with a child's motivation and ability to learn appropriate skills in school, which hinders reading acquisition (Solan, Shelley-Tremblay, Ficarra, Silverman, & Larson, 2003). Contrariwise, reading disabilities may cause school frustration, resulting in low self-esteem followed by aggressive and antisocial behavior (Solan, et al., 2003). These two pathways of reading comprehension difficulty and criminal offending may also operate cyclically, with one problem constantly influencing the other.

Cognitive deficits may manifest themselves in different ways in these adolescents. For example, visuomotor deficits affect the way in which visual stimuli are understood (Stein, 2001). Problems in the visual motor system affect an individual's ability to read quickly, efficiently, and with an appropriate degree of comprehension (Deacon & Shelley-Tremblay, 2000; Mangun & Hillyard, 1991; Shelley-Tremblay, 2003). Another way in which cognitive deficits may affect reading is through difficulty with phonological awareness (Guttorm, Leppänen, & Poikkeus, 2005). Phonological awareness is the ability to discriminate, detect, and process sounds used in understanding language (Hämäläinen, Leppänen, Torppa, Müller, & Lyytinen, 2005). Early delays or impairments in the phonological system lead to deficits in speech sound discrimination, which are associated with problems in developing the sound codes that form the basis of spoken language (Scarborough. 2005). Because basic mental processing is mediated by verbal codes, these phonological deficits contribute to problems with verbal memory, naming, and reading comprehension (Shaywitz, 2003).

These problems do not preclude improvements in reading abilities. Several studies, using various programs, have shown success in improving reading abilities in this population. For example, in a random assignment evaluation of adolescents in detention facilities, the Orton/Gillingham Treatment Program showed improvement in reading programs, as well as a decrease in recidivism, when used with juvenile offenders (Simpson, Swanson, & Kunkel, 1992). Juvenile delinquents selected to participate in the Corrective Reading (CR) Decoding program have shown repeated gains in reading ability (see, e.g., Allen-DeBoer, Malmgren, & Glass, 2006; Drakeford, 2002; Malmgren & Leone, 2000). In addition, the use of computer-assisted instruction (CAI) has shown improvement in overall reading ability (Rozalski & Engel, 2005). Finally, Houchins and colleagues (2008) found increased reading performance using explicit reading instruction using randomly selected students in multiple juvenile correctional facilities.

Despite the success of these programs, juvenile correctional schools largely fail to educate these special needs children. Juvenile correctional facilities consistently fail to provide appropriate special educational programs, and have one of the worst records of adhering to the special education requirements under IDEA (National Center on Education, Disability, and Juvenile Justice, 2003). In addition, Gagnon and colleagues (2009) found that over one-third of principals of juvenile correctional schools noted that their instructional materials were only "somewhat," "very little," or "not at all" aligned with state expectations. However, juvenile correctional schools suffer from a number of problems that normal educational systems are unlikely to encounter. In addition to educational programs, juvenile correctional facilities must also devote resources to behavioral control, rehabilitation programs, around-the-clock monitoring, as well as providing appropriate living facilities, meals, and other basic living requirements. Additionally, the system consistently deals with problems of underfunding, overcrowding, continuous movement of juveniles in and out of facilities, and a lack of qualified educators. These problems pose unique challenges to educating some of our most at-risk youth.

Current Reading Policy

Response to Intervention

The reauthorization of the Individuals with Disabilities Education Improvement Act (IDEA, 2004) allowed states to begin to use a process called response to intervention (RTI), or multitiered systems of support, to provide early intervention to prevent reading problems and also to consider a student's response to well-implemented and generally effective interventions as means for identifying learning disabilities. Historically, students could not receive interventions until they had been identified as having learning disabilities and most states required that children manifest an IQ achievement discrepancy (cf., PL 94-142). This discrepancy approach had been used since the 1960s (Bateman, 1965; Kirk & Bateman, 1962).

Researchers, teachers, parents, and policy makers became increasingly concerned that the discrepancy approach represented a "wait-to-fail" model, particularly as research was showing the efficacy of early intervention (Fuchs & Fuchs, 1986; Reid Lyon, 1989; Reid Lyon, et al., 2001). In addition, researchers demonstrated that, at least when student IQs were 85 or above, IQ did not predict how well children responded to reading instruction (Francis, Shaywitz, Steubing, Shaywitz, & Fletcher, 1996; Guthrie, McRae, & Klauda, 2007; Vellutino, et al., 1996), neither did testing to document the discrepancy provide meaningful information for teachers to guide instruction or intervention (Torgesen, 2000). Another source of criticism about the discrepancy approach was that the tests were not culturally responsive, which led to minority children being both over- and under-identified as learning disabled (Artiles, 2003; Hosp & Reschly, 2003; Klinger & Harry, 2006). Finally, too many children, particularly children from high-poverty backgrounds who arrived at school with weak language and initial alphabetic skills, had significant reading problems but were considered "garden variety" poor readers because their language was so weak that there was not a large enough discrepancy to allow them to receive intervention.

Because IDEA 2004 allowed states to provide intervention early without waiting for a discrepancy, researchers and policy makers were optimistic and intervention believing that RTI would be an important forward step in reducing the incidence of reading difficulties (e.g., Bradley, Danielson, & Hallahan, 2002; Fletcher, Coulter, Reschly, & Vaughn, 2004; Foorman, Francis, Fletcher, Schatschneider, & Mehta, 1998). The foundation for this optimism about RTI was converging evidence that explicit and systematic early reading interventions were effective (Guthrie, et al., 2007; Mathes, et al., 2005; NICHD, 2000; Reid Lyon & Chhabra, 1996; Simmons, Kameenui, Stoolmiller, Coyne, & Harn, 2003; Vellutino, et al., 1996; Vellutino, Scanlon, Small, & Fanuele, 2006). There is considerable research to support implementation of effective instruction to prevent and remediate reading difficulties in the elementary years, (Denton, Fletcher, Anthony, & Francis, 2006; McMaster, Fuchs, Fuchs, & Compton, 2005; O'Connor, Harty, & Fulmer, 2005; Vaughn, et al., 2009) and a meta-analysis conducted in 2009 (Stuebing, Barth, Molfese, Weiss, & Fletcher, 2009) provided strong evidence that IQ was not a good predictor of response to intervention (see also Ferrer, Shaywitz, Holahan, Marchione, & Shaywitz, 2010).

The implementation of RTI has become more widespread. All 50 states now encourage RTI for prevention purposes and a growing number of states allow it for identification of learning disabilities (Fuchs & Vaughn, 2012; Zirkel & Thomas, 2010). The *Institute for Education Sciences Practice Guide for RTI* written by Gersten and colleagues (Gersten, et al., 2008) reviewed the literature supporting multitier interventions. They recommended core components that included universal screening, a high-quality Tier 1 core reading program, formative progress monitoring, increasingly intensive tiers of intervention, and fidelity of implementation. These five core components have rapidly manifested in state laws or guidelines about RTI (Berkeley, Bender, Gregg Peaster, & Saunders, 2009; Zirkel & Thomas, 2010). Although there are many types of multitiered models, Tier 1 core reading instruction provides the first line of defense against reading difficulties. In the next section, we discuss current research findings for both Tier 1 general education classroom instructional interventions separately from small group supplemental interventions, which are frequently called Tier 2 or Tier 3 interventions.

National Assessment of Educational Progress

The National Assessment of Educational Progress (NAEP, 2011), provides a report card on how well students read in fourth, eighth, and twelfth grades. There were several significant changes in the 2009 NAEP reading framework. Vocabulary is tested explicitly by measuring word knowledge in context; subscales are reported for literacy and informational text. Poetry is assessed in fourth grade; and, to assess higher order processes in reading, such as inferencing and critical analysis, students respond to both multiple choice and constructed response questions (Foorman & Connor, 2010).

Students are rated in one of four categories—below basic, basic, proficient, and advanced. To achieve a basic level of reading, fourth graders should be able to make simple inferences, locate information in text, identify supporting detail, describe characters' motivations and mood, and describe the problem in narrative text. In information text, they should be able to find the topic sentence or main idea, supply supporting details, identify the authors' purpose, and make simple inferences. In contrast, to achieve an advanced level of reading, fourth graders should be able to interpret figurative language, make complex inferences, identify point of view, evaluate character motivation, and describe thematic connections across literacy texts in narrative text. In information text, they should be able to make complex inferences, evaluate the coherence of the text, explain the author's point of view, and compare ideas across texts.

The most recent NAEP results (http://nationsreportcard.gov/reading_math_2013/files/Results_Appendix_Reading.pdf) reveal that, in 2013, 67 percent of fourth graders attending public schools were reading at or above basic levels. This changed little from 66 percent in 2011 but represents an increase from 58 percent in 1998. Thirty-four percent of these students achieved at or above proficient levels, up from 32 percent in 2011 and from 28 percent in 1998. However, there continues to be an achievement gap between students living in poverty (i.e., eligible for free/reduced-price lunch, FRL) and their more affluent peers. Only 53 percent of students who qualify for FRL achieved at or above basic levels compared to 83 percent of students who were not eligible. Importantly, only 20 percent and 3 percent of students eligible for FRL achieved proficient or advanced levels, respectively, compared with 51 percent and 14 percent for students not eligible for FRL. Moreover, ethnicity and poverty are conflated so many of the students who qualify for FRL belong to ethnic and racial minorities. The achievement gap has closed somewhat since 1998 but not to acceptable levels and remains a complex and perplexing problem. Many federal and state policies, such as Race to the Top, currently, and

Reading First, previously, have targeted reforms for schools that serve high percentages of students living in poverty or who are underperforming academically.

Common Core State Standards

The Common Core State Standards (http://www.corestandards.org) are the most recent policy attempt to improve students' literacy outcomes. At the writing of this chapter, they were in the first year of their implementation with states evaluating student performance using one of two assessments— the PARCC (Partnership for Assessment of Readiness for College and Careers http://www.parcconline.org) or Smarter Balance (http://www. smarterbalanced.org). The mission of the state-initiated Common Core State Standards (CCSS) is to provide a consistent and clear understanding of what students are expected to learn at each grade from kindergarten through twelfth grade. They were designed to be relevant to the "real world" and to reflect the knowledge and skills students will need for "success in college and careers." Forty-five states have adopted the CCSS. Previously, each state had its own standards, which varied greatly with respect to expectations and content. According to the authors, the CCSS were "written by building on the best and highest state standards in existence in the US, examining the expectations of other high performing countries around the world, and careful study of what students need to know and be able to do to be successful in college and careers" (http://www.corestandards.org/ resources/frequently-asked-questions). They state that the standards are evidence based and include rigorous content and skills.

As with all such sweeping policies, there has been controversy and concerns. For example, in many states, there is not enough funding to train teachers how to implement the new practices required to meet higher reading standards required by the CCSS. State politicians complain that the federal government is too involved. In early adopting states, such as New York, students' performance on the new assessment is much weaker than on the old state assessments, which has impacted schools, adequate yearly progress, a school evaluation system, which was introduced under No Child Left Behind. Already, the CCSS have profoundly impacted reading instruction in the primary grades and will continue to do so for the foreseeable future. Most recently, parents have been opting out of testing, which will make it difficult to determine the impact of the Common Core State Standards.

Recommendations

Proper and informed legislation at the federal level can help to set the stage for effective educational policy across the country. However, navigating between states' rights and federal goals requires a high level of finesse.

States are loath to give up power traditionally reserved to their own state governments. There will likely always be pushback from the states regarding who should be setting the standards for education in the United States (Ryan, 2004). The NCLBA already tests the limits of federal power over the states (Heise, 2006). However, those who argue that federal government has no place in setting educational policy ignore the long history of the federal role in education (see, e.g., Land Ordinance of 1785, which provided one lot within every township for the maintenance of a public school within that township; the Northwest Ordinance of 1787, which encouraged schools and means of education; the Morrill Act of 1861, which promoted agricultural education and demonstrating the connection between education, business, and commerce; and the creation of the Department of Education in 1867).

Although Congress continues to face challenges in its attempts to regulate education nationally, there is a history of Congress's ability to affect many of the powers traditionally left to the states through is constitutionally granted spending power (U.S. Const. Art. 1, Sec. 8, Clause 1; *South Dakota v. Dole*, 1987). When enacting NCLBA, Congress was careful to leave enough ambiguity in the Act to largely escape constitutional challenges to many of its provisions (Salerno, 2006). However, due to a national consensus that education in the United States is not where it should be (Gallup, 2009), it may be time to test the limits of federal power in education legislation.

There are many ways in which the federal government might amend NCLB to make improvements to reading education in the United States. Greater support for the What Works Clearinghouse as well as more guidance to states as to what constitutes "scientifically based programs" in reading instruction and testing are some examples. For example, federal funding to states might require use of programs identified as effective in the What Works Clearinghouse (Francis, et al., 1996; What Works Clearinghouse, 2008). Additional effort could be devoted to making sure that the programs being used in schools today meet the already in place federal benchmark for scientific efficacy. This will also allow for additional consistency in both teaching and measurement.

However, some would argue that reform could be better achieved without federal involvement. For example, voucher programs that provide scholarships that pay for students to attend a better performing, private school. This choice would allow parents to send their children to the school of their choice. The result of the loss of students from a poorly performing school would require the school to either improve or risk losing the funding associated with the departing students. However, the shifting of students from public to private schools and the loss of funding that would follow does not decrease the financial obligations of the school, placing the poorly performing school at an even greater disadvantage.

Other critics of national educational policy contend that state and local governments are better able to effectuate change due to their more in-depth knowledge of local conditions. However, flexibility in educational planning that would allow for consideration of local circumstances and legislation at the national level are not at odds (e.g., the recently enacted Every Student Succeeds Act replacing NCLB) and it is quite likely that a number of different approaches are required.

Changing the functions and operations of entire systems of education are likely as difficult as influencing the policy that controls them. However, there are various ways in which advances in cognitive science may improve what and how we teach our children to read. Both charter schools and juvenile correctional schools may benefit from the use of empirically vali-dated reading programs. In service of this goal, charter schools and juvenile correctional schools may benefit from the creation of a database with rec-ommended programs, materials, and instruction. Juvenile correctional facilities, especially, may benefit from smaller class sizes and instruction times comparable to community schools. Students in these facilities would benefit largely from communication with community schools, as well as transitional help and support when they enter back into their community. Although these are only first steps, they are important starting points in giving our children the best possible educational opportunities.

One in three students in the United States scores "below basic" on the National Assessment of Education Progress (NAEP) Reading test (U.S. Department of Education, 2013). The United States ranks 14th in the world in reading knowledge, trailing many of our peer nations (Fleischman, Hopstock, Pelczar, & Shelley, 2010). As a nation, we are in need of proper reading instruction in our schools. In order to make the changes necessary for continued improvement in reading, the United States needs to create policy informed by the scientific community as to what works in reading instruction. Furthermore, policy must reach our various educational insti-tutions to truly effect change. As our scientists and researchers continue to advance in reading instruction, so too must the dissemination of their knowledge.

References

Allen-DeBoer, R. A., Malmgren, K. W., & Glass, M. E. (2006). Reading instruction for youth with emotional and behavioral disorders in a juvenile correctional facility. *Behavioral Disorders, 32*, 18–28.

Archwamety, T., & Katsiyannia, A. (2000). Academic remediation, parole violations, and recidivism rates among delinquent youths. *Remedial and Special Education, 21*, 161–170.

Artiles, A. (2003). Special education's changing identity: Paradoxes and dilemmas in views of culture and space. *Harvard Educational Review, 73*(2), 164–202.

Ashby, C. M. (2011). *Department of Education: Improved Dissemination and Timely Product Release Would Enhance the Usefulness of the What Works Clearinghouse.* Collingdale, PA: Diane Publishing.

Bateman, B. (1965). Learning disabilities—An overview. *Journal of School Psychology, 3*(3), 1–12.

Berkeley, S., Bender, W. N., Gregg Peaster, L., & Saunders, L. (2009). Implementation of response to intervention: A snapshot of progress. *Journal of Learning Disabilities, 42*(1), 85–95.

Bifulco, R., & Ladd, H. F. (2006). The impacts of charter schools on student achievement: Evidence from North Carolina. *Education, 1*, 50–90.

Bradley, R., Danielson, L., & R. Hallahan, R. (Eds.). (2002). *Identification of Learning Disabilities: Research to Practice.* Mahwah, NJ: Erlbaum.

Brown v. Board of Education, 347 U.S. 483, 1954.

Bush, G. W. (2001). No Child Left Behind. 20 USCA § 6301.

Common Core State Standards Initiative. (2010). Common Core State Standards for English Language Arts. Retrieved from http://www.corestandards.org/assets/CCSSI_ELA%20Standards.pdf

Connor, C. M., Alberto, P. A., Compton, D. L., & O'Connor, R. E. (2014). Improving reading outcomes for students with or at risk for reading disabilities: A synthesis of the contributions from the Institute of Education Sciences Research Centers Retrieved from http://ies.ed.gov/ncser/pubs/20143000/

Connor, C. M., Morrison, F. J., Fishman, B. J., Ponitz, C. C., Glasney, S., Underwood, P. S., et al. (2009). The ISI classroom observation system: Examining the literacy instruction provided to individual students. *Educational Researcher, 38*, 85–99.

Deacon, D., & Shelley-Tremblay, J. (2000). How automatically is meaning accessed: A review of the effects of attention on semantic processing. *Frontiers in Bioscience, 5*, 82–94.

Denton, C. A., Fletcher, J. M., Anthony, J. L., & Francis, D. J. (2006). An evaluation of intensive intervention for students with persistent reading difficulties. *Journal of Learning Disabilities, 39*(5), 447–466.

Drakeford, W. (2002). The impact of an intensive program to increase the literacy skills of youth confined to juvenile corrections. *Journal of Correctional Education, 53*, 139–144.

Ferrer, E., Shaywitz, B. A., Holahan, J. M., Marchione, K., & Shaywitz, S. E. (2010). Uncoupling of reading and IQ over time: Empirical evidence for a definition of dyslexia. *Psychological Science, 21*(1), 93–101.

Fleischman, H. L., Hopstock, P. J., Pelczar, M. P., & Shelley, B. E. (2010). Highlights from PISA 2009: Performance of U.S. 15-year-old students in reading, mathematics, and science literacy in an international context. NCES 2011-004. Washington, DC: National Center for Education Statistics.

Fletcher, J., Coulter, W. A., Reschly, D., & Vaughn, S. (2004). Alternative approaches to the definition and identification of learning disabilities: Some questions and answers. *Annals of Dyslexia, 54*(2), 304–331.

Foley, R. M. (2001). Academic characteristics of incarcerated youth and correctional educational programs: A literature review. *Journal of Emotional and Behavioral Disorders, 9*, 248–259.

Foorman, B. R., & Connor, C. M. (2010). Primary reading. In A. G. Kamhi & P. D. Pearson (Eds.), *Handbook of Reading Research* (4th ed.). Mahwah, NJ: Erlbaum.

Foorman, B. R., Francis, D. J., Fletcher, J. M., Schatschneider, C., & Mehta, P. (1998). The role of instruction in learning to read: Preventing reading failure in at risk children. *Journal of Educational Psychology, 90*, 37–55.

Francis, D. J., Shaywitz, S. E., Steubing, K. K., Shaywitz, B. A., & Fletcher, J. M. (1996). Developmental lag versus deficit models of reading disability: A longitudinal, individual growth curve analysis. *Journal of Educational Psychology, 88*(1), 3–17.

Fuchs, L. S., & Fuchs, D. (1986). Effects of systematic formative evaluation: A meta-analysis. *Exceptional Children, 53*, 199–208.

Fuchs, L. S., & Vaughn, S. (2012). Responsiveness-to-intervention: A decade later. *Journal of Learning Disabilities, 45*(3), 195–203.

Gagnon, J. C., Barber, B. R., Van Loan, C., & Leone, P. E. (2009). Juvenile correctional schools: Characteristics and approaches to curriculum. *Education and Treatment of Children, 32*(4), 673–696.

Gallup. August (2009). Available at http://www.gallup.com/poll/1612/Education.aspx

Gersten, R., Compton, D., Connor, C. M., Dimino, J., Santoro, L., Linan-Thompson, S., et al. (2008). *Assisting Students Struggling with Reading: Response to Intervention and Multitier Intervention for Reading in the Primary Grades. A Practice Guide.* Washington, DC: National Center for Education Evaluation and Regional Assistance, Institute of Education Sciences, U.S. Department of Education.

Grisso, T. (2008). Adolescent offenders with mental disorders. *Future of Children, 18*, 143–164.

Grisso, T., Barnum, R., Fletcher, K. E., Cauffman, E., & Peuschold, D. (2001). Massachusetts youth screening instrument for mental health needs of juvenile justice youths. *Journal of the American Academy of Child and Adolescent Psychiatry, 40*, 541–548.

Guthrie, J. T., McRae, A., & Klauda, S. L. (2007). Contributions of concept-oriented reading instruction to knowledge about interventions for motivations in reading. *Educational Psychologist, Special Issue: Promoting Motivation at School, 42*(4), 237–250.

Guttorm, T. K., Leppänen, P. H. T., & Poikkeus, A. (2005). Brain event-related potentials (ERPs) measured at birth predict later language development in children with and without familial risk for dyslexia. *Cortex, 41*, 291–303.

Hämäläinen, J., Leppänen, P. H. T., Torppa, M., Müller, K., & Lyytinen, H. (2005). Detection of sound rise time by adults with dyslexia. *Brain and Language, 94*, 32–47.

Hanushek, E. A., Kain, J. F., & Rivkin, S. G. (2002). *New evidence about* Brown v. Board of Education: *The complex effects of school racial composition on achievement* (No. w8741). Washington, DC: National Bureau of Economic Research.

Hanushek, E. A., Kain, J. F., Rivkin, S. G., & Branch, G. F. (2007). Charter school quality and parental decision making with school choice. *Journal of Public Economics, 91*, 823–848.

Heise, M. (2006). The political economy of education federalism. *Emory Law Journal, 56*, 125.

Hosp, J. L., & Reschly, D. J. (2003). Referral rates for intervention or assessment: A meta-analysis of racial differences. *Journal of Special Education, 37*(2), 67–80.

Houchins, D. E., Jolivette, K., Krezmien, M. P., & Baltodano, H. M. (2008). A multi-state study examining the impact of explicit reading instruction with incarcerated students. *Journal of Correctional Education*, 65–85.

Hoxby, C. M. (2004). *A Straightforward Comparison of Charter Schools and Regular Public Schools in the United States.* Washington, DC: National Bureau of Economic Research.

Individuals with Disabilities Education Act (IDEA), (2004). 20 USCA § 1400(a).

Kirk, S. A., & Bateman, B. (1962). Diagnosis and remediation of learning disabilities. *Exceptional Children, 29*(2), 73–78.

Klinger, J., & Harry, B. (2006). The special education referral and decision-making process for English language learners: Child study team meeting and placement conferences. *Teachers College Record, 108*(11), 2247–2281.

Lau v. Nichols, 414 U.S. 563, 1974.

McMaster, K. L., Fuchs, D., Fuchs, L. S., & Compton, D. L. (2005). Responding to nonresponders: An experimental field trial of identification and intervention methods. *Exceptional Children, 71*(4), 445–463.

Malmgren, K., & Leone, P. E. (2000). Effects of a short-term auxiliary reading program on the reading skills of incarcerated youth. *Education and Treatment of Children, 23*, 239–247.

Mangun, G.R. and Hillyard, S.A. (1991) Modulations of sensory-evoked brain potentials indicate changes in perceptual processing during visual-spatial priming. *Perception, 17*, 1057–1074.

Mathes, P. G., Denton, C. A., Fletcher, J. M., Anthony, J. L., Francis, D. J., & Schatschneider, C. (2005). The effects of theoretically different instruction and student characteristics on the skills of struggling readers. *Reading Research Quarterly, 40*(2), 148–182.

NAEP. (2011). *National Assessment of Educational Progress: The Nation's Report Card.* http://nces.ed.gov/nationsreportcard/

Nelson, F. H., Rosenberg, B., & Van Meter, N. (2004). *Charter School Achievement on the 2003 National Assessment of Educational Progress.* Washington, DC: American Federation of Teachers.

NICHD. (2000). National Institute of Child Health and Human Development. *National Reading Panel Report: Teaching Children to Read: An Evidence-Based Assessment of the Scientific Research Literature on Reading and its Implications for Reading Instruction.* Washington DC: U.S. Department of Health and Human Services, Public Health Service, National Institutes of Health, National Institute of Child Health and Human Development.

O'Connor, R. E., Harty, K. R., & Fulmer, D. (2005). Tiers of intervention in kindergarten through third grade. *Journal of Learning Disabilities, 38*(6), 532–538.

Plyler v. Doe, 457 U.S. 202, 1982.

Quinn, M. M., Rutherford, R. B., Leone, P. E., Osher, D. M. & Poirier, J. M. (2005). Youth with disabilities in juvenile corrections: A national survey. *Exceptional Children, 71*, 339–345.

Reid Lyon, G. (1989). IQ is irrelevant to the definition of learning disabilities: A position in search of logic and data. *Journal of Learning Disabilities, 22*(8), 504.

Reid Lyon, G., & Chhabra, V. (1996). The current state of science and the future of specific reading disability. *Mental Retardation & Developmental Disabilities Research Reviews, 2*(1), 2–9.

Reid Lyon, G., Fletcher, J. M., Shaywitz, S. E., Shaywitz, B. A., Torgesen, J. K., Wood, F. B., et al. (2001). Rethinking learning disabilities. In C. E. F. Jr., R. A. J. Rotherham, & J. C. R. O'Hokanson (Eds.), *Rethinking Special Education for a New Century*. Washington, DC: Fordham Foundation.

Rodriguez v. San Antonio Independent School District, 411 U.S. 1, 1973.

Rozalski, M. E., & Engel, S. (2005). Literacy education for correctional facilities: The "hope" for technology. *Reading and Writing Quarterly: Overcoming Learning Difficulties, 21*, 301–305.

Ryan, J. E. (2004). The perverse incentives of the No Child Left Behind Act. *New York University Law Review*, 79.

Salerno, M. (2006). Reading is fundamental: Why the No Child Left Behind Act necessitates recognition of a fundamental right to education. *Cardozo Pub. L. Policy & Ethics Journal, 5*, 509.

Sass, T. R. (2006). Charter schools and student achievement in Florida. *Education, 1*, 91–122.

Scarborough, H. S. (2005). Developmental relationships between language and reading: Reconciling a beautiful hypothesis with some ugly facts. In H. W. Catts & A. G. Kamhi (Eds.), *The Connections between Language and Reading Disabilities*. Mahwah, NJ: Erlbaum.

Shaywitz, S. (2003). *Overcoming Dyslexia: A New and Complete Science-Based Program for Reading Problems at any Level*. New York: Alfred A. Knopf.

Shelley-Tremblay, J. (2003). Hemispheric differences in the effect of selective attention on the electrophysiological response to semantic processing. *Dissertation Abstracts International. B. The Sciences and Engineering, 64*, 1519.

Shufelt, J. L., & Cocozza, J. J. (2006). Youth with mental health disorders in the juvenile justice system: Results from a multi-state prevalence study. *National Center for Mental Health and Juvenile Justice Research and Program Brief*, 1–5.

Simmons, D. C., Kameenui, E. J., Stoolmiller, M., Coyne, M. D., & Harn, B. (2003). Accelerating growth and maintaining proficiency: A two-year intervention study of kindergarten and first-grade children at risk for reading difficulties. In B. Foorman (Ed.), *Preventing and Remediating Reading Difficulties: Bringing Science up to Scale*. Timonium, MD: York Press.

Simpson, S. B., Swanson, J. M., & Kunkel, K. (1992). The impact of an intensive multisensory reading program on a population of learning-disabled delinquents. *Annals of Dyslexia, 42*, 54–66.

Solan, H. A., Shelley-Tremblay, J., Ficarra, A., Silverman, M., & Larson, S. (2003). Effect of attention therapy on reading comprehension. *Journal of Learning Disabilities, 16*, 556–563.

Solman, L., Paark, K., & Garcia, D., (2001) *Does Charter School Attendance Improve Test Scores? The Arizona Results*. Phoenix, AZ: Goldwater Institute.

South Dakota v. Dole, 483 U.S. 203, 1987.

Stanovich, K. E. (2000). *Progress in Understanding Reading: Scientific Foundations and New Frontiers*. New York: Guilford.

Stein (2001). The magnocellular theory of developmental dyslexia. *Dyslexia, 7*, 12–36.

Stewart, D. G., & Trupin, E. W. (2003). Clinical utility and policy implications of a statewide mental health screening process for juvenile offenders. *Psychiatric Services, 54*, 377–382.

Stuebing, K. K., Barth, A. E., Molfese, P. J., Weiss, B., & Fletcher, J. M. (2009). IQ is not strongly related to response to reading instruction: a meta-analytic interpretation. *Exceptional Children*, 76(1), 31.

Torgesen, J. K. (2000). Individual differences in response to early intervention in reading: The lingering problem of treatment resisters. *Learning Disabilities Research and Practice*, 15, 55–64.

U.S. Const. Amend. XIV.

U.S. Const. Art. 1, Sec. 8, Clause 1.

U.S. Department of Education, Institute of Education Sciences, National Center for Education Statistics, National Assessment of Educational Progress (NAEP), (various years) 1990–2013 Mathematics and Reading Assessments.

U.S. Department of Education, National Center for Education Statistics. (2013). The Condition of Education 2013 (NCES 2013–037), Charter School Enrollment.

Vacca, J. S. (2008). Crime can be prevented if schools teach juvenile offenders to read. *Children and Youth Services Review*, 30(9), 1055–1062.

Vaughn, S., Wanzek, J., Murray, C. S., Scammacca, N., Linan-Thompson, S., & Woodruff, A. L. (2009). Response to early reading intervention examining higher and lower responders. *Exceptional Children*, 75(2), 165–183.

Vellutino, F. R., Scanlon, D. M., Sipay, E. R., Small, S. G., Pratt, A., Chen, R., et al. (1996). Cognitive profiles of difficult to remediate and readily remediated poor readers: Early intervention as a vehicle for distinguishing between cognitive and experiential deficits as basic causes of specific reading disability. *Journal of Educational Psychology*, 88(4), 601–638.

Vellutino, F. R., Scanlon, D. M., Small, S., & Fanuele, D. P. (2006). Response to intervention as a vehicle for distinguishing between children with and without reading disabilities: Evidence for the role of kindergarten and first-grade interventions. *Journal of Learning Disabilities*, 39(2), 157–169.

Viadero, D. (2007). New breed of digital tutors yielding learning gains. *Education Week*, 26, 9.

What Works Clearinghouse. (2008). WWC procedures and standards handbook. Retrieved December, 2010, from http://ies.ed.gov/ncee/wwc/references/idocviewer/Doc.aspx?docId=19&tocId=4

Wolf, P. J. (2008). School voucher programs: What the research says about parental school choice. *BYU L. Review*, 415.

Zirkel, P. A., & Thomas, L. B. (2010). State laws and guidelines for implementing RTI. *Teaching Exceptional Children*, 43(1), 60–73.

Chapter 12

Using Cognitive Development Research to Inform Literacy Instruction and Improve Practice in the Classroom

Carol McDonald Connor

As this book has explored, teaching students how to read and write may be one of the most difficult but important endeavors facing a literate society (No Child Left Behind Act, www.ed.gov). Although, as we have discussed through this book, there are many factors that contribute to success in learning to read—including genes, home literacy environment, health, poverty, stress, preschool experiences, parenting, peers, ecological barriers, and policy (Bronfenbrenner & Morris, 2006; Duncan, Kalil, & Ziol-Guest, 2008; Pianta, Belsky, Houts, Morrison, & NICHD-ECCRN, 2007; Skibbe, et al., 2012; Taylor, Roehrig, Connor, & Schatschneider, 2010)—the contribution of how and what we teach students is not trivial. Just as there are certain parenting practices discussed in Chapter 9 that support children's early literacy development (NICHD-ECCRN, 2004), the instructional practices of teachers and the learning environment of the classroom are important influences on students' achievement as well (Connor, Spencer, et al., in press). Accumulating evidence continues to document striking differences in the quality, amount, type and content of reading instruction being offered to students in our schools (Carlisle, Kelcey, Berebitsky, & Phelps, 2011; Pianta, et al., 2007; Taylor, Pearson, Clark, & Walpole, 2000). In addition to instruction, variation in teachers' facility organizing the instructional day, planning instruction, and efficiently managing transitions and disruptions in the classroom significantly influences the amount of time available for effective instruction (Cameron & Morrison, 2004; Connor, et al., 2010; Connor, Spencer, et al., in press). Also influencing learning is teachers' support for their students' motivation to learn (Guthrie, McRae, & Klauda, 2007) and socioemotional development (Pianta, La Paro, Payne, Cox, & Bradley, 2002).

Acknowledging the importance of these other sources of influence on students' learning, the purpose of this chapter is to focus on the actual reading and writing instruction children receive. Building on Chapter 11, this chapter provides an update on the most current literacy research conducted over the past decade with greater focus on meta-analyses and new studies published after 2008, when there were appreciably more randomized controlled field trials funded and published. The chapter concludes with a discussion of common characteristics of effective classroom instructional interventions, research in children's cognitive development that is needed to further inform effective instruction, and how we might incorporate what we do know from current research findings into the classroom.

A Brief History of Reading Instruction

What counts as meaningful instruction has been debated for the past century and most recently in the "reading wars," which seem to be abating. This is evident in the Common Core State Standards (Common Core State Standards Initiative, 2010), which recognize the importance of the foundational skills (e.g., learning the alphabetic principle) as well as higher order literacy. There is also a greater appreciation of individual student differences and the importance of differentiated or individualized reading instruction—that the effect of specific instructional strategies depends on the skills and aptitudes students bring to the classroom. The reading wars do continue to bubble up with debates still evident in theory and practice. Some have contended that the reading wars reflected a larger debate in the field of education with roots in romanticism and the traditional versus progressive movements (Loveless, 2001; Ravitch, 2001). The debate has been evident in the content areas of math and science but has been most salient in reading, which has a history of contention. Of note, cognitive theories of reading and the research they inspired and continue to inspire have been highly influential in this debate.

Until the early 1800s, reading instruction in the United States relied on the Webster speller (introduced in 1782) and the McGuffey readers, which introduced the alphabet and used phonics methods (letters stand for sounds, which are combined to spell meaningful words) while commending honesty, thrift, and kindness. In 1832, John Miller Keagy introduced the whole-word method (Davis, 1987; Ravitch, 2001). The proponents of the method (following the romanticism movement) stated that learning to read should not be "tiresome drudgery" (as exemplified by the McGuffey reader) but rather should be "as natural as learning to talk" (Ravitch 2001), which sounds quite similar to the rationale for whole-language approaches of the 1980s and 1990s (Goelman, Oberg, & Smith, 1984; Goodman, 1986). In the 1930s, the Dick and Jane series, using the whole-word method, gained widespread popularity through the 1950s, until the publication of *Why Johnny Can't Read* (Flesch, 1955). With increasing criticism of public education, this book reached the national bestseller list and spurred on the bitter debate. Although characterized by the general press as the solution to reading problems, educators and educational researchers rejected the book as based on opinion rather than science (Ravitch, 2001).

In 1967, Jeanne Chall published her seminal book, *Learning to Read: The Great Debate* (Goelman, et al., 1984), that introduced the stages of reading theory, which was, at least in part, founded on cognitive development theories described in Chapter 1. Her review of the research was supposed to end the debate. However, as Chall soon discovered, comparing reading methods' efficacy was difficult. No one method completely supported all students' reading success and teachers frequently used a combination of methods. Based on her review, Chall reported that an early emphasis on decoding appeared to be critical for children's reading success.

Beginning in the 1970s researchers proposed that learning to read was like learning to talk or that it was a "psycholinguistic guessing game" (Goodman, 1970). These ideas formed the foundation of the whole-language approach that became widely implemented beginning in the 1990s. In many ways, educators' enthusiastic response to whole language was a reaction to the overemphasis on script, drill, and workbooks that was typical of the 1970s and early 1980s (Ravitch, 2001). Proponents of whole language suggested that learning to read was a natural process; children needed to be exposed to "authentic" text and "coached" by their teacher to become proficient readers (Dahl & Freppon, 1995). Whole-language approaches de-emphasized the basal reader, tended to empower teachers, encouraged the use of interesting books by professional authors, as well as an enjoyment of reading. However, in the late 1990s researchers rediscovered what Chall had found in the 1960s—that many children needed explicit decoding instruction if they were to become successful readers (Foorman, Francis, Fletcher, Schatschneider, & Mehta, 1998; Guthrie, et al., 2007; NICHD, 2000). Learning to read was not like learning to talk, because reading and writing are human inventions. This ignited the reading wars, which raged acrimoniously into and through the first decade of new millennium. The acrimony was further fueled by the National Reading Panel report (NICHD 2000) and provisions in No Child Left Behind and Reading First (http://www2.ed.gov/programs/readingfirst/index.html), which required evidence-based practice and focused heavily on code-focused instruction, the mastery of the alphabetic principal, decoding, fluency, and used of approved core literacy curriculum (i.e., basals). Reading First was discontinued in 2008 and replaced with Race to the Top, which focused attention on assessing teaching effectiveness rather than on classroom instruction. In the later 2000s, a series of studies revealed that students learn to read more successfully when instruction was balanced between meaning- and code-focused instruction and was aligned with their specific learning needs (Connor, Spencer, et al., in press; Loveless, 2001; MacArthur, Ferretti, Okolo, & Cavalier, 2001). This attempt to achieve balance along with a better understanding of individual child differences with regard to how students learn to read is reflected in the

Common Core State Standards, with standards addressing both fundamental code-focused and higher order meaning-focused achievement.

Reading Today

Two major reports have greatly influenced today's approaches to teaching reading: the *National Reading Panel Report* (NICHD, 2000) and the *National Early Literacy Panel Report* (National Early Literacy Panel, 2008). The National Reading Panel report was highly controversial when the findings were published inasmuch as the meta-analysis revealed that most students required systematic and explicit instruction in the alphabetic principle and the use of phonics methods to achieve proficient reading skills with little support found for whole-language methods. The report highlighted five core areas of instruction—phonological awareness, phonics, fluency, vocabulary, and comprehension—and many states incorporated these areas of instruction into their Reading First programs. Stuebing and colleagues (Stuebing, Barth, Cirino, Francis, & Fletcher, 2008) and Foorman and Connor (Foorman & Connor, 2010) provide excellent discussions of the report findings and the controversy.

The *National Early Literacy Panel Report* (National Early Literacy Panel, 2008) is relevant to this chapter because the report articulates the important influence of early literacy and language skills on later student reading achievement. The early literacy skills found to be most closely associated with later reading achievement include: (1) knowing the names of printed letters; (2) knowing the phonemes associated with letters; (3) phonological awareness; (4) rapid automatic naming (i.e., being able to fluently name letters, colors, numbers, or to recognize patterns); (5) ability to write name and other letters; (6) ability to retell stories and follow multistep directions (related to working memory and more complex language skills). The panel found that understanding conventions of print, recognizing environmental print (e.g., the McDonalds sign), using and understanding vocabulary, and visual processing were only moderate predictors of later reading skill. Early childhood programs that incorporate these research findings into the planning and implementation of preschool activities are more likely to support their students' readiness for primary-grade reading instruction. This means that kindergarten and first-grade instruction will have to be more responsive and accommodate students who bring a broader range of early literacy skills to kindergarten and first-grade classrooms.

In addition to these two major reports, the U.S. Department of Education, Institute of Education Sciences, What Works Clearinghouse, have published *Practice Guides* (http://ies.ed.gov/pubsearch/) on a number of subjects including response to intervention (see Chapter 10), writing, early literacy, reading comprehension, and other topics. These documents, written to provide practical solutions for teachers and educational leaders, were written by panels of experts and reviewed by other experts with the goal of providing information on the current state of best practice based on the evidence currently available. The extent to which these documents have influenced practice in the classroom or the extent to which they are used in preservice teacher education is inconsistent, but they do offer valuable insights into moving research into schools and classrooms.

Current State of Knowledge about Effective Elementary Reading Instruction

In the USA, and most nations, most children are taught how to read during the early elementary grades, kindergarten through second or third grade. There is clear evidence that children who are not reading proficiently by the end of second grade are much less likely to gain proficiency (Spira, Bracken, & Fischel, 2005), that consistently high-quality reading instruction from first through third grade provides stronger student reading outcomes (Connor, et al., 2013a), and that early effective instruction has a lasting impact on students, outcomes (Konstantopoulos & Chung, 2011). Our understanding about cognitive development, how children learn to read, and the kinds of instructional strategy and learning environments that support this learning has expanded rapidly in the past decade, as has been demonstrated in the previous chapters. There is a greater appreciation for the complexity of learning to read, the multiple cognitive and social processes that are brought to this task, and that the effect of specific instructional strategies depends on the skills children bring to the classroom (see Chapter 1's discussion of the Lattice Model).

This chapter reviews recent research, most studies published after 2008, on the cognitive, linguistic, and social processes that support learning and the kinds of instructional strategy and learning environment that are most effective in supporting learning to read specifically. For this chapter, we define reading as the ability to decode the words on a page, attach meaning to these words and the sentences they form in such a way as to form a coherent mental representation (or situation model) of the entire text (Connor, 2013; Kintsch, 1998; Rapp & van den Broek, 2005). Building a coherent mental representation (C-I model; see Chapter 1) generally depends on students' ability to accurately and fluently decode words, to inference meaning using other information in the text, as well as their academic and general world knowledge (Cain, Oakhill, & Lemmon, 2004; Snow, 2010); their ability to monitor their understanding of the text (Oakhill, Hartt, & Samols, 2005); and to use metacognitive and other strategies strategically to build meaning (Connor, Radach, Vorstius, Day, & Morrison, in review; Vorstius, Radach, & Mayer, in press). Comprehension also depends on the difficulty of the text (Hiebert & Fisher, 2007; McNamara, 2013) and the students' perceptions of why they are reading and how important it is to understand the text (i.e., motivation, purpose, enjoyment) (Snow, 2001). For this chapter, to be considered reading, text has to be involved, but we define text broadly to include both printed and digital text (for example, see Chapter 3). Writing is also an important instructional activity that emerging research indicates can be used to improve comprehension (Graham & Herbert, 2011).

Cracking the Code: Code-Focused Instruction

There are a number of excellent reviews of the literature, which show that virtually all students require at least some explicit and systematic instruction in the alphabetic principle and phonics to learn to read and that some children require greater amounts than do others (Connor, 2011; Foorman & Connor, 2010; MacArthur, et al., 2001; Reis, McCoach, Little, Muller, & Kaniskan, 2011; Stuebing, et al., 2008; Weiser & Mathes, 2011). At the same time, as Weiser and Mathes (2011) note, there has been much less research focused on encoding and spelling, and the potential benefits of encoding instruction. Emerging research indicates that there might be a reciprocal and synergistic effect for decoding and encoding instruction that might further improve students' grasp of the alphabetic principle. Their meta-analysis supports this view: they consistently found that manipulating letters and sounds or any encoding practice used to supplement phonics instruction enhanced the positive effect on student outcomes.

Most of the recent research on code-based interventions has targeted children who do not make adequate gains in reading skills even when they receive classroom instruction that is generally effective for their peers—Tier 2 and Tier 3 interventions (see Chapter 11). For example, a recent study on RTI showed that the sooner first graders who, based on assessment, were at greater risk for reading difficulties received more intensive Tier 2 or 3 interventions, the greater were their reading outcomes (Al Otaiba, et al., in press). A synthesis of IES-funded research (Connor, Alberto, Compton, & O'Connor, in press) provides several recommendations that emerge from the literature for students with, or at risk of, reading disabilities including: (1) assessment—screening, progress monitoring, assessment of English language learners, and accommodations for students with disabilities; (2) contributions of basic cognitive processes to reading; (3) intervention—increasing intensity of instruction; fluency, preschool language, and peer-assisted or collaborative learning; and (4) teacher professional development—developing specialized knowledge and combining multiple strategies.

Attaching Meaning to Text: Reading Comprehension Instruction

There is a general consensus that teaching children how to attach meaning to what they have read has been more difficult than anticipated. At one point, it was assumed that once decoding issues were resolved comprehension would take care of itself (e.g., Rayner, Foorman, Perfetti, Pesetsky, & Seidenberg, 2001). This assumption has not been upheld. Several studies have identified students who have adequate decoding skills but still struggle with comprehension (Compton, Fuchs, Fuchs, Elleman, & Gilbert, 2008; Oakhill & Yuill, 1996). That is not to say, however, that proficient decoding is not instrumental in proficient reading comprehension. Indeed, a review by García and Cain (García & Cain, 2013) revealed that, across 110 studies, decoding and reading comprehension were highly associated and the association depended on students' age (decoding had a greater effect for younger readers aged 10 years and younger) and oral language skills (i.e., listening comprehension).

Many of the current reviews of research focus on reading for understanding and reading comprehension (Block, Parris, Reed, Whiteley, & Cleveland, 2009; Shanahan, et al., 2010; Swanson et al., 2011), as well as how to meet the needs of language minority students (Melby-Lervåg & Lervåg, 2013; Slavin & Cheung, 2005) and students with, or at risk of, reading disabilities including students living in poverty (Benner, Nelson, Ralston, & Mooney, 2010; Berkeley, Scruggs, & Mastropieri, 2010; Weiser & Mathes, 2011). For example, the IES Practice Guide on *Improving Reading Comprehension in Kindergarten through 3rd Grade* (Shanahan, et al., 2010) provides a practical review of the literature on reading comprehension and offers five recommendations.

Eye Movement Studies and Comprehension Monitoring

As we saw in Chapter 3, well-designed eye movement studies provide evidence about how students process text during the act of reading and can offer insights that more typical standardized reading comprehension assessments cannot. Such studies are an important contribution of cognitive science to our understanding of reading development. For example, comprehension monitoring is one of the fundamental aspects of proficient reading for understanding listed in the seminal report *Preventing Reading Difficulties in Young Children* (Snow, Burns, & Griffin, 1998). Much of the research on comprehension monitoring has utilized think-aloud protocols and student surveys (e.g., Baumann, Seifert-Kessell, & Jones, 1992; Meyers, Lytle, Palladino, Devenpeck, & Green, 1990), which have limitations including a dependence on children's metacognitive skills (Scott, 2008). Eye movement studies offer an opportunity to examine how students process text as they are reading, do not rely on the sophistication of children's metacognitive skills (i.e., can they accurately recognize when their attention wanders?), and can offer clues as to why they might succeed or fail to attend to the meaning of what they are reading (Radach, Schmitten, Glover, & Huestegge, 2009; van der Schoot, Vasbinder, Horsley, & Reijntjes, 2009).

Moreover, improving technology is allowing eye movement research with younger children.

There are at least two aspects to comprehension monitoring: (1) detecting when a word or text does not make sense; and (2) repairing misunderstanding or confusions (meaning integration) (Connor, et al., 2015). Oculomotor viewing time measures are assumed to reflect different stages in the timeline of word processing that map onto these two aspects of comprehension monitoring. The *initial fixation* (when the eye first views the target word) represents pre-lexical and orthographic processing; *gaze duration* (the sum of all fixations before the first saccade) represents later stages of word processing, including lexical access—unfamiliar or confusing words should have longer gaze durations. *Rereading time* represents post-lexical integration of meaning (Inhoff & Radach, 1998; Radach & Kennedy, 2004, in press; Rayner, 1998; Reingold, Reichle, Glaholt, & Sheridan, 2012). Again, when readers confront unfamiliar or confusing words, they should take longer to repair their understanding than for familiar words.

Van der Schoot and colleagues (van der Schoot, Reijntjes, & Lieshout, 2012) used a narrative inconsistency task to measure students' comprehension monitoring and the extent to which they were developing and updating a strong situation model (i.e., building a coherent mental representation). Their assumption was that, as students read a paragraph, they were forming situation models. If information were included in the situation model, then later contradictory information should cause longer reading times. If the information was not included in the situation model, then contradictory information would not affect eye movements. Their participants (n = 31) included students between 10 and 12 years of age (Dutch fifth and sixth graders) who demonstrated either strong or weak comprehension skills. They found that students with weaker comprehension skills demonstrated more difficulty updating their situation models than did students with stronger comprehension skills. That is, when the inconsistency was in close proximity to the original information, their reading times were longer and similar to the students with stronger comprehension skills. However, when the inconsistency was more distal, their reading times were shorter, suggesting that they did not detect the inconsistency, were not updating their situation models, which, as a result, led to weaker comprehension when answering questions about the text.

Connor and colleagues (Connor, et al., 2015) also used an implausibility task to examine fifth graders' (n = 52) comprehension monitoring. In this task, children read two sentences with the second including either a plausible or an implausible word in the context of the first (e.g., "Last week Kyle flew to visit his family in another city. The large *plane/truck* was spacious and quickly transported them.") The task was not dissimilar to the proximal narrative task described in van der Schoot, et al. (2012). They also assessed students' reading comprehension, academic knowledge, and motivation for reading to examine whether individual child differences influenced patterns of reading on the implausibility task. They examined whether the *difference* between the plausible and implausible target words in gaze duration and rereading time would vary according to children's literacy skills, academic language skills, and/or motivation for reading.

Results showed that students gazed longer at words that were not plausible in context compared to those that were (i.e., *truck* vs. *plane*) regardless of their literacy skill, academic language, or motivation. Hence *noticing the misunderstanding* aspect of comprehension monitoring did not appear to be the culprit in poor understanding. Rather, it was what students did after they encountered the implausible word and the extent to which they attempted to repair their misunderstanding that distinguished the students— students with weaker academic language skills generally did not reread and try to repair their understanding, whereas students with stronger academic language skills did. Students with stronger reading skills processed text faster overall but there was no difference in repair time differences between plausible and implausible sentences. Motivation did not predict gaze duration or repair time differences, which was surprising (for example, see Logan, Medford, & Hughes, 2011). The results of this study point to the centrality of academic language skills in reading for understanding and indicate why comprehension may break down even when reading skills are adequate for the task (Snow, 2010; Verhoeven, van Leeuwe, & Vermeer, 2011). The standards of coherence for meaning integration that children set for themselves, their ability to develop a strong situation model, and whether or not they repair understanding for words that are implausible in context may be based on their ability to apply their academic language skills to the task of understanding (Cain, Oakhill, & Bryant, 2004; Connor, 2013; Oakhill, et al., 2005; Rapp, van den Broek, McMaster, Kendeou, & Espin, 2007).

Considering these and other studies (Connor, Alberto, et al., in press), such basic research has implications for designing and implementing effective reading comprehension instruction and interventions. Because students do appear to observe when text does not make sense—at least when the erroneous text is proximal to the context and, hence, is part of their situation model—interventions might spend more time on helping them learn to repair their understanding, strengthening their language skills, as well as building their academic knowledge. In the real world, most authors write texts that are intended to be understood, but a review of textbooks and other informational and narrative texts suggests that this may not always be the case. Attention to the quality of the text children are expected to read, and utilizing high-quality and coherent text, may aid comprehension (Hiebert & Fisher, 2007; McNamara, 2013) and will be even more important with implementation of the Common Core State Standards, which encourage use of more demanding texts.

Recent Studies on Comprehension Instruction

Randomized controlled trials (RCTs) or well-designed quasi-experimental studies are the most useful and rigorous way to investigate effective methods for teaching reading comprehension They represent the gold standard for evaluating the effect of a particular instructional strategy on students' outcomes (Shavelson & Towne, 2002) and have been used with more frequency since the inception of the U.S. Department of Education, Institute of Education Sciences in 2002 as part of the Education Sciences Reform Act of 2002 (http://ies.ed.gov/pdf/PL107-279.pdf). Three RCT studies focus on improving students' understanding of expository or informational text (Guthrie, et al., 2009; Wijekumar, Meyer, & Lei, 2012; Williams, Stafford, Lauer, Hall, & Pollini, 2009). The first, by Guthrie and colleagues (2009), tested the impact of concept-oriented reading comprehension (CORI; Guthrie, Anderson, Aloa, & Rinehart, 1999) using a quasi-experiment with fifth graders. CORI teaches reading comprehension emphasizing inferencing and comprehension monitoring. Lessons include activities designed to improve and sustain motivation using an engaging conceptual theme (e.g., ecological communities); student choice; collaboration among students; student goal setting; and use of hands-on activities. Instruction was for 90 minutes per day for 12 weeks, so it was intensive, with teaching shared between the teacher and an aide. Students participating in CORI generally exhibited stronger reading on the comprehension test and content area compared to the control group. There was no treatment effect for motivation. Hence, following cognitive development theories, CORI was able to enhance the reading development of both high- and low-achieving students by building specific cognitive skills (inferencing and monitoring). It is not clear whether focusing on motivation was an active component, because there was no effect on students' motivation.

Williams and colleagues (2009) used instruction in text structure of expository text to improve second graders' comprehension. In this RCT, students in the control condition received science instruction on the same content but no instruction on text structure and reading expository text. There were 12 lessons taught in 22 sessions each lasting 45 minutes over the course of 2 months so, again, the instruction was intensive. Using an animal encyclopedia, trade books, and researcher-developed text, teachers taught students how to use clue words, graphic organizers, summarizing, and compare-contrast strategies while focusing on vocabulary development and close analysis of text. There was also review at the end of each lesson. Results revealed that explicit comprehension instruction can be accommodated within the context of science instruction without jeopardizing students' learning of the content knowledge while increasing their understanding of expository text. Again, many of the features of their intervention relied on cognitive theories of development.

Technology has also been used to improve comprehension instruction. Wijekumar and colleagues (2012) assessed the efficacy of teaching text structure using an intelligent tutoring system (ITSS) to improve fourth graders' reading comprehension. Technology can offer a number of affordances including consistency, practice, assessment, and feedback. Structure strategy focuses on improving students understanding of text structure by identifying "signals … for text structures [i.e., clue words] in non-fiction [i.e., informational or expository text] to create strategically organized and efficient mental representations and use that knowledge to apply their memory of the text when needed" (p. 989). The signaling words help students identify one of five different text structures (i.e., compare/contrast, problem/solution, cause/effect, sequence, and description). ITSS was implemented in the computer lab 30 to 45 minutes each week for 6 months during the literacy block so both the treatment (use ITSS) and control (business as usual) received the same amount of language arts instruction. In the RCT, students in the ITSS condition achieved significantly greater scores on a standardized reading comprehension test compared to students in the control condition but the difference was modest (effect size $d = .10$) although they were larger for the researcher-developed assessments.

These three studies together demonstrate the efficacy of multicomponent instructional interventions for improving students' grasp of content knowledge, including the ability to read and learn from informational text. They also underscore the importance of strategy instruction, particularly text structure for supporting students' reading comprehension of expository and informational text. At the same time, all three instructional interventions were intensive and, at least to some extent, focused on meeting the learning needs of individual students either by supporting choice (Guthrie, et al., 2009) or through the use of technology (Wijekumar, et al., 2012). Also part of each of these interventions was a focus on building students' understanding of the text through discussion. Thinking back to Chapter 1, we see that cognitive development theories of learning are supported by these findings.

However, reading comprehension instruction that is ineffective can tell us a lot about cognitive development. For example, James-Burdumy and colleagues (James-Burdumy, et al., 2012) conducted a huge 2-year multisite randomized controlled large-scale study of four different supplemental reading comprehension interventions—Project CRISS; Read About; Read for Real; and Reading for Knowledge—which were commercially available. All four relied on "explicit comprehension instruction" (p. 347). Teachers implementing these supplemental interventions modeled the use of each strategy (e.g., summarizing was used in all four programs) and guided student practice. However, the interventions differed. For instance, Read About utilized computers and students received extensive and immediate feedback. Results after the first year revealed that none of the interventions was more effective than business as usual. In fact, Reading for Knowledge students had weaker outcomes than the control. After 2 years, only Read About improved students' social studies skills.

Thus, it appears that teaching only reading comprehension strategies is not enough. When we remember that the effective reading comprehension interventions utilized multiple strategies to teach comprehension—not just strategies—it appears that multiple strategies might be more effective. This is what McKeown and colleagues (McKeown, Beck, & Blake, 2009) found. In their RCT they investigated three different approaches to building fifth graders' reading comprehension: an intervention focusing on building content understanding; an intervention focusing on teaching comprehension strategies; and just using core literacy curriculum materials. Students in all three groups improved their comprehension with students in the content approach group achieving a bit stronger comprehension. The authors concluded that "getting students to actively build meaning while reading does not necessitate knowledge of and focus on specific strategies but rather it may require attention to text content in ways that promote attending to important ideas and establishing connections between them" (p. 245).

More evidence for the importance of using multiple strategies to improve students' reading comprehension is provided in three different studies (Block, et al., 2009; Clarke, Snowling, Truelove, & Hulme, 2010; Connor, et al., 2011a). All three used multiple strategies and showed evidence of being effective in improving students' comprehension of text. Hence we are beginning to understand how to improve students' reading comprehension but not entirely. The more effective interventions usually used multiple components that focused on developing academic language or oral language skills and strategy instruction as well as corrective feedback—either explicit or implicit. Some of these interventions were explicitly designed for students with weak comprehension skills but not all. Those studies including both higher and lower achieving students generally demonstrated treatment effects (if there were treatment effects) regardless of achievement level. Virtually all were small group interventions where teachers are more likely to be sensitive to students' individual learning needs. The What Works Clearinghouse report on RTI recommended that general classroom instruction be differentiated (i.e., individualized or personalized), which these results tend to support. The remaining studies explicitly examine the effect of differentiated instruction on students' reading comprehension.

Personalizing Reading Instruction to Improve Students' Reading Comprehension Outcomes

Research on the effect of individual child differences on the impact of reading instruction (Connor, et al., 2011a, 2013;) follows many of the cognitive development theories discussed in Chapter 1 (e.g., the Lattice Model). This instructional framework, called individualized student instruction in reading (ISI-R) relies on using assessment information to guide instruction. A key aspect of the intervention is Assessment-to-Instruction software (A2i) that uses algorithms to compute recommended amounts of teacher/student-managed or student/peer-managed and code- or meaning-focused instruction—using standardized or curriculum-based reading and vocabulary assessments. Because the language arts materials already used by the classroom teachers are indexed to the four types of instruction, teachers use materials with which they are already familiar, but use them in different ways to meet their students' individual learning needs. The second component is teacher professional development and the third is implementation in the classroom.

Connor and colleagues demonstrated that personalizing reading instruction using ISI-R in first through third grade was more effective than more "one-size-fits-all" approaches used in most classrooms. Teachers learned to provide the A2i recommended amounts using small flexible learning groups. Professional development focused on classroom management, using assessment to guide instruction, and implementing research-based reading instructional activities effectively. Using classroom observation, the investigators demonstrated that teachers in the ISI-R condition were more likely to provide individualized or personalized instruction that considered students' individual learning differences than were control teachers. Students in the ISI-R classrooms showed stronger reading comprehension than did students in the vocabulary control classrooms (Connor, et al., 2011a, 2011b). Finally, the closer the observed amounts of each type of instruction (e.g., teacher/student-managed meaning-focused small group) were to the A2i recommended amounts, the greater were students' comprehension gains. The investigators noted that the "association between students' profile of language and literacy skills and recommended instruction was non-linear" (abstract) and more complex than anticipated, which helps to explain why teachers frequently have difficulty using assessment results to guide instruction (Roehrig, Duggar, Moats, Glover, & Mincey, 2008).

Another important question is whether the effects of effective reading instruction accumulate. Correlational studies suggest that effects should accumulate (Konstantopoulos & Chung, 2011) and a longitudinal RCT demonstrates this decisively (Connor, et al., 2013). In the longitudinal efficacy study, more than 45 percent of students qualified for subsidized lunch. ISI-R was effective at each grade and the effects accumulated with students who participated in ISI-R classrooms all three grades making the greatest gains compared to students who were in ISI-R for fewer years or who were in control classrooms all three years ($d = .73$).

ISI-R was develop to test whether individual student differences in language and reading skills might influence their response to specific types of reading instruction (i.e., child × instruction interactions) and to improve achievement on the skills measured by standardized tests, which correlate with high-stakes assessments. ISI-R made the assumption that students who were better readers would also be more engaged and enjoy reading more but this was not directly tested in these studies. Following the Lattice Model there is some evidence to suggest that stronger reading skills predict engagement and not the reverse (Guo, Sun, Breit-Smith, Morrison, & Connor, 2014).

Recent research offers insights in how to support all students' reading comprehension development, use multiple strategies, personalize instruction for each child, and empower teachers. At the same time, students' reading gains were more consistent when focus was on the content and time spent in reading instruction than when enrichment was the principal goal. New research reveals that focus on both the content of reading instruction as well as the quality of the classroom learning environment (i.e., enrichment) may operate synergistically to improve students' reading comprehension outcomes (Connor, Spencer, et al., 2014). As discussed in the final chapter, cognitive science has made important contributions to our understanding of reading processes and how to develop more effective reading interventions.

References

Al Otaiba, S., Connor, C. M., Folsom, J. S., Greulich, L., Wanzek, J., Schatschneider, C., et al. (in press). To wait in Tier 1 or intervene immediately: A randomized experiment examining first grade response to intervention (RTI) in reading. *Exceptional Children*.

Baumann, J. F., Seifert-Kessell, N., & Jones, L. A. (1992). Effect of think-aloud instruction on elementary students' comprehension monitoring abilities. *Journal of Literacy Research*, *24*(2), 143–172.

Benner, G. J., Nelson, J. R., Ralston, N. C., & Mooney, P. (2010). A meta-analysis of the effects of reading instruction on the reading skills of students with or at risk of behavioral disorders. *Behavioral Disorders*, *35*(2), 86–102.

Berkeley, S., Scruggs, T. E., & Mastropieri, M. A. (2010). Reading comprehension instruction for students with learning disabilities, 1995–2006: A meta-analysis. *Remedial and Special Education*, *31*(6), 423–436.

Block, C. C., Parris, S. R., Reed, K. I., Whiteley, C. S., & Cleveland, M. D. (2009). Instructional approaches that significantly increase reading comprehension. *Journal of Educational Psychology*, *101*(2), 262–281.

Bronfenbrenner, U., & Morris, P. A. (2006). The bioecological model of human development. In R. M. Lerner & W. Damon (Eds.), *Handbook of Child Psychology: Theoretical Models of Human Development* (6th ed., Vol. 1). Hoboken, NJ: John Wiley & Sons.

Cain, K., Oakhill, J., & Bryant, P. (2004). Children's reading comprehension ability: Concurrent prediction by working memory, verbal ability, and component skills. *Journal of Educational Psychology*, *96*(1), 31–42.

Cain, K., Oakhill, J., & Lemmon, K. (2004). Individual differences in the inference of word meanings from context: The influence of reading comprehension, vocabulary knowledge, and memory capacity. *Journal of Educational Psychology*, *96*(4), 671–681.

Cameron, C. E., & Morrison, F. J. (2004, June). A structural equation model of self-regulation and early literacy development in children. Paper presented at the Society for the Scientific Study of Reading 11th Annual Meeting, Amsterdam.

Carlisle, J. F., Kelcey, B., Berebitsky, D., & Phelps, G. (2011). Embracing the complexity of instruction: A study of the effects of teachers' instruction on students' reading comprehension. *Scientific Studies of Reading*, *15*(5), 409–439.

Clarke, P. J., Snowling, M. J., Truelove, E., & Hulme, C. (2010). Ameliorating children's reading-comprehension difficulties: A randomized controlled trial. *Psychological Science*, *21*(8), 1106–1116.

Common Core State Standards Initiative. (2010). Common Core State Standards for Mathematics. Retrieved from http://www.corestandards.org/assets/CCSSI_MathStandards.pdf

Compton, D. L., Fuchs, D., Fuchs, L. S., Elleman, A. M., & Gilbert, J. K. (2008). Tracking children who fly below the radar: Latent transition modeling of students with late-emerging reading disability. *Learning and Individual Differences*, *18*(3), 329–337.

Connor, C. M. (2011). Child by instruction interactions: Language and literacy connections. In S. B. Neuman & D. K. Dickinson (Eds.), *Handbook on Early Literacy* (3rd ed.). New York: Guilford Press.

Connor, C. M. (2013). Intervening to support reading comprehension development with diverse learners. In B. Miller & L. E. Cutting (Eds.), *Unraveling the Behavioral, Neurobiological and Genetic Components of Reading Comprehension: The Dyslexia Foundation and NICHD*. Baltimore, MD: Paul H. Brookes.

Connor, C. M., Alberto, P. A., Compton, D. L., & O'Connor, R. E. (in press). Improving reading outcomes for students with or at risk for reading disabilities: A synthesis of the contributions from the Institute of Education Sciences Research Centers Institute of Education Sciences.

Connor, C. M., Morrison, F. J., Fishman, B., Crowe, E. C., Al Otaiba, S., & Schatschneider, C. (2013). A longitudinal cluster-randomized control study on the accumulating effects of individualized literacy instruction on students' reading from 1st through 3rd grade. *Psychological Science*, *24*(8), 1408–1419.

Connor, C. M., Morrison, F. J., Fishman, B., Giuliani, S., Luck, M., Underwood, P., et al. (2011a). Testing the impact of child characteristics by instruction interactions on third graders' reading comprehension by differentiating literacy instruction. *Reading Research Quarterly*, *46*(3), 189–221.

Connor, C. M., Morrison, F. J., Schatschneider, C., Toste, J. R., Lundblom, E., Crowe, et al. (2011b). Effective classroom instruction: Implications of child characteristics by reading instruction interactions on first graders' word reading achievement. *Journal of Research on Educational Effectiveness*, *4*(3), 173–207.

Connor, C. M., Ponitz, C. E. C., Phillips, B., Travis, Q. M., Day, S. G., & Morrison, F. J. (2010). First graders' literacy and self-regulation gains: The effect of individualizing instruction. *Journal of School Psychology*, *48*, 433–455.

Connor, C. M., Radach, R., Vorstius, C., Day, S., & Morrison, F. J. (2015). Individual differences in fifth graders' literacy and academic language predict comprehension monitoring development: An eye-movement study. *Scientific Studies of Reading*, *19*, 114–134.

Connor, C. M., Spencer, M., Day, S. L., Giuliani, S., Ingebrand, S. W., & Morrison, F. J. (2014). Capturing the complexity: Content, type, and amount of instruction and quality of the classroom learning environment synergistically predict third graders' vocabulary and reading comprehension outcomes. *Journal of Educational Psychology*, *106*, 762–778.

Dahl, K. L., & Freppon, P. A. (1995). A comparison of innercity children's interpretations of reading and writing instruction in the early grades in skills-based and whole language classrooms. *Reading Research Quarterly*, *30*(1), 50–74.

Davis, A. R. (1987). A historical perspective. In J. E. Alexander (Ed.), *Teaching Reading*. Glenview IL: Scot Foresman/Little Brown College Division.

Duncan, G. J., Kalil, A., & Ziol-Guest, K. (2008). *Economic Costs of Early Childhood Poverty* (Vol. 4). Washington, DC: Partnership for America's Economic Success.

Flesch, R. (1955). *Why Johnny Can't Read: And What You Can Do About It*. New York: Harper & Brothers.

Foorman, B. R., & Connor, C. M. (2010). Primary reading. In A. G. Kamhi & P. D. Pearson (Eds.), *Handbook of Reading Research* (4th ed.). Mahwah, NJ: Erlbaum.

Foorman, B. R., Francis, D. J., Fletcher, J. M., Schatschneider, C., & Mehta, P. (1998). The role of instruction in learning to read: Preventing reading failure in at risk children. *Journal of Educational Psychology*, *90*, 37–55.

García, J. R., & Cain, K. (2013). Decoding and reading comprehension: A meta-analysis to identify which reader and assessment characteristics influence the strength of the relationship in English. *Review of Educational Research*, *84*(1), 74–111.

Goelman, H., Oberg, A. A., & Smith, F. (Eds.). (1984). *Awakening to Literacy*. London: Heinemann Educational Books.

Goodman, K. (1970). Reading: A psycholinguistic guessing game. In H. Singer & R. B. Ruddell (Eds.), *Theoretical Models and Processes of Reading*. Newark, DE: International Reading Association.

Goodman, K. (1986). *What's Whole in Whole Language?* Portsmouth, NH: Heinemann.

Graham, S., & Herbert, M. (2011). Writing to read: A meta-analysis of the impact of writing and writing instruction on reading. *Harvard Educational Review*, *81*(4), 710–744.

Guo, Y., Sun, S., Breit-Smith, A., Morrison, F. J., & Connor, C. M. (2014). Behavioral engagement and reading achievement in elementary-school-age children: A longitudinal cross-lagged analysis. *Journal of Educational Psychology*, *107*(2), 1–16.

Guthrie, J. T., Anderson, E., Aloa, S., & Rinehart, J. (1999). Influences of concept-oriented reading instruction on strategy use and conceptual learning from text. *Elementary School Journal*, *99*, 343–366.

Guthrie, J. T., McRae, A., Coddington, C. S., Lutz Klauda, S., Wigfield, A., & Barbosa, P. (2009). Impacts of comprehensive reading instruction on diverse outcomes of low- and high-achieving readers. *Journal of Learning Disabilities*, *42*(3), 195–214.

Guthrie, J. T., McRae, A., & Klauda, S. L. (2007). Contributions of concept-oriented reading instruction to knowledge about interventions for motivations in reading. *Educational Psychologist, Educational Psychologist, Special Issue: Promoting Motivation at School, 42*(4), 237–250.

Hiebert, E., & Fisher, C. W. (2007). Critical word factor in texts for beginning readers. *Journal of Educational Research, 101*(1), 3–11.

Inhoff, A. W., & Radach, R. (1998). Definition and computation of oculomotor measures in the study of cognitive processes. In G. Underwood (Ed.), *Eye Guidance in Reading and Scene Perception*. Oxford: Elsevier.

James-Burdumy, S., Deke, J., Gersten, R., Lugo-Gil, J., Newman-Gonchar, R., Dimino, J., et al. (2012). Effectiveness of four supplemental reading comprehension interventions. *Journal of Research on Educational Effectiveness, 5*(4), 345–383.

Kintsch, W. (1998). *Comprehension: A Paradigm for Cognitions*. New York: Cambridge University Press.

Konstantopoulos, S., & Chung, N. (2011). The persistence of teacher effects in elementary grades. *American Educational Research Journal, 48*(2), 361–386.

Logan, S., Medford, E., & Hughes, N. (2011). The importance of intrinsic motivation for high and low ability readers' reading comprehension performance. *Learning and Individual Differences, 21*(1), 124–128.

Loveless, T. (Ed.). (2001). *The Great Curriculum Debate*. Washington, DC: Brookings Institution Press.

MacArthur, C. A., Ferretti, R. P., Okolo, C. M., & Cavalier, A. R. (2001). Technology applications for students with literacy problems: A critical review. *Elementary School Journal, Special Issue: Instructional Interventions for Students with Learning Disabilities, 101*(3), 273–301.

McKeown, M. G., Beck, I. L., & Blake, R. G. K. (2009). Rethinking reading comprehension instruction: A comparison of instruction for strategies and content approaches. *Reading Research Quarterly, 44*(3), 218–253.

McNamara, D. S. (2013). The epistemic stance between the author and reader: A driving force in the cohesion of text and writing. *Discourse Studies, 15*(5), 1–17.

Melby-Lervåg, M., & Lervåg, A. (2013). Reading comprehension and its underlying components in second-language learners: A meta-analysis of studies comparing first- and second-language learners. *Psychological Bulletin*, no pagination specified.

Meyers, J., Lytle, S., Palladino, D., Devenpeck, G., & Green, M. (1990). Think-aloud protocol analysis: An investigation of reading comprehension strategies in fourth- and fifth-grade students. *Journal of Psychoeducational Assessment, 8*(2), 112–127.

National Early Literacy Panel. (2008). *Developing Early Literacy: Report of the National Early Literacy Panel*. Washington, DC: National Institute for Literacy and the National Center for Family Literacy.

NICHD. (2000). National Institute of Child Health and Human Development, National Reading Panel report: *Teaching Children to Read: An Evidence-Based Assessment of the Scientific Research Literature on Reading and Its Implications for Reading Instruction*. Washington, DC: U.S. Department of Health and Human Services, Public Health Service, National Institutes of Health, National Institute of Child Health and Human Development.

NICHD-ECCRN. (2004). Multiple pathways to early academic achievement. *Harvard Educational Review, 74*(1), 1–29.

Oakhill, J., Hartt, J., & Samols, D. (2005). Levels of comprehension monitoring and working memory in good and poor comprehenders. *Reading and Writing: An Interdisciplinary Journal, 18*(7), 30–30.

Oakhill, J., & Yuill, N. (1996). Higher order factors in comprehension disability: Processes and remediation. In C. Cornoldi & J. Oakhill (Eds.), *Reading Comprehension Difficulties: Processes and Interventions.* Mahwah, NJ: Erlbaum.

Pianta, R. C., Belsky, J., Houts, R., Morrison, F. J., & NICHD-ECCRN. (2007). Teaching: Opportunities to learn in America's elementary classrooms. *Science, 315*, 1795–1796.

Pianta, R. C., La Paro, K. M., Payne, K., Cox, C., & Bradley, R. H. (2002). The relation of kindergarten classroom environment to teacher, family and school characteristics and child outcomes. *Elementary School Journal, 102*(3), 225–238.

Radach, R., & Kennedy, A. (2004). Theoretical perspectives on eye movements in reading. Past controversies, current deficits and an agenda for future research. *European Journal of Cognitive Psychology, 16*, 3–26.

Radach, R., & Kennedy, A. (in press). Eye movements in reading. *Quarterly Journal of Experimental Psychology.*

Radach, R., Schmitten, C., Glover, L., & Huestegge, L. (2009). How children read for comprehension: Eye movements in developing readers. In R. K. Wagner, C. Schatschneider & C. Phythian-Sence (Eds.), *Beyond Decoding: The Biological and Behavioral Foundations of Reading Comprehension.* New York: Guildford Press.

Rapp, D. N., & van den Broek, P. (2005). Dynamic text comprehension: An integrative view of reading. *Current Directions in Psychological Science, 14*(5), 276–279.

Rapp, D. N., van den Broek, P., McMaster, K., Kendeou, P., & Espin, C. A. (2007). Higher-order comprehension processes in struggling readers: A perspective for research and intervention. *Scientific Studies of Reading, 11*(4), 389–312.

Ravitch, D. (2001). It is time to stop the war. In T. Loveless (Ed.), *The Great Curriculum Debate: How Should We Teach Reading and Math.* Washington, DC: Brookings Institutional Press.

Rayner, K. (1998). Eye movements in reading and information processing: 20 years of research. *Psychological Bulletin, 124*, 372–422.

Rayner, K., Foorman, B. R., Perfetti, C. A., Pesetsky, D., & Seidenberg, M. S. (2001). How psychological science informs the teaching of reading. *Psychological Science in the Public Interest, 2*(2), 31–74.

Reingold, E. M., Reichle, E. D., Glaholt, M. G., & Sheridan, H. (2012). Direct lexical control of eye movements in reading: Evidence from a survival analysis of fixation durations. *Cognitive Psychology, 65*, 177–206.

Reis, S. M., McCoach, D. B., Little, C. A., Muller, L. M., & Kaniskan, R. B. (2011). The effects of differentiated instruction and enrichment pedagogy on reading achievement in five elementary schools. *American Educational Research Journal, 48*(2), 462–501.

Roehrig, A. D., Duggar, S. W., Moats, L. C., Glover, M., & Mincey, B. (2008). When teachers work to use progress monitoring data to inform literacy instruction: Identifying potential supports and challenges. *Remedial and Special Education, 29*, 364–382.

Scott, D. B. (2008). Assessing text processing: A comparison of four methods. *Journal of Literacy Research, 40*(3), 290–316.

Shanahan, T., Callison, K., Carriere, C., Duke, N. K., Pearson, P. D., Schatschneider, C., et al. (2010). *Practice Guide: Improving Reading Comprehension in Kindergarten through 3rd Grade.* (NCEE 2010-4038). Washington, DC: Department of Education.

Shavelson, R. J., & Towne, L. (Eds.). (2002). *Scientific Research in Education.* Washington, DC: National Academy Press.

Skibbe, L. E., Phillips, B. M., Day, S., Brophy-Herb, H. E., & Connor, C. M. (2012). Children's early literacy growth in relation to classmates' self-regulation. *Journal of Educational Psychology, 104*(3), 451–553.

Slavin, R. E., & Cheung, A. (2005). A synthesis of research on language of reading instruction for English language learners. *Review of Educational Research, 75*(2), 247–284.

Snow, C. E. (2001). *Reading for Understanding.* Santa Monica, CA: RAND Education and the Science and Technology Policy Institute.

Snow, C. E. (2010). Academic language and the challenge of reading for learning about science. *Science, 328,* 450–452.

Snow, C. E., Burns, M. S., & Griffin, P. (Eds.). (1998). *Preventing Reading Difficulties in Young Children.* Washington, DC: National Academy Press.

Spira, E. G., Bracken, S. S., & Fischel, J. E. (2005). Predicting improvement after first-grade reading difficulties: The effects of oral language, emergent literacy, and behavior skills. *Developmental Psychology, 41*(1), 225–234.

Stuebing, K. K., Barth, A. E., Cirino, P. T., Francis, D. J., & Fletcher, J. M. (2008). A response to recent reanalyses of the National Reading Panel Report: Effects of systematic phonics instruction are practically significant. *Journal of Educational Psychology, 100*(1), 123–134.

Swanson, E., Vaughn, S., Wanzek, J., Petscher, Y., Heckert, J., Cavanaugh, C., et al. (2011). A synthesis of read-aloud interventions on early reading outcomes among preschool through third graders at risk for reading difficulties. *Journal of Learning Disabilities, 44*(3), 258–275.

Taylor, B. M., Pearson, D. P., Clark, K., & Walpole, S. (2000). Effective schools and accomplished teachers: Lessons about primary-grade reading instruction in low-income schools. *Elementary School Journal, 101*(2), 121–165.

Taylor, J. E., Roehrig, A. D., Connor, C. M., & Schatschneider, C. (2010). Teacher quality moderates the genetic effects on early reading. *Science, 328,* 512–514.

van der Schoot, M., Reijntjes, A., & Lieshout, E. (2012). How do children deal with inconsistencies in text? An eye fixation and self-paced reading study in good and poor reading comprehenders. *Reading & Writing, 25*(7), 1665–1690.

van der Schoot, M., Vasbinder, A. L., Horsley, T. M., & Reijntjes, A. (2009). Lexical ambiguity resolution in good and poor comprehenders: An eye fixation and self-paced reading study in primary school children. *Journal of Educational Psychology, 101*(1), 21–36.

Verhoeven, L., van Leeuwe, J., & Vermeer, A. (2011). Vocabulary growth and reading development across the elementary school years. *Scientific Studies of Reading, 15*(1), 8–25.

Vorstius, C., Radach, R., & Mayer, M. (in press). Monitoring local comprehension monitoring in sentence reading. *School Psychology Review.*

Weiser, B., & Mathes, P. (2011). Using encoding instruction to improve the reading and spelling performances of elementary students at risk for literacy difficulties: A best-evidence synthesis. *Review of Educational Research, 81*(2), 170–200.

Wijekumar, K. K., Meyer, B. J. F., & Lei, P. (2012). Large-scale randomized controlled trial with 4th graders using intelligent tutoring of the structure strategy to improve nonfiction reading comprehension. *Educational Technology Research and Development, 60*(6), 987–1013.

Williams, J. P., Stafford, K. B., Lauer, K. D., Hall, K. M., & Pollini, S. (2009). Embedding reading comprehension training in content-area instruction. *Journal of Educational Psychology, 101*(1), 1–20.

Chapter 13

Conclusions, Future Directions, and Questions for Discussion

Carol McDonald Connor

The contributions of cognitive science to our understanding of the cognitive development of reading are substantial. In this chapter, we offer 12 observations about the state of children's cognitive development of reading today, which include salient findings from research that are discussed in this edited volume. However, we are left with questions that may help to inform future cognitive research on literacy development and how to improve the instruction we provide to all children during the early elementary years—both at home and in school.

1   Cognitive theories and research on cognitive development have been crucial in helping us understand the multiple sources of influence and the underlying processes that impact proficient reading skills. This understanding is informing the development of more effective reading interventions for elementary school-aged children. *What is the research behind the kinds of instruction and intervention you are using or observing?*

2   Genetics plays an important role in helping us understand individual differences among children and how they develop reading skills. *However, what do gene × environment interactions and polymorphism (many genes affect reading) show us about how we can optimize the environments that impact reading and help all children reach their potential?*

3   Underlying processes, including perception and memory, impact children's developing reading skills along with other cognitive skills. However, these may develop reciprocally with children's developing language and literacy skills. *How might we design instruction to take advantage of what we know about underlying cognitive processes and how they are associated with learning?*

4   Self-regulation and other critical social and cognitive skills, such as growth mindset, support children's ability to take advantage of opportunities to learn. Strategic interventions can support self-regulated learning. *What are some of the ways that interventions might promote self-regulated learning in combination with explicit literacy instruction?*

5 Children's developing language is critical to their developing reading comprehension skills and these associations appear to be reciprocal. *How can we design effective language and literacy interventions that will better support the development of reading comprehension?*

6 Children with psychological and other health issues appear to be at risk for developing weaker literacy skills. *What kinds of research and intervention would support children who are suffering from mental health and physical challenges? How can we better support them in the classroom?*

7 Parents are the first and most important teachers and yet many parents lack the knowledge to provide the kinds of learning environment that will help their child learn to read successfully. *How can we reach out to parents to provide them with the knowledge and confidence they require to become better first teachers?*

8 Supporting the learning of children living in poverty is one of the most well-researched sources of influence but continues to be a serious challenge. *How can we better meet the needs of children living in poverty who are more likely to have health issues and to have less experience to develop language and world knowledge than their more affluent peers?*

9 Ongoing policy, particularly from the U.S. Department of Education, and the newly enacted Every Student Succeeds Act, has put increasing focus on what happens in the classroom and holds teachers accountable for their students' achievement. Already, the Common Core State Standards (CCSS) have changed how teachers teach read in the primary grades and will continue to do so for the foreseeable future. The CCSS target greater use of expository and informational text across the content areas, higher order cognitive skills, and reading comprehension skills, including analysis of text, with less emphasis on the foundational skills (i.e., alphabetic principle, phonics, encoding) that are critical for students to learn, particularly during the early years of schooling. *What will the impact of CCSS be on student achievement, particularly students who are most vulnerable—those living in poverty or for whom English is a second language? And how can we use cognitive science to improve the CCSS as we learn more about the standards' impact?*

10 Research over the past few decades shows that virtually all students require at least some explicit and systematic instruction in the alphabetic principle and phonics to learn to read, and some children require greater amounts than do others. Although there is less research on reading comprehension, the research that is available suggests that decoding and reading comprehension may develop synergistically— each supporting the other. *But what about writing? What might cognitive science tell us about how children learn to write?*

11 Across studies on reading comprehension interventions, mixed results suggest that we still have a way to go before we fully understand the

multiple components and active ingredients of comprehension interventions that are effective—and this is likely to vary depending on student characteristics. In general, multicomponent interventions that include a focus on developing academic language or oral language skills as well as strategy instruction are likely to be more effective than single strategy interventions. Additionally, instruction that is specifically tailored (individualized or personalized) to each child's unique constellation of language, literacy, and cognitive skills is more effective than one-size-fits-all instruction. *But how can we better personalize instruction in the classroom? And what have we learned about cognitive development that might help us be more effective in providing optimal learning opportunities for students?*

12 Accumulating evidence suggests that the effects of effective reading instruction accumulate—at least from kindergarten through third grade and probably beyond. Efficacious instructional regimens maximize the amount of time spent in meaningful instruction and include both fundamental (e.g., alphabetic principle, phonics, encoding) and meaning-focused instruction (e.g., reading comprehension, writing, supported silent reading). In general, effective reading instruction utilizes small group assessment-informed and teacher-led instruction designed to address students' individual learning needs (i.e., flexible learning groups); provides opportunities for students to work independently and with peers; are to make key instructional decisions effective in higher poverty schools that serve many students at risk of academic underachievement; nurture students' motivation to read; use multiple strategies; and empower teachers. However, differentiating reading instruction is difficult for teachers, although they can be successful with support and appropriate professional development. *How do we bring these practices to schools? What are some of the strategies that can be used to better personalize the instruction children receive?*

We are highly encouraged by the progress we have made in improving children's reading outcomes over the past decades and are optimistic that the lofty goals of Every Student Succeeds Act might become a reality. Cognitive development theory and research, much of it funded by IES and the National Institute for Child Health and Human Development, has contributed to our understanding of how children learn to read and how we can support them effectively. How well children need to be able to read to function well in our twenty-first-century global and technological society remains an important but unanswered question. At the same time, there are important challenges and many divergent ideas about how to meet these challenges.

Our hope is that this book has helped the reader gain more insights into the importance and the complexity of learning to read. This includes how children achieve proficient reading comprehension skills and how we can help children learn this crucial cognitive skill.

Contributors

Laura K. Allen is graduate student of psychology at Arizona State University.

Amanda Chiapa is graduate student of psychology at Arizona State University.

Shayna S. Coburn is graduate student of psychology at Arizona State University.

Carol McDonald Connor is Chancellor's Professor of Education, University of California Irvine.

Greg J. Duncan is Distinguished Professor of Education at University of California of Irvine.

Nancy Eisenberg is Regents Professor of Psychology at Arizona State University.

Sara A. Hart is Assistant Professor of Psychology at Florida State University of Florida Center for Reading Research.

Annemarie Hindman is Associate Professor of Psychological Studies in Education at Tempe University.

Betty Lin is graduate student of psychology at Arizona State University.

Callie W. Little is graduate student of psychology at Florida University of Florida Center for Reading Research.

Danielle S. McNamara is Professor of Psychology at Arizona State University.

Andre Mansion is graduate student of psychology at Arizona State University.

Zorash Montano is graduate student of psychology at Arizona State University.

Frederick J. Morrison is Professor of School of Education in the Department of Psychology, College of Literature, Science, and the Arts at the University of Michigan.

Ralph Radach is Professor of Psychology at Bergische University Wuppertal.

Kristy Roschke is Graduate Student of Journalism & Mass Communication at Arizona State University.

Devin Russell is graduate student of psychology at Arizona State University.

Francis Wang is graduate student of psychology at Arizona State University.

Jennifer L. Weston is graduate student of psychology at Arizona State University.

Laurie Dempsey Wolf is graduate student of psychology at Arizona State University.

Henry Wynne is graduate student of psychology at Arizona State University.

Index